Raising
4 Dimensional Children
in a
2 Dimensional World

by
Tim McCarthy

copyright and published by 4D-2D.com, LLC
638 SE Dean Terrace, Port Saint Lucie, FL 34984
ISBN 978-1-7375447-0-8

First Edition

If you would like to purchase an individual chapter
or another copy of the entire book, please go to
www.4D-2D.com

Cover art by Jay McCarthy
jay@inyourwheelhaus.com

Introduction

I have always believed that if what you read makes sense, it should stand on its own, regardless of who wrote it. Unfortunately, in this time of social media misinformation in intentional disinformation, the source of the information has become important. Therefore, I feel compelled to tell you a little bit about myself so you can more easily accept what I have to say.

Who Am I?

I am and have been an educator for over 40 years. I have a Master's Degree (M.S.) in Education and have ten years' experience as a classroom teacher and administrator in both public and private schools. What gives me a unique perspective is that I am also a Grandmaster of the martial arts, with over 40 years' experience of teaching both children and adults. I have personally taught thousands of students of all ages using both Eastern and Western philosophies of education.

For 20 of those years I have also designed educational courses and curricula in the martial arts. I did not "invent" the idea that human beings have 4 Dimensions: The Physical, Mental, Emotional, and Spiritual. It is an Eastern way of understanding the human experience that I learned in my martial arts studies and is very different from our current Western educational system. American public schools focus on the mental dimension and provide very limited physical education. Emotional education may be provided by some exceptional teachers but is rarely part of the curriculum. Spiritual education has been forced out of the school system by lawsuits. That was why I chose to leave the school system and focus on the martial arts: I was able to teach and develop students in all 4 Dimensions and have designed martial arts programs that have been used by hundreds of schools across the U.S. and Canada, and in some other countries as well. Now I am making those same educational principles available to you.

You Don't Need a Degree in Education or Psychology to Raise Well-Balanced Children

What you do need is a desire to be the best parent you can be. I had the good fortune to be raised by good parents, and I believe there is no greater blessing in the world than to be born into a loving family. I learned a lot about good parenting from them. You can't choose your parents, so you can only play the cards you are dealt, but having good parents is a great start to a winning hand.

YOU who are reading this book, on the other hand, do have a choice. You can be that good parent who is a blessing to your children, or you can be selfish and ignorant of good parenting practices. I strongly believe in the first choice, and if you are reading this, I'll bet you do, too.

In this book I have done my best to make that first choice easy. I have spent years studying both Eastern and Western education. I have tested and improved myself in all four dimensions in my personal training. I have researched developmental child psychology. I have digested those many years of experience and research to give you a simple, easy to follow guide for raising a child balanced in all 4 Dimensions of human potential.

I apologize in advance if I occasionally get a little technical explaining what happens at each age as your child's brain develops, but I believe that information helps you understand why your child thinks and acts the way he does. If you find it too "textbook," feel free to skim over that part and get to the practical activities that will bring you the results you want. The activities are easy and fun, and each helps develop a different aspect of your child.

More experienced parents may feel that much of what I say is just common sense. If you do, I applaud you for already knowing what to do. Unfortunately, common sense is not common, so please bear with me as I explain it to the new parents and those who suffered through less-than-ideal parenting as children. This book is for every parent, beginner to seasoned expert, so please focus on the information that helps you at your own level. However, I do look forward to the day when the advice and activities in this book really are common, because that will mean that thousands and perhaps millions of children will have been raised by caring, knowledgeable parents and therefore know how to raise 4 Dimensional children of their own.

How to Read this Book

This book is not a novel intended for you to read cover to cover. You probably chose this book because you have (or you are about to have) a child, so the chapter for your child's age is the most important to you. I just ask that, after reading this introduction, you read the first chapter to understand the Foundation of the 4 Dimensions. After that, you can skip ahead to the chapter that is appropriate to the age of your child or children. If you have time, you might read the previous chapter to make sure you have done everything you can for your child's previous stage, and possibly look ahead to the next stage so you have a direction to work towards. This book is designed so you can quickly get the information and activities that you need, and then refer back to them as your child grows and your needs change. There is a lot of information packed into relatively few pages, so I encourage you to re-read and review often.

Note: I intentionally alternate the gender of the child in different sections to be inclusive, so unless I specifically identify advice for boys or girls, "he" and "she," and "his" and "her" are intended to be interchangeable.

Important: Use Your Own Judgment

While every effort to ensure the information, recommendations, advice, and activities contained in this book are believed to be reliable, the author, publisher, and owners of the copyright of this book strongly recommend you use your own judgment in following any activities, recommendations, or advice in your unique situation and do so strictly at your own risk. Always consult your doctor or health care provider where appropriate, and especially in regard to the appropriateness of any physical activities. By voluntarily choosing to undertake any activity, recommendation, or advice provided, you assume all risk and responsibility connected to that choice including any resulting physical, mental, emotional, or spiritual consequences. In no event will the author, publisher, or owners of the copyright of this book, or their related partners, agents, or employees be liable to you or anyone else for any decision made, actions taken, or results obtained in reliance on the information, recommendations, advice, or activities in this book or for any consequential, special, or similar damages, even if advised of the possibility of such damages.

Join our 4D Parents Facebook group at
4Dparents | Facebook.

You'll meet like-minded parents who are interested in raising their children in a positive way. Some parents have questions and other parents have answers. You are invited to join the conversation.

You can also follow us on Instagram at
(@4dparents) • Instagram photos and videos

and Twitter @4Dparents.

You are not alone!

Contents

Introduction i

Chapter 1	**The Foundation**	p. 1
Chapter 2	**Prenatal Care**	p. 16
Chapter 3	**Infancy**	p. 39
Chapter 4	**Toddlers**	p. 73
Chapter 5	**Early Childhood**	p. 109
Chapter 6	**Childhood**	p. 147
Chapter 7	**Middle Childhood**	p. 175
Chapter 8	**Preteens**	p. 216
Chapter 9	**Adolescence**	p. 253
Chapter 10	**Closing Thoughts**	p. 290
Appendix	**Psychological Integration**	p. 292

Chapter 1
The Foundation

"any real body must have extension in four directions: It must have Length, Breadth, Thickness, and Duration."
– H. G. Wells, *The Time Machine* (1895)

The Hills are Alive with these Timely Musings

Now, children,

"Let´s start at the very beginning:
An excellent place to start!
In math you begin with 1-2-3,
but the lesson for today is geometry.

"We start with a line – and I have to mention
that LENGTH is the name of the first dimension.
The length of a line can be short or long,
But it has no width – that would be wrong.

"When you add width, it's no longer a line,
it becomes a shape of any design:
A square, or a circle, it's all just the same,
as long as it's flat, it lives on a plane.

Raising 4 Dimensional Children in a 2 Dimensional World

*"And now you begin to see my intention,
that WIDTH is the name of the second dimension.*

*"A shape, a picture, or something between,
even add motion like a movie scene,
on a tablet, computer, a phone, or TV,
the image you see is just 2-D.*

*"No matter what screen or picture you see,
The fact is: It isn't reality.
It's just a way to represent
Something to a lesser extent.*

*"The real world requires one more extension,
and DEPTH is the name of the third dimension.*

*"The physical world isn't just flat,
there's a lot more to it than just that.
Instead of a square or a circle, you see,
It's a cube, or a globe, in full 3-D.*

*"Length and width and depth combined,
give you experience much more refined.
But any object in all creation,
must be experienced with duration.*

*"Seconds, or minutes, or hours in succession:
TIME is the name of the fourth dimension.*

The Foundation

*"You can't see, hear, feel, taste, or smell
something that doesn't last for a spell.
Unless it stays enough to perceive,
It doesn't exist in a way we believe.*

*"And this is the point of this life intervention:
Enjoy the world in all 4 dimensions.
Put down the phone and turn off the screen,
and break out of your old routine."*

Let's Start at the Very Beginning
(an excellent place to start!)

Who are You?

Did you answer with your name? Or maybe with what you do? John, Maria, a lawyer, or a musician, is only the outer layer of who you are. You can go to court and change your name, or change your profession, but that just changes the label you wear – like changing a shirt – it doesn't change the YOU inside. I want to peel back the layers and go a lot deeper.

So who are YOU, really?

This is a very important question that drills right down to the purpose and meaning of your life. Before you can wonder, "Why do I exist?" you really have to find out, "Who is it that exists?"

What makes you "YOU" and not someone else?

You might say you are the person whose eyes are reading these words, so you are defining YOU by your body – the body that can change his name, change her career, or change shirts.

Raising 4 Dimensional Children in a 2 Dimensional World

It's probably legally sound and pretty obvious to most people that YOU can be defined by your body. Your legal rights begin and end with your body. Anything outside your skin is not you, and anything inside your skin is you. That seems to make sense, but I think we need to peel back another layer and go deeper.

Does your body define who you are?

What happens if you get into an automobile accident and lose an arm or a leg? Would you still be you? If you dye your hair a different color, or gain 40 pounds, maybe get plastic surgery, or even get an organ transplant . . . are you still YOU?

Obviously, you can experience a wide variety of physical changes, and they can certainly affect your life, but they don't define YOU. Even if you could surgically change your fingerprints, you might change your legal identity, but you wouldn't really change the YOU we are talking about. So, I believe it's safe to say that YOU are not just a body with changeable physical attributes. I think we need to peel back another layer and go deeper.

Does your mind define who you are?

Maybe you say it is your mind, or consciousness. You are YOU when you are self-aware: When you realize that you are separate from the rest of the world.

OK, but what happens when you sleep? You are no longer conscious. Are you no longer YOU?

What happens if an auto accident causes brain damage? What if you grow old and suffer from Alzheimer's? Do these changes in your mind cause you to no longer exist or become someone else?

No, just like YOU can experience physical changes, the same YOU can experience mental changes and keep your individual identity. You are not just a mind with changeable mental abilities. I think we need to peel back another layer and go even deeper.

The Foundation

Do your feelings define who you are?

If a mistake makes you angry, or someone you love makes you happy, do you change your identity? Once again, YOU are separate from these emotions that you experience.

Whatever it is that is YOU is deeper than your body, deeper than your mind, and deeper than your emotions. What can we call that inner core? Through the ages, people have called it your spirit.

Without getting religious, the part of you that remains constant in the face of physical, mental, and emotional changes is your spirit. It is not physical, not mental, nor emotional. It is separate. For those of you who say, "OK, where is it? Let me touch it." I say, "OK, where is thought? Where is love? Can you touch them?"

The concepts of right or wrong and good or evil live in the moral domain of the spirit. I propose we are not bodies with a spirit, but rather spirits with a body that lives (for a time) in a physical world.

Your spirit experiences physical, mental, and emotional changes, which do have an effect on it, and therefore change it. As long as you are alive, you remain YOU, even though your body, mind, emotions, and even spirit can change during your life.

But can the spirit die? If not, what happens to it after death? Now we ARE getting religious, and I'm not going there. Your religious beliefs are yours to hold. I won't argue with them.

The bottom line is that YOU are not just the physical body, the mental processes, the emotional experiences, but the spirit that endures all of these changes. In short, there are 4 dimensions that make up who you are, each wrapped around the others in layers. None is sufficient to define who you are. It requires all 4 dimensions to make up a whole, living person.

Raising 4 Dimensional Children in a 2 Dimensional World

Dimensia

How do we experience the world? There are many ways to answer that question, but one direction we could follow is to describe the world in dimensions. Most of the time people will say we live in a three dimensional world, but I agree with H. G. Wells that it is a four dimensional world.

Let's review some basic Geometry:

A two dimensional world goes in two directions – length and width. The images on a television screen, on a computer monitor, tablet, or cell phone are two dimensional. Look at any image on the device of your choice: It has length and width. It appears to represent something in the real world, but it has no depth, not even 1/100 of an inch, because it is only a point of light on the screen. Every image on a television, computer, tablet, or cell phone screen is two dimensional, even 3-D TVs and video games have no real depth – they just trick your eyes into seeing the images as if they had depth. A good picture may look realistic and life-like, but any depth is just an optical illusion.

Depth is the third dimension, and that's what separates reality from the images on a screen. Real objects have depth. A square is two-dimensional. When you add depth, the square becomes a cube.

Most people agree that we live in a three dimensional world. In his book, *The Time Machine*, H.G. Wells proposed there is a fourth dimension to reality and that is duration (time). In order for things to exist in the real world, they have to be consistent from one second to the next, over time. Real world objects, including people, exist in four dimensions: length, width, depth, and duration.

I suspect everything I have explained so far is just a review of common knowledge. If you are smarter than a fifth grader, you may have already understood all of these ideas completely, or you may have known many of the different parts, and had never put them together quite in the way I've explained it. The important point is that these observations are self-evident – not a revelation, not a new invention of mine, just common sense.

A New Perspective

What may be a new idea to you is that human beings are four dimensional in two ways: One way is that we all have length, width, depth, and duration. The other way is that we have four dimensions of our being: Physical, mental, emotional, and spiritual. Although your body does not define who you are, you are definitely affected by it. You are a physical being that can be injured by accident or disease. You are a mental being who can learn and grow. You are an emotional being who can love or hate. You are a spiritual being who can do right or wrong, and all of these aspects affect who you become.

Now, let's move on to the focus of this book: Education. Specifically, how do we raise four-dimensional children in an increasingly two-dimensional world?

I believe that our modern world is becoming more and more two-dimensional as people spend a larger percentage of their lives in front of television screens, tablets, smart phones, and computers. According to Gregory Caremans, founder of the Brain Academy, young children spend an average of over three hours, 8- to 12-year-olds an average of over four and a half hours, and teens spend an average of over seven hours a DAY of screen time on ENTERTAINMENT.[1] That's outside the amount of time they spend on schoolwork or doing homework. Peer pressure keeps them glued to their cell phones while the gray matter in the brain begins to atrophy, they lose white matter integrity, their brains experience reduced cortical thickness, and their cognitive functions are impaired. Screen time has also been linked to obesity, lower brain development, and lower language acquisition in preschoolers, and depression in adolescents.[2]

I believe that ideas tend to move like a pendulum, and the use

Raising 4 Dimensional Children in a 2 Dimensional World

of technology has gone from the one extreme (literally 0 technology), to where we are now (just past the bottom point of the equilibrium), and has begun to rise to the opposite extreme of maximum technology (we are not even close, yet.) My goal is to make you aware of the trend and hopefully pull you back to a more balanced place where you can coax your kids off the screen and back into the real world! Technology has its place and use, but must be only one tool of many in a balanced life. Machines are wonderful servants, but terrible masters.

Because we are living in an increasingly two-dimensional world, I also believe that we need to educate ourselves and our children in all four dimensions: Not only the length, width, depth, and duration of the real world beyond a flat screen monitor, but also in the physical, mental, emotional, and spiritual dimensions of the human experience. Most people approach education from only one dimension, and that is usually mental. Schools are considered academic, in that they are designed to assist in your mental development. Test scores like the SAT measure mathematical and verbal ability. Most schools admit there is more to life than academics by offering a few required units of Physical Education, but the requirements are definitely unbalanced, with many schools barely offering courses in art and music, if at all. Good luck finding classes on managing emotions or morality.

Actually, I believe much of our education system is just plain outdated. During the agricultural revolution, society developed the apprenticeship model of education, where parents would either train their children in the family profession (where we got family names like Farmer or Miller), or send their children to a guild, where they learned a trade through hands-on training. An apprentice would work under the guidance of a master until he gained the skill of a journeyman, and eventually became a master himself. There were no classrooms, just guided work experience.

During the industrial revolution, society needed workers to work the assembly line. Students attended schools where they sat in straight rows of desks, and everyone learned how to do the same thing at the same time. The teacher lectured the students with the goal of creating carbon copies of the current workers, so that the children would fit into the industrial machine like perfect little cogs. The system itself is just the assembly line method applied to education!

Now that we have moved into the information age, the needs of our society no longer match the models of the previous generations. Of course, there is still value to the master/student relationship, and there is a place for classroom learning, but neither model is sufficient in the information age. Instead of developing skills one person at a time or creating classrooms of clones who will be happy to spend their lives on an assembly line, we need creative individuals who can solve the problems in an ever more complex world. If you have been keeping up with current events, those problems are not merely academic problems, but physical problems, emotional problems, and even spiritual problems.

So, if our current school systems are not really designed to offer a balanced four-dimensional education, what's a mother to do?

Accept responsibility. Education begins at home, and really begins with ourselves. Adults must accept responsibility for their own four dimensional education, and for the four dimensional education of their children. It is my goal to show you how, and to make it easy.

The Physical Dimension

The physical dimension is associated with our bodies. There are two aspects:

1. the building blocks, and
2. the processes.

In the physical dimension, the **building blocks** are what we put into our bodies. Please notice I did not say "food" or even "what we eat." Most of us put a lot of things into our bodies that aren't really food – take smoking and drinking alcohol as common examples. The old saying, "You are what you eat," is based in the scientific observation that we rebuild our bodies on a regular basis, cell by cell, and our only source of materials are the things we put in our bodies. It just makes sense that if you use quality ingredients, you will get a quality product. Likewise, if you use junk, it should be no surprise that you will get junk: Garbage in, garbage out.

We need to educate ourselves and our children as to what is a quality ingredient, so that we can choose the right ingredients to build a quality body. Children learn to eat what their parents eat, and most of us have fond memories of our mother's cooking. We need to establish family traditions and fond memories of healthy eating to serve us better in later life. How many times have you heard an overweight adult talk about how their parents fed them sweets when they were upset as a child, and they learned to associate these unhealthy sweets with feeling better. Later in life, they have become overweight slaves to these "comfort foods." Why perpetuate this unhealthy cycle?

In the physical dimension, one of the most common **processes** is called exercise. There are many different kinds of exercise, with different goals, but the goal of each one is to improve our bodies through the practice effect. When we practice exercises that require strength, our bodies adapt by gaining strength. When we practice exercises that require endurance, coordination, flexibility, or rhythm, our bodies adapt by improving in each of those areas. A balanced physical education program would include learning how to develop each of the different kinds of exercise, and then making exercise a habit.

Another aspect of our physical **processes** is the release of various chemicals into our systems. Some of these processes are hormonal, which may be connected with our emotions, and others are rhythmical, which are commonly known as biorhythms. We need to understand how these processes work, in order to keep them from controlling us, and maybe learn to control them.

Clearly there's more to physical education than playing softball in gym class.

The Mental Dimension

The mental dimension is usually associated with the brain and our thoughts. Like the body, there are the two aspects:

The Foundation

1. the building blocks, and
2. the processes.

In the mental dimension the **building blocks** are our thoughts. The older we get, the more power we have to choose the thoughts and images we put into our minds. We literally feed our minds with the experiences we choose for ourselves and our children. If we choose to read holy scriptures consistently, those thoughts and images feed our minds. Likewise, if we choose to watch porn or play violent video games, those images become the building blocks of our minds.

However, there is another important issue: Digital apps and programs are <u>designed</u> to grab our attention and hold it with a series of dopamine releases. Dopamine is a "feel good" hormone, so every time you get a point, reach a goal, or kill an enemy, your brain releases a small amount of dopamine. These little "highs" occur far more often online than in our four dimensional world, and literally create an addiction to gaming. In comparison, reality can become "totally boring" . . . by design. In addition, the blue light emitted by the screens interrupts sleep and that doesn't even take into account the fact in many video games you have to kill everyone else to win. How's that for food for thought?

The **processes** are somewhat controlled by the different areas of the brain, but a process is really a learned habit that can be changed. We can learn to think in different ways through practice. Although we cannot completely control what thoughts pop up in our minds, but we can choose how much energy or attention we devote to them. There is an old joke of a teen boy who approaches his pastor privately and says, "Father, I have been having impure thoughts." The reverend asks, "Have you entertained them?" to which the boy replies, "No, Father, they entertained me."

The brain is plastic – which means it learns to function in certain patterns through practice. When you "entertain" thoughts, you encourage them by dwelling on them over and over. It is simply the practice effect. If you allow yourself to be entertained by impure, negative, or evil thoughts, and become comfortable in those thought patterns, you actually ingrain that pattern into your brain. The more you practice thinking a certain way, the better you get at doing it because you actually program your brain to work that way, and it becomes a habit. Likewise, the more intention you put into positive, generous, or good thoughts, the more you will program your brain to think that way out of habit. Which way would you like your child to develop?

Although mathematical and verbal abilities are important predictors of success in college, there is certainly more to mental education than the scores on popular tests.

The Emotional Dimension

The emotional dimension is usually associated with the heart and our feelings. Like the previous dimensions, there are two aspects:
1. the building blocks, and
2. the processes.

In the emotional dimension the **building blocks** are our feelings. Feelings rarely just blow in like the wind. They are usually a response to a stimulus, triggered by things we see, hear, smell, feel, taste, or think. Like our thoughts, the older we get, the more control we gain over the triggers of our feelings, and the more control we can exercise on the feelings we invite into our hearts. We can choose which people and experiences we allow to stimulate our lives on a daily basis to provide the building blocks of our emotions.

The **processes** are also like our thoughts in that they are the results of habits. Something can happen that triggers a feeling, but there are many possible responses, and several steps that we can choose to intensify that feeling or reduce it.

Thoughts and feelings are often confused because certain thoughts cause specific feelings, and those feelings create more reactive thoughts. That second round of thoughts create new, more intense feelings, that encourage additional thoughts. They literally feed on each other. Add to that the physical dimension, where we release hormones to intensify the feeling, and it doesn't take long to work ourselves into an emotional frenzy.

These processes are habits that have been developed. Specific behaviors like the reactions to triggers were probably modeled to us by our parents, teachers, or other people we wanted to imitate. We simply learned their pattern of response to a stimulus.

For example, parents who smoke will often find that children copy what they do, not what they say. When they tell their children, "Don't smoke: It's bad for you," they soon discover that emotional education, in the form of behavior modeling, is much more powerful than mental education, in the form of lectures.

Currently there is no formal process for emotional education; it is achieved through modeling behavior in various live social groups like families, schools, and friends, and in vicarious social groups revealed in stories through books, video games, television shows, and movies.

How would you rate the choices you are making in behaviors you model for your children?

The Spiritual Dimension

The spiritual dimension is associated with matters of morality, and deals in beliefs about right and wrong. Like the previous dimensions, there are two aspects:
1. the building blocks, and
2. the processes.

The **building blocks** are the beliefs we hold. These could be religious beliefs as taught to us by any formal religion, or just personal convictions guided by our own conscience. These beliefs can change over time and due to various experiences. One of the goals of education is to constantly revise these beliefs as we learn more, to make them more accurate or more encompassing.

The **processes** involve three steps:
1. awareness,
2. evaluation, and
3. intention.

Raising 4 Dimensional Children in a 2 Dimensional World

It is the job of the spirit to make moral decisions. The first step is awareness. We must become aware that something is happening that raises a moral question. For example, a simple stimulus-response reaction is not a moral question. When you feel a pain on your arm and you immediately slap that area to kill a mosquito, that is a stimulus-response reaction. It only becomes a moral question when you perceive that it is a moral question. Until you become aware that you killed something that was alive, and you question whether that is right or wrong, it is just stimulus-response reaction – an instinct.

Once you perceive that a moral question has been raised, you step out of the instinctual behavior of animals into the spiritual dimension of humans to make an evaluation. Is it right or wrong to kill the mosquito? You compare the current perception to your current beliefs and seek to understand what principles apply. You then might propose a new interpretation (a refinement) of your beliefs. Some people believe all life is sacred (all lives matter) and would condemn the killing. Other people believe self-defense is always justified and would continue to protect themselves with a clear conscience. You can make your own evaluation to accept or reject this new proposition based on your own beliefs. My goal is to raise your awareness of what constitutes a moral question, and how you make moral decisions.

The final step is intention, which you can express in action or inaction. After you decide on the morality of killing mosquitoes, you must adapt your intention to your (perhaps new) belief. If you have recently changed your belief system to consider killing mosquitoes as immoral, then you could choose inaction by making the conscious decision never to slap a biting mosquito again – you could become the bloodmobile for hungry mosquitoes! Alternately, you could choose action, like spraying yourself with insect repellent to avoid the need to kill. You might even take your intention a step farther and become a mosquito activist, dedicated to raising the consciousness of humanity over this heinous crime against nature. Once again, the point is not what you believe about mosquitoes, but how you determine what is and what is not a question of morality, and how you change your behavior after making this determination.

The Foundation

Formal religions have done an excellent job throughout the ages of providing moral guidance for people in the spiritual dimension. From the study of ancient scriptures, to modern rites and celebrations, we have a wealth of opportunities for spiritual education. Unfortunately, people don't always draw the best conclusions from their education, and many crimes and wars have been justified by religious interpretations.

Turning the Page

Now that I have laid out the vocabulary and grammar used in this book, we can proceed together. Unless we start on the same page, and unless we speak the same language, it will be hard to communicate. Once we have a common understanding, we can develop a dialog.

I do not expect you to believe everything I tell you. I've done my best to cite research that backs up my recommendations, but I actually encourage you to question everything I say, think about it deeply, and draw your own conclusions. If you are in the field of education or psychology, I encourage you to design research to prove me right or wrong. My goal is to present a different way to look at the education of our children, which will require either action or inaction on your part. If you accept what I propose, I trust you will take the appropriate action in furthering your own education and the education of your children. If you disagree with what I propose, you can easily choose inaction, and my ideas will quietly fade away without notice. I have provided the awareness and raised the question. It is up to you to provide the evaluation and intention.

References

1. Caremans, Gregory. *"Neuroscience and Parenting."* https://www.udemy.com/course/neuroscience-and-parenting/. Unit 5, section 31. Accessed March 29, 2021.
2. *Ibid.*

Chapter 2

Prenatal Care

"It was the best of times, it was the worst of times, it was the age of wisdom, it was the age of foolishness, it was the epoch of belief, it was the epoch of incredulity, it was the season of light, it was the season of darkness, it was the spring of hope, it was the winter of despair, we had everything before us, we had nothing before us . . ."
— A Tale of Two Cities *by Charles Dickens*

A Tale of Two Kitties

Kitty Kat was a topless dancer at the Platinum Club who found herself pregnant . . . but not as you might think. She was in a secure relationship and didn't sleep around. She was faithful to her boyfriend, Karl, and he was to her, but somehow they managed to be in the 1% of people who use birth control pills that were 99% effective. Some people are just lucky.

Kitty Wadsworth was a socialite at the Country Club who also found herself pregnant . . . but also not as you might think. She didn't know who the father was as she was not in a consistent relationship and usually was too intoxicated to be concerned with birth control.

For Kitty and Karl, it was the best of times but the worst of times in that they loved one another, but they weren't ready to have a child because they couldn't afford one. Kitty made good money, but Karl was an unemployed musician. They knew that when Kitty started to show, she would lose her job and their income.

Prenatal Care

How would they survive? How could they support the child?

Kitty Wadsworth was the daughter of the Dallas Wadsworths, conservative pillars of the Baptist Church. For her it was the season of light because she was financially secure and her parents would take care of her and the baby, but it was the season of darkness because she didn't want a baby, and abortion was not an option for the Dallas Wadsworths. Up until now, in rebellion to her strict upbringing, she lived a wild life at her parents' expense. It seemed it was time to pay the piper.

Kitty Kat was not a big drinker. When she mixed with the customers, the waitresses knew to bring her non-alcoholic drinks, so it wasn't a big stretch for her to stop drinking for the baby. Neither she nor Karl smoked, and thanks to the anti-smoking laws, there wasn't any smoke in the club. Cleaning up her act for the baby didn't take much. Her challenge was going to be dealing with the financial stress of having a baby.

Kitty Wadsworth was depressed. She smoked like a chimney, drank like a fish, and took fashionable drugs to escape from the horrible life she somehow imagined she lived (of course, thousands of girls in Dallas wished they could suffer the way she did, in a mansion equipped with luxury cars, wearing the finest jewelry and clothes, and being catered to by servants – on Facebook, it looked like she lived the perfect life.) Because the cigarettes, alcohol, and other drugs were her coping mechanisms, there was little hope she would give them up for a baby she didn't want. Some people just think they are unlucky.

Karl decided to put aside his aspirations of becoming the next rock star and got a job in construction. He had no skills, so he had to do the hardest labor, and the income was only about half of what Kitty was earning at the club, but they began saving as much as they could before she lost her job. He worked days and she worked nights, but they did what they had to do for each other. They were united by love and by purpose.

Kitty Wadsworth began fighting with her parents. They wanted to know who the father was, and she really didn't know. That was an embarrassment to the family name. They started suggesting old boyfriends and sons of friends as possible husbands. Lots of fine young men would love to marry a beautiful, rich girl like her and the baby must have a father. That kind of talk only made Kitty feel more unworthy, which increased her depression, and increased her consumption of coping mechanisms. They were getting ready to "send her away" to have the baby quietly (and perhaps to a re-hab facility.) She couldn't stand that, so she went to the bank, withdrew $20,000.00, and took off on her own in her BMW.

Now, my question to you is, **"Which baby has a better chance in life?"**

The baby who is born in poverty to two healthy parents who are struggling but love each other, or the baby born into a wealthy family who has been damaged in the womb by cigarettes, alcohol, and drugs, and whose first breath of life comes with a suite of withdrawal pains that last for at least the first week of life?

Which baby would you rather have?

Which baby would you rather be?

Some things have nothing to do with luck.

When does care for your child begin?

Whenever your actions affect the health and well-being of your child.

In most cases, the attitudes you developed in your own childhood will affect your children in the way you treat them, so the physical, mental, emotional, and moral decisions you made long before you began the baby-making act can affect your child. I am not arguing directly for or against the doctrine of *karma*, but merely pointing out the logic of the long-term effects that the decisions you make will have on your children. Although it may not seem fair from a moral point of view that the sins of the father should be visited upon the son, if a father is in prison during the developmental stages of his son's life, it has an inescapable effect. Decisions you make throughout your life will affect your children on many levels.

Especially for women, who host and actually share their body with their baby for nine months, the effects of the physical dimension are easy to see. The body they have built over the months and years before conception will provide the building blocks for the new baby. Traces of drugs, alcohol, or nicotine that remain in the body since before the time of conception still affect the woman's body after conception, and therefore the development of the child. Her overall level of fitness and health will affect the growth of the baby, as will her diet, and the release of hormones that flow through not only her body, but the developing body of the baby at the same time.

So, let's get down to a game plan. What can you do?

First of all, you owe it to yourself to be the best you can be physically, mentally, emotionally, and spiritually. Get your own life in balance and get yourself healthy before you start planning to raise a family.

Just for a moment, think about it like a business: If your business is losing money, why in the world would you want to open a second location using the same business model? The second location will lose money just like the first, so your brilliant plan of expansion helps you lose twice as much money as just one location. Having a baby is basically opening a second location for your life. If your life is successful, you can hope to help another human being develop a successful life. If your life is a disaster, what kind of life can you hope to provide for the child you are bringing into the mess you are living?

Raising 4 Dimensional Children in a 2 Dimensional World

The well-planned life:

So, if you are actually planning your life, **step one** is to be the best you can be. Take action to become healthy physically, mentally, emotionally, and spiritually, which is a life-long quest. You can't wait until you have finished the project (you'll be dead), but at least set a reasonable timeline where you have invested enough time and energy in getting your own life in order before you start planning someone else's life.

Step two is to find a partner who is healthy and balanced. The more successful you are in your own quest for personal development, the more attractive you become to the opposite sex, and the better chance you will have of attracting a mate whose life is in relative balance, too. Beware of making your choice solely on sexual attraction: Falling in love (or in lust) accounts for only one dimension of your relationship. A long-term commitment will require multi-dimensional love.

Step three is to establish a stable home where both of you settle into a life with good habits. Societal convention is to get married as a formal way of committing yourselves to each other and to the mission of raising children. The reason the institution of marriage has survived for thousands of years across many cultures and continents is that it works. It is not an absolute requirement to raise children, but it is the most successful model we have come across in human history. People have tried other ways to raise children successfully, but the enduring model of success is the family. The choice is yours, but why not follow the plan that works?

Step four is to prepare for the act. I am not aware of any research that tracks the relationship between the emotional state during the act of conception and the result it has on the development of the child, but why take the chance? If you have accepted the premise that human beings have an emotional and spiritual dimension, why not put those dimensions to work in your favor while making the baby? Be as giving, loving, and generous as you can, making love and making the baby the result of love. It just stands to reason that that situation would be ideal.

Now, what happens if your life isn't a perfect plan?

For most people, life is what happens while you are making other plans. So, what do you do if you find you made a baby before you believe you are really ready for it?

Well, welcome to the human race.

Chances are that you, your parents, and your grandparents were all born as a little bit of a surprise, before the parents believed they were really ready for it. Some fortunate couples actually set out to make a baby, and they can follow the plan described above. For the rest of humanity, the pregnancy may be the result of birth control that didn't work, bad judgment (possibly impaired by drugs or alcohol), or even rape. You can learn from the past, but you can't change it. You just have to deal with it.

Here's what to do:

Once you realize you are pregnant, you need to consider some changes. For example, if you consider your life a disaster, the baby may be just the reason you've been waiting for to turn your life around. You may have bad habits that include anything from drugs, to smoking, to living on a roller coaster of emotions, but you can choose to change all of that.

If you are reading this book as an expecting parent, you have already shown that you are interested in providing the best life for your baby. That life requires you to clean up your act. It's no longer just about you. Now it's about the baby, too, whether you like it or not. As the mother, everything you put into your body goes through the baby's body. Every emotion you feel and every hormone you release into your bloodstream flows through the baby, too. Every period of guilt or depression is shared with the baby, essentially training the baby to feel that way. So, let's get all that under control to provide the best environment for your baby.

Raising 4 Dimensional Children in a 2 Dimensional World

Physically

People generally agree that quitting a chemical dependency cold turkey is extremely difficult for adults. Just imagine what it would be like for a baby to be born to a mother addicted to cocaine, alcohol, or even nicotine. Her first experience of the world, of being separated from the warmth and security of her mother's womb, is a week of withdrawal symptoms. The baby has no knowledge of the cause of the pain, nor what to do to make it go away. All she can learn is that the world, and this new life, is not a very pleasant experience. How hard will it be to help the baby feel secure when her first week of life was ruled by constant craving, shakes, and pain? This is a difficult recipe for success.

Now compound that with physical developmental problems caused by the chemicals. The National Institute of Drug Abuse cites several experiments that document that babies born of mothers addicted to drugs can be physically smaller, have a smaller head size, may be born prematurely, and have different learning abilities than babies born of mothers not addicted to drugs.[3] You can find dangers such as still birth and lasting consequences for lung and brain function of your baby when you smoke during pregnancy on the American Lung Association website.[4] Drinking alcohol has its own set of issues that have been named Fetal Alcohol Spectrum Disorders (FASD) and include mental retardation, birth defects of the skeleton or major organs, and nervous system problems.[5] Add to that the recent evidence that adverse physical and psychological traumas can be passed down to future generations,[6] and you begin to understand the enormous effects your choices have not only on your child, but possibly her children.

Even marijuana, which is becoming legal in many states, has been shown to cause long-term issues with cognitive and executive functioning,[7] and THC, the psychoactive component, has been found to linger in breast milk 6 weeks after the mother's last use.[8] Just because it's legal, doesn't mean it's healthy for you or your baby.

If it is within your power to take these pains and handicaps away from your baby, what kind of a parent would you be if you were unwilling to do it? All you have to do is clean up your act – quit smoking, quit drinking, quit doing drugs, and both you and the baby have a new beginning. If you ever had a reason to change your life, this is it!

Although these addictive substances are the worst things you can do to your developing baby, if you are not addicted to drugs, and maybe just a social drinker or smoker, the same reasons apply, and it should be a no-brainer for you to quit.

In addition to these obvious changes, take a closer look at the other chemicals you are putting on and in your body. Makeup, nail polish, cleaning supplies, sunscreens, and even water can contain chemicals dangerous to a developing baby. Something is definitely going on in our modern society that is changing our children: In 1990s, 1 in 2,500 children were diagnosed on the autism spectrum.[9] According to the CDC, in 2014 (the most recent figures I could find) it was roughly 1 in 59.[10] Granted, we have probably changed the criteria for diagnosis, but not THAT much. I'm not suggesting that any of the following chemicals directly cause autism or any other disease or disorder, but I am recommending you consider cleaning up your personal environment the best you can to reduce the toxic bucket that may affect your baby.

For example, the California Safe Cosmetics Program website shows that since 2009, 604 cosmetics manufacturers have reported using chemicals in more than 85,000 products that have been known or suspected of causing cancer or reproductive harm,[11] and those numbers are updated regularly, so they may be larger by the time you read this.

Some of these chemicals can find their way into your breast milk,[12] so even after your baby is born, you could be passing on toxins.

What can you do about it? Fair warning: Researching all the toxic chemicals in our modern environment is a rabbit hole that once you go down, you may never come back out the same. They are everywhere! Just don't get overwhelmed. Educate yourself on the most dangerous and easiest to avoid by searching the internet for "toxins during pregnancy" on sites like https://theperfectpregnancyplan.com/toxins-to-avoid-during-pregnancy/. Make a plan to start eliminating or at least reducing them, step-by-step. Just because you can't avoid everything doesn't mean you shouldn't avoid something. I recommend focusing on one major source of toxins each week to make it manageable, but you can take it at whatever pace suits your personality.

Here are some recommendations:

1. **Pesticides** and other actual poisons. Stop using them on or near your body and search for natural alternatives if you have a serious bug problem that must be addressed. Wash all non-organic fruits and vegetables in water and vinegar, as they may have been sprayed with pesticides before you bought them.
2. **Mercury.** Mercury is common in large fish as well as in some mascaras.[13] Eating fish, especially for the Omega 3 content, is important during pregnancy, so don't necessarily avoid all fish, just the really big ones. There are natural mascaras that don't contain mercury, but they don't give you the maximum volume. I believe that is a sacrifice you can endure.
3. **Lead.** Many public water supplies have lead leaching from the pipes into your drinking, cooking, and bathing water. Get a report from your water utility and consider investing in a filter. Bottled water is not a great alternative as plastic bottles may leach BPAs. Lead can also be found in some toys made overseas and in the paint in homes built before 1978. Do what you can to protect your child from lead both during pregnancy and after birth.
4. **BPAs.** Bisphenol A is a hormone disruptor that can affect both your own and your baby's hormones.[14] BPAs are common in plastic containers and food cans are often lined with BPAs. They leach into food when heated, so get drastic with plastic: Avoid buying or storing food in plastic containers whenever possible, and never microwave food in a plastic container.
5. **Phthalates.** Phthalates (the Ph is silent) are also hormone disruptors that can alter gene expression[15] and cognitive outcomes[16] in your baby, and are common in plastics and

Prenatal Care

commercial beauty products like nail polish, hair sprays, and many artificial fragrances. Reduce or avoid using perfumes, air fresheners, scented candles, scented shampoos, laundry detergents, and especially dryer sheets unless you can determine they are phthalate free – and understand that most companies do not have to reveal the contents of their fragrances, so if it says "fragrance" it may contain phthalates or other undesirable chemicals.

6. **PFCs**. Perfluorinated chemicals (PFCs) are used on plastic coated nonstick cookware and in some anti-aging skin products.[17] Polytetrafluoroethylene (PTFE) can leach from your cookware into your food when scratched or heated above 325°, and perfluorooctanoate (PFOA) can also leach into your food, possibly contributing to a variety of growth issues for your baby.[18] Stop using your nonstick cookware if you can – at least during your pregnancy. Stainless steel is a good alternative.

7. **Parabens**. Several parabens are banned in Europe,[19] but some are common in cosmetics and hygiene products sold in the US. They act like estrogen in the body and disrupt your hormones.[20] Look for ingredients like methylparaben, butylparaben, or anything else that contains the word paraben in the name.

Start your research by reading labels but understand that the US Government allows the multi-billion dollar cosmetic industry to regulate itself, and they have no legal obligation to test for safety.[21] Most fragrances fall under the heading of trade secrets and do not have to be revealed or identified. Also realize the terms *natural* or *organic* can be misleading in that they may contain only one natural or organic ingredient to qualify. Look for USDA Certified Organic products to be sure they contain only organic ingredients. Once again, just because it's legal doesn't mean it's healthy for you or your baby.

Another potentially dangerous influence that many people don't realize is the effect of EMFs and wireless communications on the developing baby. Some of the studies show clear developmental problems on mice, but there are others that do show significant issues on human babies – even from extensive cell phone use.[22] Why take a chance? Keep your cell phone, tablet, and laptop away from your body

and your baby just to be safe. You can read more about it at https://www.babysafeproject.org/science.
   Also realize that children and developing fetuses can be more susceptible to the effects of these toxins than full grown adults. Just because you haven't noticed the effects of these toxins on yourself doesn't mean your baby won't be affected.

   On a more positive note, you need to eat healthy foods. By healthy, I mean natural. Anything packaged in cans or plastics is subject to the chemical issues listed a above, so eating raw fruits and vegetables or cooking fresh food is the preferred recommendation. Fast food is usually not health food, so try to avoid it. I know it's going to be hard to make dramatic lifestyle changes, so do whatever you can as often as you can. You don't have to be perfect to do better.
   Pregnant women should gain about 20% of their ideal weight (which would be 26 pounds for a 130-pound woman) to insure healthy growth for their baby. Don't stuff yourself, but don't starve yourself either. That requirement generally translates to about 300 extra calories a day, including 10 to 12 extra grams of protein.[23] You should also probably take a prenatal vitamin or at least a good multivitamin as certain vitamins like folic acid have been shown to reduce neural tube defects by as much as 60%.[24] You might even take some additional Vitamin D, as low levels of vitamin D have been linked to autism and even schizophrenia.[25] In addition, make sure you are getting plenty of iron and Omega 3 acids, because your baby will need both from your breast milk, so "pre-load" your supply. Generally, listen to your body. Your cravings are probably your body telling you what it needs. If you eat too little in an attempt to keep your girlish figure, your baby may be pre-programmed for a scarcity of food. When she is born into a healthy family with adequate food, her pre-programming may lead to obesity as her body built itself to survive on minimum nutrition.
   An interesting side note is that later in the pregnancy your baby will taste and smell the foods you put into your body. Your baby will be born with a predisposition, created by what you eat during pregnancy, to like what you eat.[26]

Prenatal Care

If you haven't thought about it yet, you will need some bigger clothes as your pregnancy progresses. Stretchy leggings will come in handy, but especially if you are working, you will need something reasonably stylish. If you can't afford a whole new wardrobe, consider buying used clothing at yard sales, consignment stores, or thrift stores. You will need the clothes for only a short while, so you may not be able to justify the expense of new ones. If you are beginning to see varicose veins or feel pressure from increased blood volume, consider getting compression socks or compression leggings.

Also, exercise regularly. Consult your doctor or other health care provider as to the best forms of exercise for you and your baby, but just remember: You are not training for the Olympics, you are just trying to keep yourself as healthy as possible in order to keep your baby as healthy as possible. Get off the couch but delay the "iron woman" training until after the baby is born.

If you are having trouble sleeping, especially later in the adventure, a pregnancy pillow can offer some relief. Pillows you have around the house can help you see if the pillow will help, but sleep is so important that the small investment in a practical pillow designed for your needs may be worth it.

Mentally

Read as much as you can about pregnancy, childbirth, and caring for your infant. You want to be as prepared as possible for what you are facing on a day-to-day basis, but also thinking ahead to what you will need to know in the near future.

A nice idea is to start a journal, where you write down your thoughts, feelings, and questions. This journal can become a treasure to share with your child when she gets older. It might also be extremely useful when speaking with your doctor, to help you remember which questions to ask.

At about 7 months into the pregnancy, begin to attend birthing classes like Lamaze, the Bradley Method, the Alexander Technique, or even HypnoBirthing. You can research all of these options and more, and discuss them with your doctor, but a good place to start is WebMD.[27] Make a birthing plan: Your doctor probably has a form to fill out with your preferences during labor and childbirth, plus make a personal plan that includes a packed bag for the hospital, a list of phone numbers you need to call, transportation to the hospital, etc. When the time comes, it will probably happen fast, so you want to grab-and-go instead of trying to figure out what to do and what to bring.

      One specific decision you want to consider in advance is the choice between natural birth and a cesarean section. My recommendation is natural whenever possible, but definitely talk it over with your doctor because each case is different and can change rapidly during childbirth. There are too many circumstances to discuss effectively in this chapter, so search the Internet for more information, especially on a site like https://www.birthinjuryguide.org/2019/04/doctors-c-section-natural-birth/.

      Another decision you might consider in advance, if you choose a c-section (or you end up needing one during the delivery), is whether or not to "seed" the baby. When the baby passes through the vagina, it gets coated with the mother's vaginal secretions, which contain bacteria that help the baby's digestive and immune systems develop. Research has shown that c-section babies tend to have different microbiomes than babies born vaginally.[28] Some parents have chosen to "seed" a baby born through c-section by gathering vaginal secretions from the mother and immediately wiping the newborn baby with them. Current research has yet to show a clear benefit to this practice, so you will want to do some up-to-date research on your own and discuss it with your doctor, especially if you have something like syphilis or herpes that may be spread to the baby in the seeding process. Learn more at https://www.whattoexpect.com/pregnancy/c-section-seeding.

      It's also a good idea to attend parenting classes, when available, to learn the basics of childcare from a person, rather than a book or tablet. You are bound to have a hundred questions about childbirth, feeding, sleeping, and more, and it's great to have an experienced person to answer those questions and the other ones you didn't realize you should ask. If you can afford it, look into finding an experienced advisor like a doula.

Be mentally prepared to make changes. Childbirth rarely goes according to plan, so have a flexible attitude. You may have everything planned out in your head, but when the time comes, you may have more pain than you imagined, or the baby may be in the wrong position, or any of a thousand other unforeseen variables. Make up your mind ahead of time to do whatever it takes and cut yourself some slack if you (or your spouse) don't live up to your superhero expectations. You may have to improvise, adapt, and overcome. Focus on the reward (the baby), and everything else will become secondary.

One of the things many expecting mothers neglect to think about is the "fourth trimester," which is the time immediately after childbirth. In addition to making a birthing plan, you should make a postpartum plan where you not only prepare yourself, but your home and your relationships for a massive change of life. Generally, two conversations of about 40 minutes or so should be enough if you have some guidance, like that available in various articles from Kimberly Johnson on https://kimberlyannjohnson.com,[29] and especially in her book, *The Fourth Trimester*. One important note is that the mother should plan to rest for at least three weeks after the birth, so it's important for a team of others to pick up the slack on housework and her other normal responsibilities.

Emotionally

In addition to the hormones flowing through the mother's body, the baby is literally surrounded by her feelings and learning her way of reacting to the world. Granted the baby cannot see what she sees, but the baby can hear most of what she hears and feel what she feels. The baby is a sponge, learning as much as it can as fast as it can. The baby's brain is literally building itself according to the input from its mother. Through habit, the baby sets its emotional thermostat according to the mother's emotional thermostat. If peaceful and happy are the normal range for the mother, the baby will be born with peaceful and happy programming. If fearful or depressed are the normal emotions of the mother, the baby will be pre-programmed to be fearful or depressed. Too much cortisol (the stress hormone) from the mother has been shown to have negative effects on mental and motor development.[30]

Therefore, do what you can to be as happy as you can. Don't just wait to react to whatever happens in your life: Plan your day to include happy activities, positive relationships, and quiet "me time." When you fail to plan, you plan to fail. Be proactive instead of reactive to create happy times.

Take time to talk to your baby, read out loud, massage it, sing some favorite lullabies, rock or gently dance to soothing music. The time you invest now in soothing emotions can pay off greatly after your baby is born. When she cries, you can help her "return" to these happy and secure times with the same song, sounds, and rhythms.

Spiritually

If the mother has spiritual experiences through prayer, meditation, or attending religious services, the baby's spirit (and body) will be present during those events and can be born with those expectations ingrained in her spirit.

If you meditate, continue to do so. If you pray, pray out loud speaking affirmations to your baby. Read scripture, say prayers, or sing hymns that you can continue to say and sing after your baby is born. If you don't pray, simply speak positive affirmations to your baby and read positive thoughts and stories out loud in place of scriptures. Her spirit will absorb what your spirit teaches her.

What about the father?

First of all, the father needs to be present. According to (then) Senator Barak Obama in his infamous Fatherhood Speech at the Apostolic Church of God in Chicago, "children who grow up without a father are five times more likely to live in poverty and commit a crime; nine times more likely to drop out of schools, and twenty times more likely to end up in prison."[31] Those are not good odds! If you made the baby, your first job is to be there for the child – not just during the pregnancy, but for the formative years of his life.

If you are a single mother with an uncooperative father, find alternative support systems. Get emotional help from your parents, if possible. Enlist as much help and support as you can from your girlfriends. Join a group of other single mothers. Look to your church, temple, or mosque for resources. Sure, it's a lot easier with a loving husband, but sometimes no husband is better than a bad husband. You and the baby can do just fine if you need to.

Back to the father: While the mother is pregnant, you cannot continue to blow secondhand smoke into the lungs of the mother, and therefore to the baby. It's not fair. The American Lung Association clearly says that secondhand smoke can damage the baby, too.[32]

And you can't continue to be addicted to drugs or alcohol. Of course, you can rightfully say that what goes through your bloodstream does not go through the baby's bloodstream. However, your actions affect the mother. If your addiction causes her stress, anxiety, fear, or anger, all of those emotions affect the baby.

Your actions are a major contributor to the emotions of the mother. Your obligation as the father is to provide a healthy, secure environment for the mother, in order to provide a healthy, secure environment for the child. You should do whatever it takes (legally) to provide for the physical, mental, emotional, and spiritual well-being of the mother. Obviously, tobacco, drugs, and alcohol are not in her best interest, so you must quit or reduce your consumption around her for the sake of the baby. You should encourage her to eat good food and share those foods with her, to make it easier for her to follow the plan. You should not subject her to mental, emotional, or spiritual duress by doing things to upset her – whether that be yelling at her or cheating on her. You must take extra care not to do anything that will cause a flood of negative emotions to surround your baby.

Face it, her hormones will be raging enough due to the pregnancy. She will barrage you with a constant series of illogical requests (actually demands) due to cravings for specific foods, bouts with loneliness and depression, and the actual physical pain and discomfort of carrying the baby. Why push this emotional strain on the both of you to another level by being a jerk?

As a father, you can no longer be concerned about your own needs and desires first. You cannot even be primarily concerned with the needs of your wife. You now have to consider the baby's needs first, your wife's second because what happens to her happens to the baby, and that leaves your needs and desires in third place. That's how being a man is different from being a boy.

Actively plan some happy "couple time" every day, where you can just enjoy each other's company and the positive emotions of the family you are preparing to have. Plan some special treats of activities during the week like your "date night" and maybe a special little trip (a "babymoon") during the second trimester when mom still has enough energy to enjoy it. As pointed out in the mother section, don't just react to what life hands you; be proactive and create the life you want to live.

Spend some "baby time," too. The baby can hear your voice, so if you read, sing, and massage the baby while he is still in the womb, he can recognize your voice and the songs you sing after he is born.

Summary

Childcare really begins well before the moment of conception, as the mother's body already contains the building blocks that will be used for the baby's body, and the processes that assemble those raw materials. Many of the habits and attitudes of both parents that will affect the child throughout his life have already been established.

In addition, beginning at the moment of conception and continuing for the nine-month term, whatever happens to the mother, happens to the child. Both parents must be careful and take responsibility for the physical, mental, emotional, and spiritual well-being of the mother, as any chemicals or feelings that wash over the mother, wash through the child.

Prenatal Care

For the Mother:
1. Quit smoking, drinking any alcohol, and doing any drugs. If your doctor has you taking medicine, ask if you can reduce or remove that drug from your system safely during your pregnancy. Do not discontinue prescriptions on your own; follow your doctor's advice.
2. Eliminate as many toxins from your environment as you can. You probably won't get rid of them all, but the more you can avoid, the better your chances will be for a healthy baby.
3. Eat the healthiest foods you can find. Read about nutrition, take vitamin and mineral supplements, and drink plenty of water.
4. Exercise regularly. Exercise for pregnant women is different than exercise for fitness models, so consult your doctor or health care provider for appropriate exercises.
5. Learn as much as you can about prenatal care. Read books, magazines, Internet articles and websites, and watch television programs. Direct your mental effort to the goal at hand – making a healthy baby.
6. See your doctor as often as he or she recommends. Attend classes to prepare for the childbirth – learning and practicing what to do – and make a birthing plan.
7. Make a postpartum plan for yourself, your home, and your support team.
8. Try to stay calm and happy. Realize that it's bad for your baby when you get upset, so make an intentional effort not to get upset. In other words, don't sweat the small stuff – and compared to the health of your baby, it's all small stuff.
9. Continue to work if you can. Take leave when your doctor recommends or when you feel that working is hurting the health of your baby. Some women can be working in the fields, take a few hours off to have a baby, and continue working in the fields the next day. Other women have to stay in bed for months at a time to prevent a miscarriage. Use your best judgment and do whatever you have to do for the sake of the baby. Period.
10. Sing to your baby. Move rhythmically or rock in a chair. Your baby can hear and feel the motion, so sing a favorite song or

lullaby over and over when you are feeling happy and calm to create a "happy tune" that you will be able to use to calm the baby after he is born.
11. Continue your spiritual journey. Go to church, or temple, or mosque: Pray, or meditate, or do whatever you do to feed your spirit. Your spiritual well-being will help you deal with the surprises and challenges that may come up.

For the Father:
1. Quit smoking, drugs, and drinking in a way that might upset the mother. You can have a social drink without harming the baby, but if your drinking tempts the mother to drink, you are hurting more than you are helping.
2. Join in on researching how to reduce and eliminate as many of the toxins in your immediate environment as you can. Two heads are better than one.
3. Eat the healthiest foods you can, to encourage the mother to do the same. Be an active part of the team by sharing as many of the mother's projects as possible. It's not fair to eat foods she can't eat and drink drinks she can't drink. Eat healthy foods together to show her you care about her health and the health of your baby.
4. Exercise with her. If your exercise regimen requires a little more intensity, you may have to do a little extra, but be the motivator for her. As in all areas, you may have to sacrifice some of your own goals and priorities to a more important priority – the health of the baby.
5. Do your best to learn about prenatal care. You can read the same information or read separately to learn twice as much. Share what you learn and put it into practice.
6. Attend doctor appointments with the mother, if possible, but make a point to attend any birthing and childcare classes so you know what to expect and what to do. Most of the birthing plan will rely on you, so make your preparations and know your role.
7. Be part of the postpartum plan, as you will have to do a lot of extra work, but don't try to do it all. Get some help from friends

and family.
8. Do your best not to upset her, and to console her when she is upset. Chances are she will be able to find fault with the behavior of a saint while her hormones are erupting, but do your best to be that saint to reduce the stress on her and the baby. She will appreciate it when she returns to normal.
9. Plan positive time and activities to keep your connection strong.
10. Continue your spiritual journey, hopefully sharing it with the mother. Attend religious services together, pray together, and do as many things as possible to feed not only your spirit, but the spirit of the family unit you have created.

Remember that the child developing within the mother will become a human being with physical, mental, emotional, and spiritual dimensions. Pay attention to all four of these dimensions during the pregnancy to predispose the baby for a positive life after birth.

Also please use your own good judgment in following any advice I offer and consult your doctor or other health care provider at all stages of pregnancy. Research is subject to change and my advice may be based on research that has changed or been updated since this publishing. Choose your actions based on your own beliefs, experiences, research, and judgment, especially during extenuating circumstances (like a pandemic.)

Recommendations for further research:

www.zerotothree.com
www.nida.nih.gov
www.lungusa.org
www.webmd.com
www.americanpregnancy.org
www.kimberlyannjohnson.com
www.child-encyclopedia.com
https://www.babysafeproject.org/
https://parentsasteachers.org/
https://theperfectpregnancyplan.com/
https://www.babygaga.com/

https://www.bellybelly.com.au
https://www.whattoexpect.com/
https://ewg.org
https://naturalfamilyliving.com
https://fda.gov

References

3   National Institute on Drug Abuse; National Institutes of Health; US. Department of Health and Human Services. "Substance Use in Women Drug Facts." https://www.drugabuse.gov/publications/drugfacts/substance-use-in-women. Accessed May 31, 2021.

4   American Lung Association; Health Effects of Smoking and Tobacco Products. "Nicotine." https://www.lung.org/quit-smoking/smoking-facts/health-effects/nicotine. Accessed May 31, 2021.

5   American Pregnancy Association; Fetal Alcohol Syndrome. https://americanpregnancy.org/pregnancy-complications/fetal-alcohol-syndrome/. Accessed May 31, 2021.

6   Sokolowski, Marla B, PhD; and Boyce, W Thomas, MD. "Epigenetics and the Role of Developmental Time," 2017. http://www.child-encyclopedia.com/epigenetics/complete-topic, p. 23. Accessed May 31, 2021.

7   Fried, PA; Watkinson, B; and Gray, R. (1998). "Differential effects on cognitive functioning in 9- to 12-year-olds prenatally exposed to cigarettes and marihuana." *Neurotoxicol Teratol*. 20(3): p. 293-306.

8   Wymore, Erica M, MD, MPH; Palmer, Claire, MS; Wang, George S, MD; *et al*. *JAMA Pediatrics*. Published online March 8, 2021. doi: 10.1001/m=jamapediatrics.2020.6098 Study: THC and Pregnancy | Children's Hospital Colorado (childrenscolorado.org). Accessed May 31, 2021.

9   Autism Science Foundation; What is Autism; How Common is Autism? https://autismsciencefoundation/what-is-autism/how-common-is-autism. Accessed May 31, 2021.

10 Baio, J; Wiggins, L; Christensen, DL; *et al*. "Prevalence of Autism Spectrum Disorder Among Children Aged 8 Years — Autism and Developmental Disabilities Monitoring Network, 11 Sites, United States, 2014." *MMWR Surveill Summ* 2018;67(No. SS-6):1–23. DOI:http://dx.doi.org/10.15585/mmwr.ss6706a1.

Prenatal Care

11. Cal. Dep't of Pub. Health; Cal. Safe Cosmetics Program; Current Data Summary. https://www.cdph.ca.gov/Programs/CCDPHP/DEODC/OHB/CSCP/Pages/SummaryData.aspx. Accessed May 31, 2021.

12. Matta, MK; Zusterzeel, R; Pilli, NR; *et al.* "Effect of Sunscreen Application Under Maximal Use Conditions on Plasma Concentration of Sunscreen Active Ingredients: A Randomized Clinical Trial." *JAMA.* 2019;321(21):2082–2091. doi:10.1001/jama.2019.5586.

13. Adams, Rebecca. "There's Mercury in Your Mascara, and the UN is OK with That." *Huffington Post* 10/18/2013. There's Mercury In Your Mascara, And The UN Is OK With That | HuffPost Life.

14. Rochester, JR. "Bisphenol A and human health: a review of the literature." *Reprod Toxicol.* 2013 Dec; 42:132-55. doi: 10.1016/j.reprotox.2013.08.008. Epub 2013 Aug 30. PMID: 23994667. Accessed May 31, 2021.

15. Grindler, NM; Vanderlinden, L; Karthikraj, R; Kannan, K; Teal, S; Polotsky, AJ; Powell, TL; Yang IV, Jansson T. "Exposure to Phthalate, an Endocrine Disrupting Chemical, Alters the First Trimester Placental Methylome and Transcriptome in Women." *Sci Rep.* 2018 Apr 17;8(1):6086. doi: 10.1038/s41598-018-24505-w. PMID: 29666409; PMCID: PMC5904105. Accessed May 31, 2021.

16. Dzwilewski, K L C; *et.al.* (2021) "Associations of Prenatal Exposure to Phthalates with Measures of Cognition in 7.5-month-old Infants." *NeuroToxicology.* doi.org/10.1016/j.neuro.2021.03.001. Accessed May 31, 2021.

17. Wilhelm, Erika. "Chemical Linked to Breast Cancer Found in Popular Anti-Aging Skin Care Products." *Campaign for Safe Cosmetics,* October 14, 2015. Chemical linked to breast cancer found in popular anti-aging skin care products - Safe Cosmetics. Accessed May 31, 2021.

18. EPA Health Advisory. Drinking Water Health Advisories for PFOA and PFOS | Ground Water and Drinking Water | US EPA. Accessed May 31, 2021.

19. Commission Regulation (EU) No 1004/2014 of 18 September 2014 amending Annex V to Regulation (EC) No 1223/2009 of the European Parliament and of the Council on cosmetic products Text with EEA relevance. EUR-Lex - 32014R1004 - EN - EUR-Lex (europa.eu). Accessed May 31, 2021.

20. Nowak, K; Ratajczak-Wrona, W; Górska, M; Jabłońska, E. "Parabens and their effects on the endocrine system." *Mol Cell Endocrinol.* 2018 Oct 15;474:238-251. doi: 10.1016/j.mce.2018.03.014. Epub 2018 Mar 27. PMID: 29596967. Accessed May 311, 2021.

21. Food and Drug Administration; Cosmetics Laws & Regulations; Cosmetics & U.S. Law. Cosmetics & U.S. Law | FDA. Accessed May 31, 2021.

22. The Babysafe Project; Science; "The Science of Wireless Radiation." https://www.babysafeproject.org/science . Accessed June 1, 2021.

23. Zero to Three; Resources and Services; "How does nutrition affect the developing brain?" https://www.zerotothree.org/resources/1372-how-does-nutrition-affect-the-developing-brain. Accessed June 1, 2021.

24. Zero to Three; Resources and Services; "What are neural tube defects (NTDs)?" https://www.zerotothree.org/resources/1374-what-are-neural-tube-defects-ntds. Accessed June 1, 2021.

25. Ali, AA; Cui, X; Pertile, RAN; et al. "Developmental vitamin D deficiency increases foetal exposure to testosterone." *Molecular Autism* 11, 96 (2020). https://doi.org/10.1186/s13229-020-00399-2. Accessed June 1, 2021.

26. NPR.org; Ted Radio Hour; "When Does Learning Begin?" April 25, 2013. https://www.npr.org/templates/transcript/transcript.php?storyId=179022386. Accessed June 1, 2021.

27. WebMD.com; Pregnancy; References; "Types of Childbirth Classes." https://www.webmd.com/baby/childbirth-class-options#1. Accessed June 1, 2021.

28. What to Expect; Pregnancy; Fetal Health; "Can Vaginal Seeding benefit Babies after a C-Section?" What Is Vaginal Seeding After a C-Section, and Are There Benefits for Baby? (whattoexpect.com). Accessed June 1, 2021.

29. KimberlyAnnJohnson. Articles - Kimberly Ann Johnson. Accessed June 1, 2021.

30. Huizink, Anja C; Robles de Medina, Pascale G; Mulder, Eduard JH; Visseer, Gerard HA; Buitelaar, Jan K. "Stress during pregnancy is associated with developmental outcome in infancy." *The Journal of Child Psychology and Psychiatry* 44, 6 (2003), pp. 810-818. https://doi.org/10.1111/1469-7610.00166.

31. Transcript from "Obama's Father's Day Remarks," *The New York Times*, June 15, 2008. Obama's Father's Day Remarks - The New York Times (nytimes.com). Accessed June 1, 2021.

32. American Lung Association; blog. "An Amazing Journey: How Young Lungs Develop." https://www.lung.org/blog/how-young-lungs-develop. Accessed June 1, 2021.

Chapter 3
Infancy
Year One

"I'm selfish, impatient and a little insecure. I make mistakes, I am out of control and at times hard to handle. But if you can't handle me at my worst, then you sure as hell don't deserve me at my best."
– Marilyn Monroe

Baby Henry

Ooooooh! Bright!

Cold . . . . Lonely!!

Ohhhhhh . . .HUNGRY!!

"WAAHH!   WAAAAAAAAHHHH!"

Ohhh . . . . Comfort. Warm. Familiar. Secure.

Mmmmmmmm. Food.
Mmmmmm. Mmmmmm. Mmmmmm. Mmmmmm. Good.
Mmmmmm. Mmmmmm. Mmmmmm. Mmmmmm. Good.
Mmmmmm. Mmmmmm. Mmmmmm. Mmmmmm.
Mmmmmm. Mmmmmm. Mmmmmm. Mmmmmm. Full.

Pretty Face. Beautiful eyes. Secure.

"Uhh. Uhh" Uncomfortable. "Uhh. Uhh." (Burp)

Ahhhhhhh. Warm. Secure. Pleasant words. Rocking . . .

Tired . . . . feel . . . very . . . tired . . . .

Raising 4 Dimensional Children in a 2 Dimensional World

Baby Edward

Ooooooh! Bright!

Cold . . . . Lonely!!

Ohhhhhh . . .HUNGRY!!

"WAAHH!   WAAAAAAAAHHHH!" HUNGRY!!!

"WAAHH!   WAAAAAAAAHHHH!" HUNGRY!!!

Cold. Lonely. HUNGRY!!

"WAAHH!   WAAAAAAAAHHHH!" HUNGRY!!!

"WAAHH!   WAAAAAAAAHHHH!" HUNGRY!!!

Cold. Frightened. HUNGRY!!!

"WAAHH!   WAAAAAAAAHHHH!" HUNGRY!!!

"WAAHH!   WAAAAAAAAHHHH!" HUNGRY!!!

Noise. People. Warmth.

"WAAHH!   WAAAAAAAAHHHH!" HUNGRY!!!

"WAAHH!   WAAAAAAAAHHHH!" HUNGRY!!!

Mmmmmmm. Food.
Mmmmmm. Mmmmmm. Mmmmmm. Mmmmmm. Good.
Mmmmmm. Mmmmmm. Mmmmmm. Mmmmmm. Good.
Mmmmmm. Mmmmmm. Mmmmmm. Mmmmmm.
Mmmmmm. Mmmmmm. Mmmmmm. Mmmmmm. Full.

Ringing Noise. . . Separation . . . Lonely.

Infancy

"Uhh. Uhh" Uncomfortable. "Uhh. Uhh."

"URGGGGGGGG!" Uncomfortable. Lonely.

"URGGGGGGG!" (Burp)

Distant words . . . Lonely.

"YAAAAHHHHH!" Lonely. "YAAAAHHHHH!"

"YAAAAHHHHH!" Insecure. "YAAAAHHHHH!"

"YAAAAHHHHH!" Lonely. "YAAAAHHHHH!"

"YAAAAHHHHH!" Disappointed. "YAAAAHHHHH!"

Tired . . . . Lonely . . .

"YAAAAhhhhh!" Frightened. "Yaaaahhhhh!"

"Yaaahhhh!" Lonely. "Yaaahhh!"

Tired . . . . Miserable . . . very . . . tired . . . .

Which baby would you rather have?

Which baby would you rather be?

You Write the Program

The first year of life is a time of tremendous growth. Your baby learns how to interact with the world around him, and literally organizes his brain according to what he learns. Your baby is born with about 86 BILLION brain cells,[33] but they are not connected yet.

Interaction with people will determine how they are connected. Brain cells that fire together, wire together. The connections will be made at an amazing rate: At about 5 weeks of age, your child's brain will grow at about 250,000 neurons per minute.[34] At its peak, the cerebral cortex creates an astonishing two million new synapses every second.[35] There won't be a test on these numbers, but the point is that infancy is a crucial time for brain growth, and it happens almost unimaginably quickly. Your baby's brain gets built only once, so do your best to build it right.

For the first six months, your child's interaction is linear – face to face or person to person between you and him. During the second six months, interaction will move to a triangle, with some person or object like a toy or some food being the third corner.

Your job during this time is primarily meeting the baby's three basic needs (according to Maslow's Hierarchy): Physiological, safety, and love/belonging.

Children derive security from routines, so especially at the beginning try to create routines and adapt them to the changing needs of your child. Establishing rhythms of wake time, feeding time, play time, and nap time will make your baby secure and make your life more predictable . . . and therefore more comfortable. During the first few months, your baby does not easily respond to praise or punishment, so expect to follow more than you lead.

Because your child is developing so rapidly, we will take a closer look at several stages and his specific needs, but first let's take a look at some postpartum needs of the parents.

Parental Needs:

Immediately after the baby is born, you'll experience an intense wave of love and devotion. You'll quickly forget the pain of childbirth in the ecstasy of seeing the most beautiful baby in the world. The joy of that moment is worth all the blood, sweat, and tears, and it's important to spend as much time bonding with the baby as possible, both at the hospital and at home.

Once you get home, be aware that one out of five women are diagnosed with a postpartum mood disorder like depression, and 50% of women have a pelvic floor dysfunction.[37] If you have pelvic floor

Infancy

issues, look into kegel exercises. You also may experience an average of 700 hours of sleep deprivation during the first year of the baby's life, and that's when your risk for depression doubles.[38]

Forewarned is forearmed. If you are feeling down, you are not alone. Consult your health care provider about taking bio-identical progesterone for your depression. However, never doubt that your baby loves you and needs your love, so keep on keeping on. Postpartum mental care can be expensive, but not having it may be even more costly. Consider help if your depression lasts more than two weeks and you feel you need it.

You really need to rest for three weeks after childbirth. You can get out of bed to take short walks to the kitchen and bathroom, but take it easy. Stay warm, use oil internally and externally, and eat and drink enough. Breastfeeding takes a lot of nutrients, so don't starve yourself (and your baby) by trying to lose weight too soon. There will be plenty of time for that. Maintain your own sleep as well as you can to keep yourself physically and mentally healthy.

On the other hand, it's not fair for dad to take on the responsibilities of care for the mother and the house all by himself. Get help from friends and family. A new mom should

5 Universal Postpartum Needs

1. **An Extended Rest Period** – 30 to 60 days: 5 Days in the bed, 5 days on the bed, and 5 days around the bed. Minimize movement. Avoid carrying the baby before you have core strength.
2. **Nourishing Food** – every culture has some: Mineral rich, nutrient dense, and easy to digest.
3. **Loving Touch** – all cultures have traditions. The mom needs a loving touch and so does the baby.
4. **Presence of Wise Women** – take pressure off parents to know everything.
5. **Contact with Nature** – everything has a time and season. Don't rush things.

from Kimberly Johnson – *The 4th Trimester*[36]

not be alone for more than a few hours at a time. It's also important to plan time to re-bond as a couple, because couples experience a 67% decline in marital satisfaction after the birth of the first child.[39] Know that there is light at the end of the tunnel, and your child will begin sleeping through the night at about 6 months. Focus on the joy of spending quality time with each other and catch a nap whenever you can. You will make it!

Pets

Children love animals, but make sure your animals love children. If you have pets, be extra careful: Don't leave your child alone with the pet. Your infant doesn't know how to treat animals, so he may do something offensive. Be ready to intercede if needed.

There is a strong argument for having pets in the home. Research has actually shown that children raised with dogs, and to a lesser extent with cats, have stronger immune systems.[40] Parents who own furry pets (dogs and cats) even before the child's birth have babies with more robust gut microbiomes,[41] and children exposed to pets in the first year of life tend to have fewer asthma and allergies than those without pets.[42] Of course, you must use your own good judgment depending on the pet and the infant.

One neat trick for the pets is to bring the scent of the new baby home to the pet before the baby arrives. Hospitals often provide a "hat" for the newborn. If you have a pet, ask for the hat (they would otherwise throw it away) and have someone take the hat home to your pet to create familiarity.

Now, let's get back to the child. Here's a more detailed breakdown of needs and developments by age:

0 to 2 months

Your baby will spend most of her time (about 16 hours a day) sleeping, but she won't sleep through the night, so neither will you. Do not try to wake her or keep her awake – let her sleep except for feeding. Put her to sleep as soon as she shows signs of being tired: Rubbing her eyes, yawning, looking away from you, and fussing.

After the first month, try to separate feeding from sleeping with a quiet, fun activity.

Major Lessons: learning to regulate eating and sleeping patterns, and emotions.

Physically

Be careful to support her head whenever lifting her – her head is very large in comparison to her body, and her neck muscles are not strong enough to support it. You can seriously injure your baby just by lifting her improperly.

Consult your doctor for the latest schedule of vaccinations. Vaccinations save lives. If you have been scared away from vaccines by Internet chatter, please check your sources carefully. Much of the anti-vaccine rhetoric is outdated or based on opinion rather than solid, peer-reviewed research. Please check sites like the CDC at https://www.cdc.gov/vaccines/parents/why-vaccinate/vaccine-decision.html or Parents.com at https://www.parents.com/health/vaccines/controversy/8-reasons-parents-dont-vaccinate-and-why-they-should and make an informed decision.

Feeding

After birth, your baby's brain growth depends critically on the quality of her nutrition. Breast milk offers the best mix of nutrients, hormones, antibodies, and healthy bacteria for promoting all growth, so breast feed her if possible. There is a clear link between the amount of Omega 3 acid in your milk and later academic success, even better than national income or amount of dollars spent per pupil in schools,[43] so continue to take your Omega 3 supplement to pass it on to her.

If you can't breast feed, don't feel guilty, but use formula. Cow's milk is healthy for baby cows, but hard to digest for baby humans. Formula is much easier to digest and is designed for humans.

Raising 4 Dimensional Children in a 2 Dimensional World

Avoid heating the bottle in the microwave: Plastic bottles may contain BPAs and phthalates, and even glass bottles may be heated unevenly. Use the stove.

For the first two months you may have to wake her during the night for feeding. You should not let her go four hours without eating. After that, if she is gaining weight properly, you can let her sleep as long as she will, especially if you feed her sufficiently during the day.

After the first month don't let her fall asleep while you are feeding her. If she dozes off and stays asleep, stop feeding and put her to bed. You won't get her to sleep longer by feeding her too much. Separate feeding from naps, even for a few minutes, so she learns to fall asleep on her own.

<u>Warning</u>: Never prop a bottle in her mouth while she is sleeping – it's a choking hazard.

Sleeping

NEVER put your baby to sleep on her stomach – always on her back, on a firm surface with no loose blankets, pillows, or toys. She should be in the same room with you, but not the same bed. Learn as much as you can about SIDS (Sudden Infant Death Syndrome) on websites like www.SIDS.org.

Change the baby's position in the room. If there is anything to look at on the ceiling or walls, she may turn her head in that direction, which can cause stiff neck muscles or even affect the shape of the still solidifying bones of her head. Every other day simply lay the baby in the crib with her head at the opposite end, so she leans her head differently every day.

Establish the same nap time every day and not late in the afternoon, as that will make bedtime more challenging.

Avoid naps "on the go" (in cars or strollers) whenever possible, as it does not lead to quality sleep, but you may "do what you have to do" if she's crying and nothing else seems to work.

Starting at about 6 weeks of age, start to establish a bedtime routine. Reserve active games to daytime hours and quiet games for the evening. Keep activities in the same order every night. Save her favorite activity for last and do that one in the bedroom to associate sleep with something enjoyable. Keep the lighting and other conditions in the bedroom consistent so that if she wakes during the night, everything is the same as when she fell asleep.

Activities

Gaze: Look at your baby close-up (her field of vision is only about 8 to 15 inches). She wants and needs to see your face and learn from your expressions. Make faces, sing, and clap her hands.

Smile: At the beginning your baby will smile when she is happy, but not respond to you. By three months of age, she will smile in response to your smiles, and soon smile to get you to smile back at her.

Present Objects: Move your hands and objects across her line of vision. She will track them with her eyes, learning to follow them. Soon she will start to turn her head to follow them, strengthening her neck muscles.

Grasp: Infants have a grasping instinct. Offer your fingers to be grasped and pull gently to exercise her grasp.

Reach: Offer interesting (safe) objects. She will start reaching toward them and grasping at them, but probably not be able to coordinate grasping them or even touching them. If possible, place a mobile of dangling objects out of reach above the crib.

Massage: Massage is not only soothing for both you and your baby, but the stimulation helps her brain form connections with the different areas of her body.

Tummy Time: Roll your baby over on her tummy for very short periods of time, until she fusses, to get her used to the position. She will adjust better to longer periods of tummy time when she is older if she is familiar with the position.

Mentally

Your baby's brain is learning and growing, and one affects the other. According to the stimulation you provide, the brain will adapt and adjust to potentially form lifetime patterns.

Variety of stimulation is important. Present different colors and shapes (always safe objects, in case she actually touches or grasps them) within her field of vision for her to look at.

All areas of the brain seem to be linked, so stimulation will tend to increase your baby's cognitive abilities as well as her success in school and later in life, while lack of stimulation can impair your baby's physical, mental, and emotional health.[44] Children of nurturing mothers have been found to have a 10% larger hippocampus (the area of the brain associated with memory) than children whose mothers are not as nurturing.[45]

How does a nurturing mother stimulate her baby's brain? Use what the Center for the Developing Child at Harvard University calls the "Serve and Return" method, where – just like in a game of tennis – the baby will serve up a stimulus (a look or a sound) and you will return with a responding look or sound. This back-and-forth communication helps the brain wire successfully for human interaction.[44]

Communication

Your baby will use facial expressions and cries from day one. She will use a different cry to express hunger, tiredness, or boredom. Try to learn your baby's "language." She will indicate boredom by looking away, arching her back, frowning, or (of course) crying. Just be ready when your baby "serves" you with any kind of communication, to "return" the attempt with a loving response. With practice you will learn her language before she learns yours. Attentive parents are not parents who teach their infants, but parents who learn from them what they need.

Infancy

Activities

<u>Talk to your baby</u>. It really doesn't matter what you talk about at this age – tone of voice is probably more important than content.

<u>Sing. Dance</u>. Give her an appreciation of music by singing, listening to happy music, and moving in rhythm. If you play an instrument, play soothing music for her.

Emotionally

Your baby may seem to be born with a temperament – an attitude toward you or even the world. As discussed in Chapter 2, much of what happened in the womb as far as the emotions and hormones flowing through the mother and the baby have helped form the baby's brain up to this point. In addition, if the baby inherited any addictions from the mother, the first week or so of life going through withdrawal was not pleasant. There may even be some genetic "hard wiring" that is inherited through the parents' DNA: There is research to support inherit-ability of temperament in adults,[46] but there is currently no direct evidence for children. Just realize that

---

Ways to Soothe a Crying Baby
- Offer a pacifier.
- Swaddling your baby in a blanket reminds her of the womb, so make her into a baby burrito.
- For gas pain, cradle your baby on her belly by wrapping your forearm across one shoulder, down the belly, and holding her bottom with your hand.
- Hold her close to your chest and gently move her with rocking motions.
- Reduce stimulation by lowering lights, sounds, and smells.
- Massage your baby, especially her stomach to relieve gas.
- Introduce low-level white noise in the background with a vacuum cleaner, a fan, or radio static.
- Say, "Shhhhhhhh," into the baby's ear.
- Sing the same song or lullaby you sang during pregnancy.

If you are truly worried that your baby cries too much, consult your doctor.

your child's brain is extremely plastic at this age, so the kinds of experiences you provide from this point forward can go a long way in shaping your baby's future temperament. You cannot control the nature (which has already happened), but you can strongly influence the nurture (the present and the future), so do your best to be present, attentive, and loving to help your baby develop into an emotionally balanced individual.

At the beginning, your baby is learning how to react to the world. Is it a safe and secure place, or a dangerous place full of threats? The emotional support you provide will establish patterns in your child's emotional make-up that set the stage for future relationships throughout her lifetime. Specifically, lack of physical contact during infancy seems to lead to emotional problems later,[47] so hold and hug your baby as often as you can.

Your baby's brain has four basic emotions at this age: Flee, Fight, Freeze, and Fine. Not all crying is a call for comforting. When she has a messy diaper, she will want to flee and make one kind of sound. When she is hungry, she will probably be angry and make a different sound. When she is frightened or lonely, she will make a different sound, and when she is fine, she may actually smile.

When she cries, she is reaching out to communicate one of these needs. When you respond, you teach her that she can count on people to help her in need. If you are nowhere to be found when she cries, or you provide the wrong response, she learns that she can't trust that anyone will help her in need. This is how children learn to feel secure or insecure.

When you try to soothe her, and she continues to cry, and you don't give up in frustration but continue to try different strategies, she learns that she is important and that her parents will care for her. While you are learning which cry means which need, she will also learn to soothe herself from the methods you use to soothe her.

Note: Even good caregivers get it right only 50% of the time, but they repair and restore. Inattentive caregivers are ones that react inappropriately or create emotional discomfort, which causes a lack of attachment for their babies.

Warning: NEVER shake a baby. As mentioned earlier, her head is large and her neck muscles are weak, so you can cause severe damage and even death by shaking her. If you get frustrated, pass the baby to someone else or just let her cry while you take a break to recover. Frustration can lead to serious mistakes.

Spiritually

Although your baby's brain limits what can be learned mentally, the spirit is always complete. Your spirit can communicate love and care with her spirit – not on a physical, mental, or emotional level, but on a purely spiritual level.

Begin to initiate the practices of your family's faith – reading scriptures, attending services as soon as manageable, bedtime prayers, religious songs and music, and age-appropriate ceremonies like baptism and/or circumcision. If you meditate, perhaps chanting your mantra will establish a connection of calm with this sound, especially if you practiced chanting and meditation during the pregnancy.

2 to 6 months

Your baby will be awake and actively learning how to live. He will sleep for 6 hours at a stretch – maybe even all night — don't wake him to feed him. Set patterns now for a successful life.

Major Lessons: learning to reach out and touch the world, and learning that he has some power to affect and even control it. He is also learning to coordinate the use of his hands.

Here are some ways to foster this development:

Physically

Movement is the first key to develop your child's brain. The reason we have a brain is for movement . . . plants don't have a brain because they don't move; animals do. Get him to move as much as possible with different activities when he is awake.

Raising 4 Dimensional Children in a 2 Dimensional World

Feeding

Continue breast feeding or formula throughout this period. In the later months, if you start to introduce other foods, expect him to explore everything with his hands as well as his mouth. If you use a spoon, he will want to hold it.

Never give an infant honey for fear of botulism. Adding any sugar to the bottle, including fruit juices, can cause tooth decay. The less sugar you give him, the better. Wipe his gums and brush his teeth (when he gets them) to remove residual sugars.

Teething may start – causing crying without apparent cause. Teething rings will help. A simpler remedy is gently rubbing the gums with a clean finger. Do not use teething gels on children younger than 2,[48] and do not give aspirin to children.[49] Always check the label on over-the-counter medicines for age limitations.

Sleeping

Do your best to establish a sleep pattern, but be aware it may be the baby's pattern, not yours. Look for signs that he is tired before he gets cranky because an overtired baby has more trouble falling asleep.

Your baby will start to follow circadian rhythms (night and day) at about 3 – 4 months. Reinforce this natural development by being more stimulating and active during the day and more laid back at night. Continue developing your bedtime routine. Warm baths are a good activity to introduce to help your baby relax and get ready for bed.

Activities

<u>Grabbing:</u> Your baby will be able to grab safe objects. At about 3 months old, lay him on his back and offer objects to be grabbed. One at a time, present a variety of colors, shapes, and textures. Be aware that much of what he grabs will go into his mouth, so choose the objects within reach carefully – usually objects too large to fit entirely in his mouth. Remember to keep your hair tied back to avoid some personal pain.

Infancy

Rattles: Safe noise makers are great toys, as he will be able to connect his action (shaking) with a real-world result (noise).

Tummy Time: Place him on his tummy for 30 minutes a day (not all at once) and encourage him to lift his head and chest. Present interesting (safe) objects to look at. Take a scarf and blow it over his head and let it settle on his back, then slowly slide it off. Dangle it in front of him for him to follow with his eyes before you blow it over his back again. Gently roll him over from tummy to back. At about 4 to 6 months of age, start encouraging him to do it himself.

Encourage baby push-ups during Tummy Time by raising and lowering a rattle over his head so that he lifts his head and even shoulders to look at it.

Sitting: Sit him up with support but watch carefully. It will be easy to fall over and possibly off of the couch or wherever you have placed him.

Play "How big? So big!" Sit your child on your lap and ask, "How big is (baby's name)?" Then lift his arms up and say, "Sooo Big!" Soon he will learn to lift his own arms.

Exercise: Starting at about 3 months, lay your child on his back and move his legs in a running motion. This motion will increase his heart rate and exercise his leg muscles. If you can smile and connect happiness and fun with this exercise, you may be programming him to enjoy exercise later in life. Please note, you are not simulating running a marathon – you are just doing short bursts of motion and attaching it to fun and positive feelings. You can alternate the leg motions with arm motions, and light stretching, like touching his toes to his nose and laughing.

Tickling: About the fourth month, your baby will become ticklish. Be careful to keep tickling as a fun experience and possibly a reward for good behavior – excessive tickling may cause your baby to feel out of control at a time when he is learning to control his environment.

Raising 4 Dimensional Children in a 2 Dimensional World

Mentally

Your baby is beginning to learn how to initiate action to get what he wants. He is learning not only to reach out and manipulate the world around him by touching objects, but soon to request objects by communicating with you. Help him understand this process by offering an object, and when he reaches out, giving it to him. Then ask for it back, to see if he will return it. Continue this give and take process as long as he finds it fun.

Ring a bell and wait for your baby to look at it, connecting the direction of the sound to the object. Move the bell and ring it again.

Communication

Learn to read your baby's expressions: Looking away means he is shifting to Flight mode and wants to avoid something; clenching his jaw or crying louder when you try to comfort him probably means he is in Fight mode and angry about something; lack of response or apathy might mean he is in Freeze mode and afraid. With a little time and patience, you will learn what he is saying before he can speak a word.

Activities

Imitation: Your baby will imitate you, but at this age, he will love it when you imitate him or otherwise respond to what he does, as that confirms that he has some affect or even control over his environment. Make faces, stick out your tongue, and when your baby imitates you, you imitate him to set up the pattern of back-and-forth communication.

Talking: Your baby will start to babble. Respond to him as if you understood, to establish that communication is a back-and-forth activity. Now is a great time to hold your baby on your lap and read children's books to him. Point to pictures and repeat their name, encouraging him to do the same. Babies can learn the meaning of many words (receptive vocabulary) that they cannot speak (productive vocabulary).

Infancy

<u>Mirrors:</u> Offer safe mirrors for him to look into. At about four months of age, he should be able to recognize himself in the mirror. Point to body parts and identify them. Move away from the mirror and ask, "Where did baby go?"

Emotionally

At this age, your baby will also start to laugh. Do what you can to make a happy baby, but don't expect to see evidence of a sense of humor until the second year.

At about 4 months you may notice that your child is either high-reactive or low-reactive. High reactive children tend to have high levels of movement and distress, while low-reactive children tend to have low levels of movement and crying. These two personality types tend to express themselves in an inhibited or uninhibited child in the second year and may remain constant throughout their lives. High-reactive adolescents are at a slightly higher risk of anxiety and depression, but also tend to become good programmers, scientists, and mathematicians. Low-reactive adolescents tend to be more socially outgoing, spontaneous, risk-takers, but also tend to be good communicators, salesmen, and leaders.[50]

These personality types are tendencies, not destinies. As you notice which way your child leans, you may choose to encourage development in the opposite direction to create a more balanced personality, or you may choose to let your child develop on his own, patiently suggesting choices that might suit him.

Peek-a-boo is a great game to communicate emotionally. At this age, your baby doesn't understand object permanence. When you disappear, you are simply gone, which can be terrifying to a baby. By playing peek-a-boo, your baby will learn that when you go away, you always come back. This can be emotionally reassuring in the middle of the night when he wakes up and you are not there.

As you and your baby have fun with the game, start to stay hidden for a few seconds longer, to allow him to learn to anticipate what will happen next.

As your baby learns the power of intention (being able to get what he wants), he will also experience frustration when he can't get it. This new emotion could be powerful and learning to deal with it will be challenging. However, remember that infants younger than 6 months do not respond well to praise or punishment, so just comfort him.

Spiritually

Continue introducing your faith to your child. You can choose books with religious themes for reading time. Once again, what his brain is not ready to understand, his spirit may assimilate.

6 to 9 Months

At this age, your baby will become mobile. Baby-proof your house, as it only takes a few seconds of inattention for a child to get into trouble. Learn more about the most important childproofing at https://www.webmd.com/parenting/guide/childproof-home#1. In addition, be very aware of nearby water: Drowning is a leading cause of death for children 1 to 4 years old, but once your baby is on the go, she is an accident looking to happen. Fence off your pool and keep doors locked to prevent your baby from going out of the house and into danger. Fence off or block stairs to prevent accidents, as beginning crawlers cannot judge how safe a slope or stairs are.

Developmentally, your relationship will transition from two to three: Instead of being just direct communication between the two of you, your baby will start to communicate about objects or other people.

Major Lessons: learning to crawl and learning to communicate about objects.

Infancy

Physically

Feeding

Parents determine when and where a baby eats. The baby determines how much. Don't try to force feed your baby . . . respect her wishes (unless your doctor recommends otherwise.) At 6 months, you can start to mix breast feeding with other foods. It is important to add some iron and Omega 3s to your baby's diet at this age, especially if breast feeding. Take supplements to keep your own levels up. Most infant cereals and formulas are fortified with iron but check on the Omega 3s. If they seem low, squeeze some oil out of supplement pills into the formula to be sure your baby won't have potential cognitive deficiencies.

Offer new foods. Your baby will want to touch and taste them, attempting to help feed herself. Encourage exploration, even though it can be messy. She may want to help hold the spoon during feeding as a way of eventually learning to feed herself. Don't fight for control; cooperate – it's her mouth.

When introducing a new food, expect as many as fifteen contacts with the new food before acceptance. Don't give up too early. Data gathered from eleven countries on children from 6 to 23 months of age show a positive association between dietary variety and nutritional status. Exposure to fruits and vegetables in infancy have been associated with acceptance of these foods at later ages, so start good habits early.[51]

Sleeping

Try to establish 2-hour naps during the day, and avoid naps "on the go" because the quality of sleep will not be good.

Now is the time to establish a "fall asleep by yourself" bedtime routine. By now, you should have a fairly well-developed and consistent routine of the same activities every night. Bathing is a relaxing activity, and reading in a calm voice is a good choice. Choosing a favorite activity for last, which can be done in the crib, helps your baby look forward to going to bed. Finally, when she is sufficiently drowsy, let her drift off to sleep. This will help her become accustomed to falling asleep in the crib, not in your arms (you can see how this could become a problem in the future).

When you put your baby into her crib and she cries, she is now old enough for you to try the Ferber method[52] of walking away, waiting a short amount of time, then returning to comfort her, but not picking her up (don't let her equate crying with picking up if you ever want her to stop crying at bedtime). Leave again after a few minutes, and possibly return again. Each time wait a little longer before you return as you develop the routine. The short-term pain of hearing your baby cry may be well worth it in avoiding long-term crying if you can teach her to soothe herself early. Expect it to take about a week to establish the pattern – don't give up too soon.

Activities

Your baby may learn to crawl or move in a variety of interesting ways (some babies never crawl and move directly from scooting to walking). Encourage the development and progress.

Get it: Play a human version of "fetch" by rolling a ball a few feet away and encouraging your baby to crawl after it.

Feel it: Place different textures on the floor for your baby to crawl over or to stand on with your support to encourage sensory awareness. You can also make a texture book (different textures) and bind them. Let the baby touch them while you describe the texture, color, and even shape.

Sit: Your baby should be able to sit without support, so this position provides a whole new angle to experience the world and interact with you. Get her to clap her own hands and blow kisses.

Stand: Encourage but don't force standing with support.

Explore: Consider taking your baby out into the yard to play in the grass (beware of pesticides on your lawn). Beware of insects. Your baby may learn to grasp clumps of grass and eventually individual blades of grass (and probably put them in her mouth). The sandbox and the pool are other outdoor alternatives, as well as trips in the carriage for different stimulation. Use your good judgment to keep her from getting hurt in these lower-control environments.

Warning: Do not hold hot drinks with a child in your lap – sudden movements can cause burns.

Mentally

Start to introduce toys with a purpose, like ones that show physical relationships. Play games that incorporate your baby's newfound physical skills.

Your baby is beginning to understand she can affect the world by requesting what she wants. When she points to an object, at first, move it within reach so she can get it for herself. Eventually, help her crawl to get it for herself.

When she is holding a toy in each hand, offer a third toy and patiently watch as she figures out how to grasp the new toy – possibly without letting go of the other two.

Communication

Your baby may start to put vowels and consonants together. Imitate her sounds and encourage her to make another sound, then imitate it. At first, "Mama" and "Dada" will probably not be connected to you, but eventually they will. A fun word to teach is, "Uh, Oh!"

Your baby will learn to respond to certain words, like her name, and to "No." Narrate your child's life by saying things like, "You are eating a big banana." Her vocabulary will continue to grow, even if she can't speak it. Continue to hold your baby on your lap and read children's books to her. Point to pictures and repeat their name, encouraging her to do the same.

Continue to play peek-a-boo and say, "Bye" just before you disappear, and then, "Hi!" when you appear. Soon your baby may start to say the words during the game.

Raising 4 Dimensional Children in a 2 Dimensional World

Play, "Where's your nose?" "Where's your toes?" to teach a combination of vocabulary and body awareness.

Activities

<u>Memory</u>: Play games like Patty-Cake and The Itsy-Bitsy Spider to encourage not only physical coordination but mental memory of physical patterns.

<u>Shapes</u>: Offer toys that fit inside each other to learn physical relationships. Use blocks for stacking. Get one of those toys where you stack rings on a pole. Provide shape puzzles where the circle fits into the circular space, and the square fits into the square space, etc.

<u>Hinges</u>: Provide toys with hinges like cardboard boxes or sturdy books. Children this age love cabinet doors, but there's usually something dangerous inside, so cabinets are not one of your better options. Use childproof locks for safety.

<u>Tools:</u> Encourage understanding of tools. For example, filling a cup with water in a bathtub, then pouring out the contents. Spoons are also tools to learn about while eating.

<u>Push Buttons</u>: Introduce cause and effect toys like the jack-in-the-box. You push the button, and the toy reacts. After you show her how to push the button, patiently wait for her to push the button, as her brain works very slowly at this age.

<u>Which one</u>: Present 2 toys. When the child points to one, let her touch it. Next, name the toys. Then ask, "Which one is the duck?"

Emotionally

Learning the meaning of, "No" is an important crossroad. As a parent you must decide how to use this powerful tool. On one hand, a loud, "No!" may save your baby from burning herself on something hot. On the other hand, children who are told, "No!" too often tend to grow up focused more on what they can't do, as opposed to what they can do. Once she learns the meaning of, "No!" use it judiciously. However, fully expect your child to occasionally test the limits by ignoring a stern, "No!" just to learn what happens when she does ignore it. Later in life, explanations will help, but at this age she doesn't have the vocabulary to understand your explanation.

Encourage mimicking faces as a way to learn how to express different emotions.

She may be shy and pull away from new people and new situations. If you offer emotional support, you will teach her that you understand her communication, understand her needs, and respect her feelings. With a little patience and soothing, chances are she will slowly (at her own pace, not yours) be curious about the new person or situation and reach out to it.

Begin identifying emotions to help her understand her feelings. Say things like, "What made you angry?" or "That makes you happy!"

To develop confidence, use words and facial expressions to encourage your baby when she is working on a task and even more so when she succeeds. Offer slightly challenging tasks and let her learn to succeed on her own (or at least with minimum help.)

At this age your child's temperament will begin to show more clearly. If she smiles and laughs a lot, and readily reaches out to touch objects you present, these are early indicators of an extroverted personality. Extroversion and introversion are two different personality types, each with advantages and disadvantages, and neither one is "better" than the other. In addition, this tendency can still develop either way based on her future interactions with people and objects, but these are early hints.

Following the "goodness of fit" theory by Thomas and Chess: Shy children benefit from being encouraged by parents to explore, and will remain shy and inhibited if you are overprotective. Aggressive children benefit from more restrictive control and lower parental negativity. Children who have difficulties with self-regulation benefit from firm, consistent parental discipline.[53] Don't blindly follow your parents' methods, and don't just do the opposite if you didn't like how they treated you. Your baby is not you, and you are not your parents.

The fact that you are reading this book shows you want to be the best parent you can be. Tailor your parenting to the needs of your child.

Spiritually

Continue introducing your faith to your child. Don't expect to see any noticeable changes but believe that your efforts have an effect. Her brain development will limit what she understands and expresses, but her spirit is always whole.

Studies have shown that fearful children tend to develop an early conscience, and do best under parental warmth and gentle discipline that promotes internalizing the difference between right and wrong. More fearless children do their best under maternal responsiveness and secure attachment. In the long run, warm, supportive parenting appears to predict higher levels of effortful control of attention and impulses than cold, directive parenting.[54]

9 to 12 months

Your baby is transitioning from infant to toddler. He is beginning to understand cause and effect relationships. He may begin experiencing the "9 Month Revolution," when he begins to understand intention and will eventually realize that a ball rolled to him is expected to be rolled back. When he points to something, he will expect mommy to look at it. He will start to help you get him dressed.

Major Lessons: walking, understanding intention, and (soon) talking.

Here are some things you can do to foster development:

Physically

Much of the physical advancement at this age will center around learning to walk. Encourage your baby to walk by holding himself up with furniture or by you holding his hands for balance as he takes a few steps. Use a "walker" if available, and push toys with a handle to help him stand.

Infancy

When he's ready, set up short walks from mommy to daddy with lots of enthusiasm upon success, and encourage quick recovery after the unavoidable falls. Encourage your baby from the beginning to "try, try again" with positive (not negative) reinforcement.

Feeding

For the first two years of life, a baby should get 50% of his nutrition from fat, which is the balance provided in breast milk and baby formula.[55] When introducing more adult options, don't feed him "fat free" foods. Avocados, for example, contain good, nutritious fats.

Your baby will develop the "pincer grasp" using the thumb and index finger. Let him practice by picking up Cheerio style cereals to feed himself.

Model good eating habits and proper table manners without trying to enforce them at this age. Count on your baby to naturally want to do what you do but expect him to have limited fine motor skills. He will also enjoy exploring every aspect of his life, including food, by handling it and seeing where it looks and feels good. Continue to introduce new foods patiently. Don't force him to eat – trust his instincts that he will eat what he needs when he is hungry, unless he begins to look and act weak – then consult your doctor.

Activities

Shake Toys: Fill some water bottles with different stuff – colored liquids, glitter, shells, marbles, coins, etc., for shaking. Be sure to glue the tops shut so your child can't open them and swallow the insides.

Continue the activities from the previous section like cause/effect toys with draw strings or push buttons, stacking toys, and shape toys.

Continue to encourage an appreciation for music and rhythmic movement by singing, dancing, rocking, and playing music (a musical instrument or bang-able object).

Raising 4 Dimensional Children in a 2 Dimensional World

Mentally

At this age, your baby may begin to "Pretend Play" by copying you and using objects, like talking on a phone. Model simple behaviors you want him to emulate, especially when playing with toys or getting dressed.

Communication

Be a good listener: look at your child and pay attention to what he says or is trying to say.

Most babies can speak by 1 year old, but the range is enormous – some don't speak at all yet, while others speak in short sentences. Don't be alarmed but encourage communication. Constantly talk to him – children learn language from people, not video games.

He will begin to point at objects that he wants. Encourage speech to go along with this communication, but understand it is communication, nonetheless. Encourage your baby to request what he wants either by pointing or asking, whichever comes easier, to encourage the request/response model as a way of fulfilling his needs.

Constantly talk to your baby about what you are doing, where you are going, and what will happen when you get there.

Your baby may follow your gaze, but don't be surprised if he does not look at the object at the end, yet. He'll get there.

Activities

<u>Find it</u>: Play "find it" by hiding a favorite toy under a cloth or burying it in the sand as he watches you. Teach him to remove the cloth (or the sand) to find the toy.

<u>Close your eyes:</u> Let your baby touch an object, then get him to close his eyes and still feel the object to reinforce the concept of object permanence.

<u>Read:</u> Read to your baby and ask questions: Who is this? Where's the doggy?

Infancy

<u>Count</u>: Count everyday items that you come across.

<u>Identify</u>: Name colors and shapes.

<u>Wave</u>: Teach him to wave "bye-bye."

Emotionally

The primary emotions available at this age are interest, happiness, anger, fear, surprise, sadness, and disgust.[56] Fear needs comforting; anger needs time to play out and you taking away the cause of the anger. Interest and happiness should be encouraged as often as possible as a way to avoid sadness. Offer emotional support during attempts to accomplish any task with words and/or facial expressions, and then celebrate success. This is a good age to start "high fives."

Try to avoid saying, "Good Boy!" or, "Bad Boy!" when attached to an action. Instead, say something positive like, "You did it!" to create the joy of achievement. The goal here is to focus on the skill, and not place a value judgment on the child. Your child wants and needs your approval, but congratulations like, "Great job" or "Well done!" supply the approval without a judgment. We certainly don't want to start labeling the child, "Bad Boy!" even when he does something you don't like, as you will be programming him to believe he is a bad boy because you told him so. Stay positive!

Be a role model – your baby will watch you intently to learn how to handle surprises and setbacks. When your baby falls, if you get upset, he will learn that is the proper response. If you just encourage him to get up again as if nothing happened, he will learn that is the proper response. The same role modeling will apply to many other events, both big and small, that happen every day. Children learn persistence (grit) from their parents.

At this time in your baby's development, natural tendencies toward fear and inhibition to new things and people may start to appear. Be supportive to help him develop confidence, but, again, at his pace, not yours. On the other hand, if he shows low levels of self-regulation (impulsiveness), exert patient, firm control.[53]

Spiritually

At this time, your baby's brain begins to develop the executive attention network, which is the ability to maintain focus for longer periods of time and inhibit emotional and physical responses. Effortful control is strongly related to the development of empathy and guilt or shame.[54] Don't expect an overnight change, but begin to work on helping your baby focus and inhibit instinctive responses over the next four years and beyond.

Continue introducing your faith to your child. Read children's stories based on your scriptures, to model proper moral behavior. The first year is not a time of noticeable spiritual advancement, but as explained earlier, the spirit should not be measured by physical, mental, or emotional standards.

Activities

<u>Wait:</u> Make a game out of teaching your child to refrain from touching a prohibited toy: Don't touch for a count of five, then celebrate. Later, don't touch for a count of ten.

Summary

Pay attention to your child. Emotionally, all she ever wants is your attention. Gaze at her, then play with her, communicate with her, and then support her as she begins to explore the world.

At first, you will provide everything for your baby. As she grows, you will step back to a role of helping rather than providing. Be aware of her frustration level so you can provide the minimum help necessary in instances where she can learn to do things for herself, but try to avoid her feeling the frustration of not being able to do something she is not yet ready to do. You want her to develop the "I can do it" attitude by taking "baby steps" in successfully accomplishing a variety of age-appropriate tasks.

Infancy

Set routines. Children enjoy doing things over and over and need lots of practice to master skills. Let them.

Provide a variety of interesting stimulation. Break routines occasionally for special treats and events.

Screen Time

The American Academy of Pediatrics recommends no screen time before the age of 18 months.[57] Yet, according to the *Huffington Post*, in one study 50% of parents in Arizona believed their children learn as much watching television as being with their parents.[58] Don't fool yourself! Setting them in front of a TV may be easier, but it will not have the long-term benefits of personal interaction. And don't believe the claims made by the marketers of infant learning apps and games. They have little or no independent research to back them up as yet.[59] Many of the bells and whistles they add actually tend to distract the child from learning, so don't be one of the 40% of people who let their 3-month-olds get hypnotized by a video screen in the name of digital education.

Another survey showed that the average age regular media is introduced to infants in the U.S. is 9 months,[60] and I believe that is way too soon. You are better off using an old-fashioned paper book and not only reading, but questioning, commenting, and interacting. Your child needs education in all four dimensions of living, not the two dimensions of an electronic device, so start her off right!

Even background television distracts the child from the person-to-person learning that is most effective at this age. Plus, the TV is distracting you, the adult, from paying full attention to your child. No screen time for the first 18 months means turn off the TV when the child is in the room so you can pay full attention to each other.

Child Care

This entire chapter assumes you will spend time with your child throughout the first year. Unfortunately, we are not all able to do so. Economic realities require some mothers to work and seek childcare. The best option, if available, is a relative who can spend time interacting with your baby, like a grandparent. If you absolutely must employ day care, understand that recent research shows that children are somewhat more likely to develop insecure attachments to their mothers and higher body mass index (are fatter) when they go to day care more than ten hours a week during their first year of life, especially if it is low quality day care.[61] If you need to use day care, seek out the highest quality center you can find. Look for the ratio of caregivers to children, the qualifications of the staff members, the amount of physical activity they do during the day, the quality of the snacks they provide, and the amount of screen time provided. Then, just observe how the staff members interact with the children over longer than a five-minute visit. Additionally, be sure to invest as much time as you can at home connecting with your child because the parent child interaction during this time frame has lasting effects on the child's development and is very difficult to make up later in life.

Note: As all children are unique and develop at different rates, I recommend you read the next chapter to prepare for your child's growth and in case your child happens to develop more quickly in one area or another.

Because children's abilities vary greatly, don't panic if your child seems a little slow in one area or another. If you are seriously concerned, speak with your doctor or other health care provider to make sure your child is developing within the normal range.

Also please use your own good judgment in following any advice I offer. Research is subject to change and my advice may be based on research that has since changed or been updated since this publishing. Choose your actions based on your own beliefs, experiences, research, and judgment, especially during extenuating circumstances (like a pandemic.)

Infancy

Recommendations for further research:

www.Zerotothree.com
www.WebMD.com
https://pathways.org/us/
http://education.com
www.SIDS.org.
https://parenting-ed.org/parenting-information-handouts/early-childhood/
www.child-encyclopedia.com/
www.littlehumans.com/
https://abc.fpg.unc.edu/
https://www.who.int/topics/early-child-development/en/
https://parentsasteachers.org/
https://www.holisticmommd.com
https://www.cdc.gov/vaccines/parents/why-vaccinate/vaccine-decision.html
https://www.parents.com/health/vaccines/controversy/8-reasons-parents-dont-vaccinate-and-why-they-should/
https://www.vaccines.gov/getting/for_parents/five_reasons
https://www.AAP.org
https://www.EPA.gov
https://healthyenvironmentforkids.ca

References

33. Azevedo, FAC; Carvalho, LRB; Grinberg, LT; *et al.* "Equal numbers of neuronal and nonneuronal cells make the human brain an isometrically scaled-up primate brain." *J Comp Neurol.* Published online April 10, 2009:532-541. doi:10.1002/cne.21974. Accessed June 5, 2021.

34. Brynie, Faith Hickman. *101 Questions Your Brain has Asked about Itself but Couldn't Answer . . . until Now.* Twenty-First Century Books, Minneapolis, 2008. pp 30-31.

35. Zero to Three; Resources and Services; "What are the most important changes in the brain after birth?" https://www.zerotothree.org/resources/1379-what-are-the-most-important-changes-in-the-brain-after-birth. Accessed June 5, 2021.

36. Johnson, Kimberly Ann. "Recovering from Birth Requires these 5 Universal Needs – for Every Woman." Motherly; Life. August 29, 2018. https://www.mother.ly/life/postpartum-recovery-needs-for-every-woman. Accessed June 5, 2021.

37. Johnson, Kimberly Ann. Interview in *Little Humans* series https://littlehumans.com/. Accessed June 5, 2021.

38. Howard, Pierce Johnson. *The Owner's Manual for Happiness – Essential elements of a Meaningful Life.* Center for Applied Cognitive Studies, 2013, p. 36. https://paradigmpersonality.com/wp-content/uploads/2017/08/OMH-Ch-2-Boosters-Downers-Myths.pdf. Accessed June 5, 2021.

39. American Psychological Association; Monitor on Psychology; 2011;10. "Must babies always breed marital discontent?" https://www.apa.org/monitor/2011/10/babies. Accessed June 5, 2021.

40. Study from the Henry Ford Hospital in Detroit quoted by Dr. Susan Lynch of the UC San Francisco dept of Medicine, in the Netflix series *Babies*, Episode 2.

41. Tun, HM; Konya, T; Takaro, TK; *et al.* "Exposure to household furry pets influences the gut microbiota of infants at 3–4 months following various birth scenarios. *Microbiome* 5, 40 (2017). https://doi.org/10.1186/s40168-017-0254-x. Accessed June 5, 2021.

42. Hesselmar; Alberg; Alberg; Eriksson; Bjorksten. "Does early exposure to cat or dog protect against later allergy development?" *Clinical & Experimental Allergy* 29,5 pp 611-617 (1999). https://doi.org/10.1046/j.1365-2222.1999.00534.x Accessed June 5, 2021.

43. Caremans, Gregory, *"Neuroscience and Parenting."* https://www.udemy.com/course/neuroscience-and-parenting/ Section 2.7. Accessed March 29, 2021.

44. Harvard University; Center on the Developing Child; Key Concepts. "Serve and Return." https://developingchild.harvard.edu/science/key-concepts/serve-and-return/. Accessed June 5, 2021.

45. Castro, Joseph. "How a Mother's Love Changes a Child's Brain." *Live Science*, January 30, 2012. https://www.livescience.com/18196-maternal-support-child-brain.html. Accessed June 5, 2021.

46. Rothbart, Mary K. "Early Temperament and Psychosocial Development." Encyclopedia on Early Childhood Development; Temperament; November 2019, p.9. http://www.child-encyclopedia.com/temperament/according-experts/early-temperament-and-psychosocial-development. Accessed June 5, 2021.

Infancy

47. The Urban Child Institute; Research. "Enhancing Development through the Sense of Touch." May 23, 2012. http://www.urbanchildinstitute.org/articles/research-to-policy/research/enhancing-development-through-the-sense-of-touch. Accessed June 5, 2021.

48. Murkoff, Heidi. "Are Teething Gels Safe?" What to Expect; First Year; Teething. April 23, 2020. https://www.whattoexpect.com/first-year/ask-heidi/are-teething-gels-safe.aspx. Accessed June 5, 2021.

49. Duda, Kristina. "Why Kids Shouldn't Take Aspirin." Verywell Health; Kids Health; Cold & Flu. December 1, 2019. https://www.verywellhealth.com/why-kids-shouldnt-take-aspirin-770789. Accessed June 5, 2021.

50. Temperament. In: Tremblay, RE; Boivin, M; Peters, RDeV, eds. Rothbart, MK, topic ed. Encyclopedia on Early Childhood Development; Updated June 2012, p. 14. https://www.child-encyclopedia.com/sites/default/files/dossiers-complets/en/temperament.pdf. Accessed June 5, 2021.

51. Black, Maureen M, PhD; and Hurley, Kristen M, PhD. *Helping Children Develop Healthy Eating Habits,* University of Maryland School of Medicine, USA. September 2013, 2nd rev. ed.

52. Sleep Baby; The Ferber Method. https://sleepbaby.org/ferber-sleep-method. Accessed June 6, 2021.

53. Rothbart, Mary K. "Temperament." Encyclopedia on Early Childhood Development; p.6. www.child-encyclopedia.com/temperament/complete-topic. Accessed June 5, 2021.

54. *Ibid,* p.9.

55. Zero to Three; Resources & Services. "How does nutrition affect the developing brain?" How does nutrition affect the developing brain? • ZERO TO THREE. Accessed June 6, 2021.

56. Lifespan Development; Chapter 3: Infancy and Toddlerhood; "Infant Emotions." Infant Emotions | Lifespan Development (lumenlearning.com). Accessed June 6, 2021.

57. Zero to Three; Resources & Services. "Screen Sense: What the Research Says about the Impact of Media on Children Aged 0-3 Years Old." https://www.zerotothree.org/resources/2536-screen-sense-what-the-research-says-about-the-impact-of-media-on-children-aged-0-3-years-old. Accessed June 6, 2021.

58. Mastergeorge, Ann. "The Importance of Everyday Interaction for Early Brain development." The Huffington Post, February 3, 2014. https://www.huffpost.com/entry/the-importance-early-brain-development_b_4696877. Accessed June 6, 2021.

59. Courage, Mary L, PhD; and Troseth, Gerogene L, PhD. "Infants, Toddlers, and Learning from Screen Media." 2016, p.8. http://www.child-encyclopedia.com/technology-early-childhood-education/complete-topic. Accessed June 6, 2021.

60. Cardon, Greet, PhD; *et al*. "Physical Activity in Infants and Toddlers." Encyclopedia on Early Childhood Development, 2011, p 30. http://www.child-encyclopedia.com/physical-activity/complete-topic. Accessed June 6, 2021.

61. Belsky, Jay, PhD; *et. al*. "Child Care and Its Impact on Young Children." Encyclopedia on Early Childhood Development, 2020, p 37. http://www.child-encyclopedia.com/child-care-early-childhood-education-and-care/complete-topic. Accessed June 6, 2021.

Chapter 4
Toddlers
Years 2 and 3

"Always be a first-rate version of yourself and not a second-rate version of someone else." – Judy Garland

The Carpenter and the Gardener

The Carpenter begins with the end in mind. He takes a piece of wood, cuts it, shapes it, and assembles it into something useful. If he is a good carpenter, his creation is both functional and beautiful. His work is consistent, so that if he makes a set of four chairs, they all look exactly alike.

The gardener creates an environment that helps his garden grow. He provides the seeds, the fertilizer, and the water, but the plants must grow on their own according to their nature. He prevents interference from weeds and insects, and occasionally needs to trim the plants, but each plant grows differently and is beautiful in its own way.

The Carpenter and the Gardener are also two styles of parenting.

Which parent would you rather have?

Which parent would you rather be?

The Second Year

After the traumas of interrupted sleep, nasty spit-ups, and seemingly endless, mysterious bouts of crying, the second year of life

Raising 4 Dimensional Children in a 2 Dimensional World

will be a welcome relief. Your little monster is starting to act like a real person, but don't let that fool you: She doesn't yet understand what you think she does, and she can't always do what she wants to do, which leads to fits of frustration.

Now that she's learning to walk, you have to be extra vigilant: Where can she go? What can she find? What can she reach when she starts to climb? Where can she fall?

If you haven't already done so, take some time now to control your space – unless you want the stuff you own to start owning you. The first birthday is a great time to de-clutter your house and your life. Invest a little time in creating the environment you want for yourself and your child. You should have already child-proofed your house, so now you can set-up some safe play zones, perhaps keep other areas securely off limits, and make storage of toys quick and easy. You probably don't need as many toys as you already have, so give some away to friends with younger children or to charity.

If you are familiar with Maslow's Hierarchy of Needs, you are already providing your child's need for the physiological, safety, and love/belonging levels. During this year you also need to be aware of meeting your child's needs for esteem. These first 4 levels will keep you busy until adolescence, when some children may advance to the fifth level before adulthood.

During the first half of this year, play will increase between you and your child, but that will probably decrease in the second half of the year. Don't feel rejected; it's normal for children to begin to be more interested in other children as they approach their second birthday.

Major Lessons: Becoming aware of the world outside her immediate grasp and walking.

Note: Please read the previous chapter(s), as all children develop at different rates and many of the advances at this age are built upon earlier developments. In case your child is a little slower in one area, or in case you missed some of the activities in the previous section, it is always a good practice to review where you are coming from before advancing into new territory.

Also realize that over the twelve months from age one to two, your child will advance in many areas. The following descriptions of abilities are not all meant for the one-year-old, but rather show the progression made over the course of the year. Use these guides as a general direction you are working toward. Don't rush her progress and don't sweat it if she needs more time to develop certain skills.

Here's a breakdown in the four dimensions:

Physically

Your child will be moving more, with a desire to explore. If he is not yet walking, provide a walker, push toys that encourage walking, and hold his hands as he attempts to walk. Once he is walking freely, provide a pull toy for him to pull around (it could be something as simple as a shoe box with a string attached). As he gets better at walking, ask him to carry small objects. Soon enough he will be running.

Allow plenty of time for movement and physical activity. Try not to make him sit still for more than an hour at a time (except when sleeping) to prevent a build-up of energy that may release itself in bad behavior. There are currently no US guidelines for the minimum amount of activity, but other countries have suggested a minimum of 180 minutes (three hours) of moderate to vigorous physical activity for one-year-olds, spread throughout the day.[62] Use your judgment in defining moderate and vigorous, but the sample activities I have provided on the following pages all qualify as moderate to vigorous.

Drowning is the leading cause of death for this age group[63] – lock your doors, fence your pool, and never take your eyes off of him for more than 30 seconds at a time, but places like the tub require constant vigilance. If you own a pool, consider early swim lessons as one of many ways to reduce the risk of drowning.[64]

If you have stairs, fence them off until he can safely climb not only up the stairs, but down as well. Always position yourself below him – in case he does fall, you can catch him before he falls too far.

Follow the law when riding in cars, which usually means placing him in a rear-facing car seat until he outgrows the manufacturer's size guidelines, and then graduates to a front facing car seat. Never leave your child alone in a car, truck, or van. Not even for a minute. EVER.

Feeding

Although you may continue breast feeding, he will want to participate in family meals. By the middle of the year, he should learn to drink from a cup and eat with a spoon.

Whole cow's milk can start to be introduced into the diet after his first birthday, and a good way to do so gradually is to mix it with breast milk or formula. A toddler still needs a high level of fat content in his diet (50%) until about 2 years of age to help with the myelination in the development of his brain.[65]

Avoid getting your child hooked on sugar early in life. Not only does it create a lifetime of problems, even at this age it makes him hyper and rots his teeth, plus it leads to cognitive and memory deficiencies, and reduces impulse control.[66]

Continue to introduce new foods patiently, without forcing, and model proper eating etiquette. He will naturally follow your lead, but he will still be experimenting with what food feels like, tastes like, looks like when swirled around, and what happens when he throws something on the floor. Don't get upset – it's part of the learning process.

Sleeping

Continue your well-established bedtime routine, including reading. Make sure your child feels safe, knows he belongs where he is, and is loved by you.

During this year he will want to help undress himself before bed and help put on his bed clothes. Be patient and supportive of his efforts, letting him do what he can, and helping out before he gets frustrated. The goal is for him to gain confidence in his abilities.

Toddlers

Activities

Continue to use any activities from the previous chapter that your child found either difficult or particularly enjoyed, plus add these:

<u>Blow bubbles</u>: Let him pop them.

<u>Ask for help:</u> For simple tasks like opening doors, drawers, and turning pages in a book.

<u>Play catch</u>. At this age his brain probably can't communicate quickly enough with his hands to catch a ball tossed to him, so play rolling catch, where you roll the ball to him, and he rolls it back. Another option is to play catch with balloons. . . they are slower.

<u>Get it:</u> Point to an object and ask him to get it.

<u>Make some noise</u>: Give him noisemakers like small pots, drums, or even a xylophone.

<u>Do the Hokey Pokey</u>: To develop mind/body coordination.

<u>Building Blocks:</u> Stacking and knocking down blocks are simple physical challenges. A set of plastic mixing bowls that fit inside each other can be more fun than much more expensive toys.

<u>Patty-Cake:</u> Play Patty-Cake to develop coordination, rhythm, and cooperation.

<u>Fill'er Up:</u> Get two small boxes (shoe boxes?) or buckets and a group of different safe objects like balls or small toys. Move the objects from one box to another, and then invite your child to move them back. If he can walk, separate the boxes by a few steps. Of course, shower him with affection when he moves every item into the second box. Add a mental dimension to the game by saying, "In" and, "Out" at the appropriate times. Play it outdoors by placing a hula hoop (or any container) in the yard and asking him to gather various toys or objects and place them in the hoop.

Go Outside: Increase sensory stimulation by going outside the house/apartment.

Sponge Fun: Give him some sponges to squeeze, stomp, and use to wash stuff (outdoors).

Kickball: Help him learn how to kick a ball.

Parks: Go to the park to swing on swings, slide down the slide, and interact with other children. Beware of the dangers of falling. If he plays with other children, at this age it will primarily be parallel playing, where they play side-by-side. Most children won't play with each other (face to face) until they are a little older.

Note: Use your good judgment in these and any physical recommendation I make. Take whatever precautions you think necessary for your child in your unique situation (like a pandemic) to keep your child and everyone else safe.

Mentally

Her brain is growing at an amazing rate. By the age of two, her brain has twice as many connections between neurons and uses twice as much food energy (proportionately) as an adult's.[67] She is also learning to see the world differently, sometimes month by month. For example, by 12 months of age most toddlers will follow your gaze and look at what you are looking at. They can copy movements like putting a ball in a cup, and can even reverse roles in simple tasks, so that if you touch her nose, she may touch your nose.[68]

A 13-month-old can detect whether you can see something, and can use that information to predict what you will do. A 14-month-old can tell the difference between things done by accident and things done on purpose.[69]

At about 18 months she can determine what others want as opposed to what she wants.[70] She will begin to understand intention, so that if an adult drops something, she may pick it up and hand it to him, or if a ball is rolled to her, she will understand she is supposed to roll it back. If the adult tries to do something simple and fails, then she will do it correctly, showing she understood the intention over the action.[68] This is a great time to ask her to begin helping with simple chores around the house.

By Age 2, toddlers understand that one person's intentions are not the same as another's (some recognize this as early as 9 months.)[70]

Over the year, she will also graduate from what Piaget called the sensorimotor stage (primarily a stimulus/response way of dealing with the world) to the pre-operational stage of cognitive development, where she understands one thing can represent another.[71] The development of language is a clear sign that she understands words can represent ideas and objects. This stage will soon advance to the magical thinking of tea parties and imaginary friends.

Communication

Verbal and emotional growth will dominate your child's development this year, as your child really begins to talk to you – picking up new phrases, words, and inflections at an amazing rate and gradually substituting language for tears and physical expression. She might even start negotiating for more of what she likes and explaining why she is angry.

But let's not get too far ahead. Around her first birthday she will most likely point at things she wants. When she points, she will expect you to look at what she's pointing at. She is trying to show you something and using a combination of words and gestures to communicate. Remember that she can understand (her reflective vocabulary) more than she can say (her productive vocabulary), so you can help her learn by looking at what she is pointing at and asking, "Do you want the Teddy Bear?"

Soon, she will try to say the words. If she says, "Bu" and points to a book, don't try to make her repeat the word properly. Instead, say, "Do you want to read the book?" and then open it and start to read. She will learn the correct pronunciation at her own pace, as her brain and vocal control continue to grow. Just be as positive as you can and model the correct speech. If you use "baby talk," she will try to speak as you do. Soon she will also learn to raise her voice at the end of a word to indicate a one-word question like, "Book?"

At this age, most children will learn to say the word, "No!" and perhaps shake their head if they have seen you do that. It's not only cute and entertaining, but a way for her to establish control of the world by expressing what she wants and doesn't want.

Another breakthrough milestone will be the concept of "Me," which shows she understands that she is a unique individual separate from the rest of the world. This brilliant new understanding will lead to her declaring that certain things are, "Mine!" and all the trouble that will lead to throughout the rest of her life.

Realize that her brain does not yet operate "up to speed," so you should ask only simple, direct questions, and allow time for an answer. Always state things positively, as she may not process, "Don't Run!" as easily as, "Walk slowly."

Continue to build her vocabulary by narrating what you do throughout the day, and especially during walks, point out objects, sizes, colors, etc.

Sometime between 18 months and 2 years, she'll begin to form two- to four-word sentences. As your baby makes mental, emotional, and behavioral leaps, she'll increasingly be able to use words to describe what she sees, hears, feels, thinks, and wants.

At this age she will also be able to learn more than one language, so if you have a bilingual household, begin teaching her in both languages. There are two thoughts on raising bilingual children: 1) speak one language in the home and the other language in public, or 2) have one parent speak one language and the other parent (or a grandparent) speak the other. At this age, there won't be much "public" exposure, so I recommend option 2 until she goes to school. At that point you could transition to option 1.

Activities

Continue to use any activities from the previous chapter that your child found either difficult or particularly enjoyed, plus add these:

Toddlers

<u>Mirrors:</u> Look into safe mirrors so that she can learn to recognize herself, then continue the activity from the last chapter of touching and naming various body parts.

<u>Play Dough:</u> Is good for manual dexterity and for creativity to create shapes and animals.

<u>Play with tubes:</u> Paper towel tubes, wrapping paper tubes, etc. provide imaginative play. Drop a small ball through the tube, look through it, or bang it to make noise.

<u>Who's This?</u> Ask her to identify people she knows in photos.

<u>Puzzles:</u> Introduce simple shape and color puzzles, or cut up magazine photos into two or three pieces and put them back together. You can also present 3 objects (an apple, a banana, and a cucumber) and ask, "Which one is round?" "Which one is yellow?"

<u>Open it:</u> Take a small jar (like as spice jar) and put some favorite cereal in it. Hand it to your child and let her figure out how to get the cereal out.

<u>Water:</u> Outdoors, in a pool, or in the tub, fill cups and other containers with water and pour the water from one to the other.

<u>Follow Instructions:</u> Make a game out of following instructions first, by asking her to do one thing, and later, seeing if you can ask her to do two things (pick up the ball and hand it to me) and she can accomplish both. Be patient, as it may be later in the year before she can follow a two-step request.

<u>Stuffed Animals:</u> Are fun to touch and hold, but later in the year, will also be useful to stimulate her imagination as she pretends to feed the teddy bear or have conversations with him. The older she gets in this age group, the more you should encourage pretend play. You might even learn some interesting things about yourself and your parenting from the things she says as she feeds the bear or puts him to bed.

Raising 4 Dimensional Children in a 2 Dimensional World

Shadow Fun: Use a flashlight to create shadow images on the wall.

Art: Provide crayons and paper to draw. At first, she will just scribble. One at a time, show straight lines, circles, and other basic shapes and encourage her to copy them.

Music: Sing, dance, or play an instrument (any noisemaker).

Freeze Dance: Play music, dance, and when the music stops, you and your child must freeze.

Shell Game: Play the classic shell game, first with one cup to see if she can find the ball or other toy. When she understands how to find it, add another cup and move them around. When she gets good at finding it with two cups, add a third.

Order it: Take pictures of favorite activities (making cookies?) at the beginning, middle, and end. Show the child the pictures, ask her to identify what you are doing, and to put them in order. (Do not do this on your phone as the relationship between the pictures is easier to connect side-by-side than when you can see only one at time.)

Scavenger Hunt: Walk the neighborhood with a basket and collect interesting (safe) stuff. Describe the shapes, colors, textures, smells of the things you collect. Increase her vocabulary by naming and describing each item. Play around the house by asking her to help you find certain items.

Work it: As she approaches two years of age, challenge her imagination by presenting something new and saying, "I don't know how this toy works," and let her figure it out.

Imagine it: Ask her to imagine something she can't physically see, like a blue elephant. Then it's her turn to ask you to imagine something.

Emotionally

During the second half of the year, after the mental understanding of "me" emerges, your child will start to develop the "exposed self-conscious emotions": Embarrassment, jealousy, and empathy.[72] At this point you can add these new emotions to the primary emotions identified in the previous chapter in your discussions about emotions.

Be ready for the occasional temper tantrum as a result of a breakdown in communication (one word cannot convey the meaning of what he wants, and that is frustrating). Compound that with this new overwhelming emotion he has no experience in regulating, and you have a recipe for an eruption.

As part of his understanding of his separate identity, and his newfound ability to control things with his hands and sometimes with his words and gestures, he wants to learn what he can do and what he can't do. His best tool is trial and error, so he will test boundaries not necessarily to show you who's boss, but more likely to find out what happens when he does. If he is frustrated, he will experience a range of emotions, and if you teach him that he can get his way by throwing a tantrum, then that's the lesson he will learn.

Remember that children want your attention more than anything. If he gets more attention by being bad than by being good, then you literally reward him for being bad.

Continue to teach him about emotion by describing feelings . . . but you may have to wait for a "teachable moment" to discuss it. Say things like, "That makes you feel happy!" or "Are you feeling frustrated?" Notice that the word "feel" is used to separate the emotion from the identity. "You are feeling angry," teaches him about an emotion. "You are angry" labels him.

Talking during a tantrum will probably not get through, so wait. Instead, offer a hug, and if he declines, tell him it will be available when he wants it. Be aware that he will model your behavior, so if you display anger, he will copy you. Instead, deal with his moods calmly and patiently. Some experts even say that "time out" is more for the parent than the child.

Raising 4 Dimensional Children in a 2 Dimensional World

During this year he should begin to show affection with hugs and maybe kisses. As he gets older, encourage empathy: Practice with toys by saying, "Teddy bear fell down and got a boo-boo. Can you give him a hug?" Later, when you see another child who is sad, you can encourage him to give her a hug and he will know what to do.

Toward the end of the year, he will begin to develop effortful control, which means he may be able to direct his attention and to stop his first, instinctual response and replace it with a better option. This breakthrough comes from the brain developing the executive attention network, which will continue to develop over the next few years, but early signs of effortful control predict the ability to maintain focus, develop social norms, and later develop empathy and shame.[73] Although effortful control seems to have a hereditary basis, warm, supportive parenting is associated with its development.[74]

Discipline

Teach your child what, "No" means with a firm voice . . . it could save an injury. However, children this age have a problem with impulse control and have difficulty connecting actions with consequences. To a child this age, "Put on your shoes," doesn't necessarily mean right now. Even when he hears you, his brain works slowly, so it could take some time to register what you want, and then some more time to connect that with action (or stopping). Understand he is not being defiant, just doing the best he can with the tools he has.

Use consequences directly connected to the action. Yelling and spanking can be confusing, as the child may learn, "Mommy doesn't like me" instead of, "I shouldn't run into the street." Unfortunately, long explanations will probably not be understood. Use short, direct sentences like, "Don't hit mommy. That hurts. Don't hit. Don't hit." Short time-outs serve more as a redirect of attention than a punishment, but can be very effective.

Prevention is better than cure. When you see frustration building, distract and re-direct before it becomes a tantrum, because then it is too late. Praise positive behavior much more than you focus on negative behavior by at least 4 to 1. As I recommended in the previous chapter, don't be one of those parents who "No!" too much,

Toddlers

and have children who grow up saying, "I can't" rather than, "I can."

Give a warning whenever you see trouble brewing, like, "I'm counting to three, and if you don't stop, you're going to time-out. One, two, THREE!" If he doesn't listen, take him to the quiet and safe spot you've designated for time-outs, and set a timer for 30 seconds (which will seem like 30 minutes to him). When it goes off, ask him to apologize and give him a big hug to convey that you're not angry and you still love him . . . and whenever possible, practice the behavior you want a few times.

Allow him to assert his independence by offering two positive choices. Instead of asking, "Are you ready for your bath?" (a possible, "No!"), ask, "Would you rather take your bath first or brush your teeth?" He feels in control, and you win either way.

Help him anticipate. At the park, say, "We're going home in 5 minutes," so he has time to adjust to the idea.

Discipline is a matter of habits. Practice the good habits and praise him for doing them well. When he does the wrong thing, distract and re-direct him to do a good thing. He has a very short attention span, so use it to your advantage.

Activities

Continue to use any activities from the previous chapter that your child found either difficult or particularly enjoyed, plus add these:

<u>Making Faces:</u> Make faces that display different simple emotions and label them. Invite your child to make the same face and repeat the name of the emotion. Another variation is for you to draw the faces and put them in a bowl, then take turns pulling them out and naming the emotion.

<u>Emo-Charades:</u> Act out different emotions then ask your child to do the same. Later, make it into a game of charades, where you show an emotion and he has to guess which emotion it is, and then he acts out the emotion and you have to guess. You can eventually involve other family members and play on teams.

Wait: Now that you understand what effortful control is, continue playing this game where you teach your child to refrain from touching a prohibited toy: Don't touch for a count of ten, then celebrate. Later, don't touch for a count of twenty or even thirty.

Calm: Teach your child a simple form of meditation to calm down. Ask him to close his eyes and pay attention to his breathing while not moving for 10 seconds. At first, you count out loud to ten, but soon just be quiet. With success, increase the quiet time to twenty, then thirty seconds.

Gardening: Plant seeds if the weather permits. Kids love shovels, dirt, and water, but you can also introduce the idea of caring for something and taking responsibility.

Spiritually

As your child's vocabulary increases, it provides greater opportunity to increase the kinds of books you read and the content. Look for books that reveal simple moral messages, as well as age-appropriate books that contain stories and lessons about your own religion.

Help your child participate in prayers: Say things like, "Dear God, we thank you for _____ (ask your child to identify things she is grateful for – make suggestions, where needed) and please take care of _____ (ask your child to name the people she would like to pray for – again, make suggestions, where needed.)

Even if you don't pray or believe in God, it is still a positive practice to review the things you are grateful for at the end of the day, including the people who are important in your life. An attitude of gratitude goes a long way in creating and maintaining happiness.

Continue to attend religious services and explain what you can based on your child's level of understanding. Don't sweat about the details; just feed her spirit like you feed her stomach, mind, and heart.

The Third Year (the "Terrible Twos")

Your young man's personality will begin to show during this year. Don't be surprised if you see several different versions: They try on different personalities before one sticks. Do your best to encourage the one you like.

According to Dr. Maureen O'Brien, author of *Watch Me Grow I'm Two*, "the central dilemma for both child and parent in the third year springs largely from the normal unevenness of the two-year-old's mental, physical, and emotional development . . . many of the difficulties . . . even tantrums on the child's part – are a result of this mismatch between a parent's or child's expectations of the child's abilities."[75] In other words, he just can't do what you want him to do (or even what he wants to do.)

He is becoming aware of other people's viewpoints, yet still has a short attention span, a limited ability to control impulses, and very little practice at controlling emotions. He is still learning how to control everything about his body, from the use of his fingers to the release of hormones. You need to be patient with him, as he will grow out of it, but you also need to help him become patient with himself by modeling proper behavior.

Here are two tricks to help you deal with the inevitable "traumas" you will experience during this year: (1) Imagine yourself ten years in the future – will you even remember this event? If so, will you be laughing about it? (2) Imagine how it could have been much worse. Both of these tricks will take you out of your emotional dimension and into your mental dimension, and give you a little healthy perspective.

Major Lessons: Taking turns, playing make believe, and potty training.

Physically

She will be developing a variety of gross motor skills and fine motor skills. In addition to walking, she will begin running, climbing, squatting, spinning, jumping, pedaling a tricycle, and even somersaulting. For finer skills, expect to see her use tools like a hammer on a toy bench, a spoon to eat and not spill food, and crayons to color within the lines. Once again, this is a range of activities that will not all appear at her second birthday, but develop over the 12 months from two to three.

At 24 months the average child can climb and descend stairs, dance, stack three or more blocks, and begin to show a hand preference. By 27 months, she may run and play chase, pedal a tricycle, walk up and down stairs, try to jump off everything, unscrew lids, turn knobs, and unwrap packages. At 30 months she may be able to start experimenting with galloping and hopping, be able to kick a ball in an intended direction, use chalk, crayons, and kids' scissors. By 33 months she could be able to throw a ball, eat an ice cream cone while walking, alternate feet when climbing stairs, and swing a bat to hit a baseball off a tee.[76]

This is a good age to start to share simple chores, like picking up toys when done, working in the garden, putting dishes in the sink or dishwasher, and taking care of pets. It's probably too young to assign the chores to her to do on her own, but she will most likely enjoy helping you do whatever you do because she wants to be like you.

Feeding

After two years of age, children should begin transitioning to a more heart-healthy level of dietary fat (no more than 30 percent of total calories), including lower-fat cow's milk (1 or 2%).[65] Toddlers are curious, but tend to resist new foods. Expect fifteen contacts with the new food before the she accepts it. Don't force her. At this age of establishing an independent identity, the more you push, the more she will push back. Instead, model good behavior and stimulate curiosity by discussing the food's colors, textures, smells, and tastes, and then answer questions. When you eat it, she is more likely to try it, so you can feed her appropriate foods off your plate. Make it cooperation, not a contest. As she gets older and understands language better, you can even tell her that if she doesn't like the taste, that is because that food is for adults. (How's that for motivation?)

Eat at mealtimes or structured snack times and teach her to sit while eating. Do what you can to get her to chew thoroughly to prevent choking.

Judge the amount of food she eats by the week, not by the meal. Let her eat when hungry and not eat if not hungry. Don't bargain about food. Don't reward her for "good eating" or even "good behavior" with sugar: You will only be setting up a lifetime of dependence on sugar and an addiction to comfort foods that will cause weight and health problems well into adulthood.

If you are sending her to day care, ask if they have healthier snacks and drinks. If they don't, supply your own. Don't have sugary treats around the house. Kids want what they eat all the time, and children who are not exposed to sugar do not crave sugar, so you have a real life-altering choice here.

2-5% of children under age 3 suffer from food allergies, resulting in a range of reactions from skin rashes, diarrhea, watery eyes, sneezing, or a swollen throat, to spasms or difficulty breathing.[77] Pediatricians agree that most children outgrow the majority of these allergies by around age three, but it's important for you to be aware of these issues, monitor them, and consult your doctor when you think necessary.[77]

Potty Training

When do you start toilet training? As with most other milestones, it's best to take the cues from your child. When she begins showing an interest in the potty, being aware of peeing and pooping, and expressing the need to go, she is probably ready. Pique her interest with discussions, stories and potty books, and asking at the most likely times if she wants to go potty. Role modeling is important, so watching the appropriate parent should also create desire.

Raising 4 Dimensional Children in a 2 Dimensional World

By age two, most children are at least physically able to control elimination voluntarily – and the two-year-old's need to be a "big kid," especially when combined with new "toys" like her own potty or toilet seat, is a powerful motivating force. Just realize that toilet training is probably possible this year, but it certainly isn't necessary.

Two-year-olds love the step-by-step process, so turn it into a ritual: Pull down your pants, sit on the potty, do your business, and wipe off. (For you fathers who may not have been raised with sisters, girls always wipe down the front, not up.) Expect three to six months of daily attention to achieve your goal.[78] There will still be accidents for years to come whenever she is upset, preoccupied, or in an unfamiliar place. Even after successful days, most children need more time to establish the unconscious control needed to sleep through the night. If you don't already have one, invest in a water-proof mattress pad.

Don't over-react to accidents. They are usually not done on purpose. Punishment can have negative effects, and if you react strongly enough, she may do it again just for the attention.

If you find that your child has lost interest or is actively resisting your efforts, simply drop the subject until the next time she complains about her dirty, uncomfortable diaper. Don't expect consistency right away. Praise success, but don't overdo it. Also expect that if she or any member of your family is going through an emotional trauma, she may revert until a more emotionally stable time.

Note: Preschool by three is possible, but potty training is often required.

Sleeping

Continue to reinforce and revise your bedtime routine. Model behaviors. If you want her to brush her teeth, do it together: You brush yours and she brushes hers. Alternately, you can offer choices: Do you want to brush your nose, your eyebrows, or your teeth? Do you want me to brush your teeth, or do you want to do it yourself?

This age is also a good time to add some steps to the bedtime routine, like breathing exercises. With the child in your lap so you can feel each other's heartbeats, read a calming story. Dr. Becky Baily has wisely said that it's not the book you are reading, but the lap you are sitting on that counts. When the story is finished, teach your child to take deep breaths to calm down and get ready to sleep. As you both take one deep breath at a time together, say something like, "I breathe for you; I breathe for us; and I breathe for all that surround us."[79]

Then, develop your attitude of gratitude by praying or just being thankful by recounting the good things in your life, the good things that happened today, and the important people in your lives.

Finish up with some questions: "How do you want to wake up tomorrow?" "What do you want to feel like when you wake up?" Help your child pre-program herself for a good day.

Activities

Continue to do the activities from the previous year as long as they are fun, plus you can upgrade the activities or increase the skill level with some of these ideas.

Art: Develop fine motor skills by drawing, coloring, and cutting paper with safe scissors.

Balance: Help her develop her balance by standing on tip toes, jumping, galloping, and standing on one foot. Challenge her to combine two actions at a time like standing on one foot and clapping.

March: Play some music and march around the house in a musical parade. Add an instrument if you can.

Follow the Leader: Take turns being the leader and the follower. You can face each other and do fun and funny movements, or you can march, gallop, and dance around the house one following the other.

Fill'er Up: Upgrade the game by adding the concept of sorting: Put all the objects on the floor and ask her to put all the red objects in one box (or bucket) and all the blue objects in the other. You can sort by big and small, shape, noise or quiet, etc. You can also play outdoors.

Walk: Go for walks outdoors to enjoy nature in your neighborhood or at a park for a variety of stimulation. Get a little sun (not too much),

Raising 4 Dimensional Children in a 2 Dimensional World

breathe the fresh air, and look at plants, houses, people, insects, and other animals.

Run: You probably won't need a game; she will just run for the joy of running. It becomes more fun if you chase each other or she chases a playmate. Be wary of things she will bump into while indoors or dangers like moving cars outdoors.

Tricycle: If you can afford one, this is a good age to learn how to pedal and steer a tricycle.

Shadow Dancing: When outdoors, show your child her shadow, then ask her to make the shadow dance, jump, and do other activities.

Paint the House: Give your child a paint brush and water, and let her paint the driveway or outside of the house (with water, not paint!)

Parks: Go to the park to swing on swings, slide down the slide, and interact with other children. Use your judgment to prevent injuries. She should start actually playing with the other children, face to face playing the same game, which will lead to conflicts. Be a good referee and anticipate trouble before it happens.

Sport Skills: Some time during this year she should be able to throw a ball overhand, swing a bat, or kick a ball in an intended direction. Catching may still be challenging and hitting a ball will probably be limited to hitting it off a Tee, but she can begin learning the build-up skills she will need to play team sports.

Note: Use your good judgment in these and any physical recommendation I make. Take whatever precautions you think necessary for your child in your unique situation (like a pandemic) to keep your child and everyone else safe.

Mentally

Between the ages of 2 and 3 your child will transition from being able to picture something in his mind that isn't present (Piaget's symbolic thought phase) to asking, "Why?" and, "How come?" (Piaget's Intuitive thought phase). He will also use Transductive Reasoning, which connects two events without reason or logic.[80] This faulty way of connecting people and events can lead to emotional problems.

In his mind, everything is alive, so don't be surprised if he thinks his food can talk. At 24 months, he will understand some broad references of time like "later" or "soon," but specific concepts like "in ten minutes" or "Next Monday" have no meaning. At 27 months he should begin to be able to classify objects and may begin counting, and by 30 months he should be able to sort objects by color or shape and follow a story line. However, don't be surprised at 33 months if he has trouble distinguishing between what's real and what's pretend. By 36 months of age, he should have enough spoken vocabulary to enjoy describing events (real or imaginary), narrating his own actions, and should be able to draw a simple face.[76]

He will also be more aware of what is happening and what is being said around him, so your job is to protect him from information that is inappropriate or emotionally overwhelming. Be careful NOT to have the TV on in the background because chances are good it will include loud noises and violent images in shows, movies, or even the news.

As part of his desire to learn, he will repeat words and actions, and ask you to, "Do it again!" over and over, not in an attempt to annoy you, but as a pure scientist, performing an experiment, and then verifying the results by performing the same experiment again and again. He is learning by repetition.

As part of his new ability to classify items, he will acquire his gender identity. Don't be alarmed at minor confusions: Physical gender seems to be a black and white fact (you have one or you have the other), but mental and emotional gender traits have many shades of gray. Most men have some "feminine" traits or tendencies, and most women have some "masculine" traits or tendencies, which are defined more by society than by nature. None of us is 100% male or female when viewed this way, and a balanced person would probably be closer to 60/40 than 100/0. Don't overreact if your son likes to play with dolls or your daughter likes to play with trucks. Chances are it's not a life sentence. Give it time.

In addition, recent research shows that sexual identity and sexual preference may form in the womb at different times than the physical sex glands, and occasionally they don't all match up.[81,82] If that research is correct, sexual identity and sexual preference may not be matters of choice, but more likely matters of genetic wiring.

Most children will sort it out over time, including those who have a "change of heart" during the hormone releases of puberty, but if your child seems outside these general guidelines, speak with several qualified psychologists to get sound, child-centered advice.

Communication

Two-year-olds can typically speak between 200 and 250 words.[83] By age 3 they are able to put three and four words together into sentences, but still have trouble with describing feelings, which can compound into frustration.

At 24 months they are putting two-word sentences together like, "Daddy come?" and learning to use pronouns like I, me, and you. At this age they will be more interested in what they want than what you have to say, but as the year progresses, they become better listeners. By 33 months they should start to use prepositions like over and under, but they are very literal, so be careful about making jokes that might be misunderstood ("If you don't stop drinking juice, you're going to explode!").[84]

Activities:

Continue to do the activities from the previous year as long as

Toddlers

they are fun, plus you can upgrade the activities or increase the skill level with some of these ideas.

Describe it: Anywhere – either in the house or outside – point out an object and ask multi-sensory questions like, "What color is it?" "What sound does it make?" and then add some new adjectives and descriptions of your own to increase his vocabulary.

Follow directions: Give your child two consecutive directions like, "Jump then run to the couch." When he can successfully follow two directions, add a third.

Your Turn: Play games like Go Fish that require taking turns. As he gets older, try easy board games.

Songs: Teach your child some simple songs or nursery rhymes. As he learns them, ask him to finish the sentence or complete the rhyme. You can do the same thing when reading a familiar book.

Art: He should be getting better at drawing simple shapes. Ask him to draw something specific, like a dog. Alternately, you can start to draw something, and ask him to guess what it is.

Puzzles: He may enjoy taking apart simple toys and putting them back together or assembling simple puzzles. Ask him to name each piece of the puzzle or toy.

Order it: Review sequences of familiar routines, like, "What happens after bath time?" or, "How do we set the table?"

Organization: Ask, "Where do toys go?" "Where do shoes go?" and put them in their proper place. When he gets good at organizing, occasionally put his shoes in the toy bin and let him correct your "mistake."

Match it: Place 20 playing cards on the floor (face up) with two of each kind. Mix them up and ask your child to put the two matching cards together (if you don't have a deck of cards, you can make your own with stickers or even crayons and paper).

The Director: Let your child direct the play. Ask him questions about what he is doing and why. Encourage his imagination by asking more questions.

Make Believe: Have a dinner party for your stuffed animals. Use paper plates, plastic spoons, cups, etc.

How many uses: Take a simple object, like a ball, and ask him to identify how many ways he could use the ball. Give some suggestions, or take turns offering uses.

Identity: As soon as possible, get him to say his full name, your phone number, and his home address (one step at a time) in case he gets lost.

Emotionally

In addition to the exposed self-conscious emotions that developed last year, this year your child will develop the "self-conscious evaluative emotions:" A different kind of embarrassment, plus shame, guilt, hubris, and pride, which require an understanding of the cultural rules of her family and society. Last year the embarrassment was due to the attention of others; this new kind is an embarrassment from not following the rules of the culture.[72]

All children have three emotional needs: Your attention, your affection, and your acknowledgment. Keep this in mind during the wild outbursts that are sure to come. This is also a critical age for developing self-worth, and therefore self-confidence, so be aware of the messages you are sending.

Different children have different temperaments, and each is associated with a different style of parenting that seems to be more effective. The three broad temperaments are (1) Extroversion, (2) Negativity, and (3) Effortful Control. Extroverts tend to be more positive, active, and take more risks, which leads to more behavior problems. Negative kids tend to be more afraid or sad, but also can be more angry, and can become anxious and depressed or even aggressive later in life. I discussed effortful control earlier in the chapter, and the good results that can be attained.[85]

The important thing is for you to understand the differences and adjust yourself accordingly. If you are unaware of the possibilities, a negative child naturally draws some negative responses from not

Toddlers

only other children, but parents. Don't let yourself be controlled by your baby. Instead, listen to your baby's needs, but respond in the most effective way to meet those needs as described in Chapter 3.

She will take her emotional cues from you: Whenever she encounters something new, she will look to you for the proper reaction. If you freak out, you will teach her to do the same. If you are calm and collected, she will try to be like you. However, certain fears and anxieties will appear on their own as the result of her developing imagination: Monsters in the closet or under the bed. Don't try to combat these fears with logic (a mental solution for an emotional problem.) Instead, listen to understand the source of fear, and then address that.

Another fear you may encounter is fear of separation. A two-year old is asserting her independence, but only so far. She will run away, but at a certain distance, she will come back, depending on the local distractions. Get her used to being separate from you in a place where she doesn't notice you, but you can still watch her, like the park or playground. As she spends time with other children and even with another adult, you will prepare her for times when you leave her with someone else, like a relative, preschool, or day care.

Because of her Transductive Reasoning, she will connect two events that have no logical connection, and may feel responsible for things she has no control over. For example, if she is drinking juice when Daddy comes home angry about traffic, she may think that drinking juice makes Daddy angry. When you discover these odd fears, ask, "Why do you not want to drink juice?" Then do your best to show (not tell) her that Daddy likes her to drink juice.

Once again, think prevention. When she looks tired, head off a problem by saying, "You look tired; let's read a book." Help her to identify her emotions by labeling them. Name it to tame it. Help her become aware of her body by asking, "Where do you feel it?" What does it feel like?" Offer suggestions if she doesn't have the vocabulary. Is she breathing fast or slow, deep or shallow? Ask questions like, "How big is the feeling?" "What color is it?" "What shape is it?"

Raising 4 Dimensional Children in a 2 Dimensional World

These questions not only acknowledge the feeling, but help her move out of the emotional dimension into the mental dimension where feelings have less control.

Offer different ways to handle upset feelings and calm herself, like taking a few deep breaths or counting (if she is too young to count, maybe recite a favorite nursery rhyme or song, especially if it is a happy song). Alternately, you can ask her to change the color, size, or shape of the feeling using her new-found imagination. Another calming method is to change her focus. Take advantage of her short attention span by getting her to think about something she likes to do (again, NOT something she likes to eat.) In addition, if it is a powerful emotion, try to offer physical outlets like running to release the emotional energy (play tag or chase).

Be confident that the turmoil of the early months that give this age the label of The Terrible Twos will subside as the two of you learn how to work together on better ways of expressing feelings (words instead of actions), and how to find acceptable ways to deal with these new emotions. Later in the year she will understand that her feelings aren't the only feelings, and other people can be hurt by her words and actions. You just have to persevere until her brain develops that ability, with your guidance.

Discipline

At this age, discipline is primarily prevention and re-direction. Punishment is a double-edged sword because children easily draw the wrong conclusions. When your child is finished with an encounter with you, what conclusion will she draw? Unfortunately, one of the most common conclusions is, "I'm not good enough." Too much discipline leads many children to believe they are not worthy, need permission to do anything, and they become too submissive and dependent.

Create frameworks where experimentation is possible, but rules are clear and enforced. Give most of your attention to positive behavior and very limited attention to negative behavior. Use the guidelines provided earlier in this chapter to prevent, distract, and re-direct with positive choices, always affirming your love for your child.

Toddlers

The rules are the rules, and have consequences, but help her understand that she made a mistake and learned a lesson, rather than she made a mistake because she is a loser or a bad person. Self-confidence is an important lesson this year.

An important concept in discipline is Minimum Consequences: You want to use the minimum consequences to get the job done. You don't want to use a bazooka to kill flies when a fly swatter will do the job just as well without the collateral damage. Any punishment you use should be just enough to stop the unwanted behavior. Excessive punishment has collateral emotional damage, so do your best to get the best behavior with the minimum punishment.

One new issue that may arise at this age is aggression, especially now that she is beginning to play with other children. Be on the lookout for trouble brewing and stop it before it rears its ugly head. It is not constructive to allow a two-year-old to hit another child and then punish her for it. The more often it happens, the more it becomes a pattern that can be hard to break. Chances are that her aggression is at least as upsetting to her as it is to you. Instead, intervene with redirection when you see it coming. Not only will you prevent the fight, but you will also demonstrate how to handle aggressive feelings in the future.

As recommended earlier, give a warning to end activities to allow her some control but still be obedient.

When going out into public, bring quiet games to restaurants or doctor's offices to occupy your child. Preparation wins the day. If you get stuck, at the doctor's office, open a magazine and identify different animals or point to different body parts to review vocabulary. Alternately, you can look at pictures and make up stories . . . maybe even taking turns to advance the story.

Activities

Continue to do the activities from the previous year as long as they are fun, plus you can upgrade the activities or increase the skill level with some of these ideas.

Raising 4 Dimensional Children in a 2 Dimensional World

Breathe Fast: Create awareness of breathing by intentionally breathing fast and breathing slowly. How do you feel when you breathe fast? When you breathe slowly? Practice breathing slowly by choice.

Name it: Name emotions whenever you notice them. As her emotional vocabulary increases, ask, "How do you Feel?" and even, "Why do you feel that way?" She may identify the events that led up to the feeling, but you might also ask her to feel her heart rate and breathing as physical causes of the emotion.

Control it: Once you have a common vocabulary of emotions, start working on how to control them. Normally you don't need to control positive emotions unless they start getting manic. Smiles, hugs, and happy dances are all cool. However, negative emotions tend to hurt, so controlling them is a good thing. Practice deep breathing and singing a happy song or reciting a happy nursery rhyme. When she can count, practice counting to ten when angry.

Stop it: Rehearse how to control impulses by making a game of "freeze." Have your child play or dance or run around, but when you say, "Stop!" she must freeze in place. Play often and as long as it's fun for her, to program her to stop when you see danger.

Change it: Teach your child to be mentally flexible by exploring different ways to do things. Ask her to play with a specific toy a different way. Start with something simple like a ball. Once she can think of one way, challenge her to show another, or even two or three different ways to play with it. Expand the game to other activities like bathing, brushing teeth, and getting dressed.

Acting Class: Make your own play or movie. You and your child (or two children) can act out a scene like sharing a doll. Your child grabs the doll and says, "Mine!" You say, "Let's share. You make her dance and then give her to me so I can make her dance." Then switch roles. If your child is old enough, you can record your movie on your phone or tablet and play it back. Use this activity to rehearse conflicts you anticipate or even ones you have seen occur, and offer a constructive solution.

Better Way: Act out an unacceptable emotion, like a temper tantrum, and then act out a "better way" to express the emotion, like saying, " I get angry when you don't listen to me." Alternately, you can use dolls or plush toys as puppets to act out the bad way and the better way.

Who's the Best? Several times a day ask your child a positive question like, "Who's the best?" or "Who's a smart girl?" to build her confidence. You might even ask the question after she does something well, as a way of building her confidence while complimenting her.

Spiritually

As your child connects to his feelings, he will become fascinated with all parts of his body and all sensations. When he finds his genitals, distract him but do not shame him. As he is not sexually developed yet, this isn't really a sexual activity. If you give a big emotional response, that only encourages him to push for another emotional response. Calmly teach him that certain things are private, and others are for company. Teach him when, where, and who it's OK to touch, and when, where, and who it is not, and remind him when necessary. Emphasize that if someone else touches him there, he should always tell you.

Unfortunately, learning to talk will also bring with it learning to lie. Most children will naturally lie when they realize they have done something wrong. Remember, they don't have much experience dealing with feelings, and when they realize they have done something they know is wrong, they will first try to hide it, and then try to lie about it. It probably isn't a moral issue, yet, just a stimulus/response way of avoiding a bad feeling or maybe avoiding the bad consequences.

Start by identifying the feeling and naming it. Then identify your own feelings about what happened, and clearly state that you are not happy about the broken plate, but lying about it makes you more unhappy. Finish up with something like, "I know it's hard to behave all the time, but everybody makes mistakes. The important thing is to learn from your mistake and do better next time. When you lie about it, you are not learning. You are making another mistake. Now tell me the truth," and give him a hug for telling the truth. Don't expect miraculous success the first time or every time, but with persistence you should win in the long run, especially if you make the consequences for lying worse than the consequences for whatever he did.

    Discipline comes from habits. Whatever the problem, whenever possible, give him a chance to practice doing it right.

Activities

What would you do? Make a game out of discussing situations like:
    "What would you do if you saw Mary start to cry?"
    "What would you do if you were playing with Billy, and you had two trucks?"
    "What would you do if you ate my grapes and I asked, 'Who ate my grapes?'"
    "What would you do if you lied to Daddy, and he didn't know it?"
Be aware of his limited ability to hold more than one idea in his mind at once before you start piling on, "What if this, and this, and that?" Keep it simple, practical, and related to his everyday life.

Summary

    The toddler years are exciting for both the parents and the child. The parents will have to decide what kind of parent they want to be: A carpenter or a gardener. Dr. Shefali Tsabary says that we need to understand that we do not own our children, but that they are unique, sovereign beings. She tends to look at things spiritually, and goes so far as to say, "The child was put here for the education of the parent, not the other way around."[86]

    Your child will learn to walk, run, skip, and play. She will learn to talk, graduating from gestures and single words, to short sentences, speaking hundreds of words, and probably to lying. She will become aware of her own separate identity, recognize herself in a mirror, and

Toddlers

recognize pictures of significant people in her life. She will experience a new wave of intense emotions with no idea how to deal with them. With help, she can begin to understand those emotions, and learn to manage them successfully.

She will change her diet from breast feeding and formula, with about 50% fat content, to more table food and about 30% fat content. She can learn to control her bowels and emerge from messy diapers to being mostly or even fully housebroken and ready to attend day care or preschool.

She will become more affectionate, more stubborn, more frustrated at her inabilities, and seemingly defiant as she tries to figure things out. She will experiment in an attempt to learn and repeat things over and over that she wants to remember. She will model her behavior after you, so be as calm and understanding as you can.

She can now participate more fully in getting dressed, reading stories, and saying prayers. She can imagine things that aren't real, and make faulty connections between things that happen, sometimes drawing childishly harmful conclusions. She will also start to question everything.

Enjoy this magical time of tea parties and imaginary friends. Encourage her thinking outside the box, to become a unique individual. The range of abilities during these years is immense, so don't be surprised if your child doesn't match exactly what I have said, but if you are worried about any serious differences, consult your doctor.

Screen Time

The American Academy of Pediatrics has revised its 1999 guideline of no screen time for children under 2 to "caution" for kids under 2.[87] Generally, before 18 months they may not understand that what is on the screen is supposed to represent something else. After 18 months you can try some simple, age-specific games and learning activities like those reviewed on www.commonsensemedia.org to help them learn to use technology, but be involved so that you can direct their attention, ask questions, and talk about what you both see. Video chats with relatives are different, as they involve human serve and return interaction. After their second birthday you may allow one hour a day of carefully reviewed and highly recommended activities that improve vocabulary, especially if you are raising a bilingual child.[88]

Using two dimensional technology can seemingly put your child into a trance, where she is so engrossed in the screen that the real, four dimensional world seems to disappear. Dr. Ellen Wartella of Northwestern University describes it as being "hypnotized" by technology, causing the child not to interact with her as she would be if she were sharing a book with her.[89] In fact, there is research that shows children this age have difficulty transferring the skills learned in two dimensions into their 3-dimensional experience.[90] In addition, there is evidence that the amount of screen time young children spend is associated with poorer executive functions and self-regulation.[91]

I strongly recommend avoiding television completely, as many of the commercials are designed for children and specifically to make them feel they need something, which undermines their confidence. Even background TV can be upsetting because of the loud noises and violence. It also distracts you, the adult, away from your child and from providing the four dimensional person-to-person interaction that she needs. Certainly, do not use the TV as a babysitter. Wait until after you put your toddler to bed to watch the news or even a good movie.

Child Care:

I recommend that, if at all possible, you spend these early years paying full-time attention to your child, as the investment in time and teaching you make now will have far reaching results in the child's future. If the real world gets in the way of your ideal life and you simply must work and use childcare, the first choice is still a family member who can interact with the child as recommended here. If you need to go to a professional childcare facility, look for the highest quality you can find (not necessarily the highest price, but price often represents investment in quality staff.) Review the recommendations in the previous chapter to help you decide.

Bullying: At this age your child may experience a simple form of bullying at childcare or even during play dates and park fun. A simple solution is to teach your child to sternly point his finger at the bully and say, "No! No! No!" That may be all that is necessary, but a submissive child may need some coaching and practice on how to do it. Another successful tactic is to invite the bully over for a supervised play date, where your child and the bully can become friends. This ploy can not only stop the bullying for your child, but may even help the bully find better ways to interact with other kids.

Note: As all children are unique and develop at different rates, I recommend you read the next chapter to prepare for your child's growth and in case your child happens to develop more quickly in one area or another, and the previous chapter in case your child happens to develop more slowly in one area or another. Specifically, some of the activities might well be continued into the older years.

Also please use your own good judgment in following any advice I offer. Research is subject to change and my advice may be based on research that has since changed or been updated since this publishing. Choose your actions based on your own beliefs, experiences, research, and judgment, especially during extenuating circumstances (like a pandemic.)

Recommendations for further research:

www.Zerotothree.com
www.WebMD.com
https://pathways.org/us/
http://education.com
https://parenting-ed.org/parenting-information-handouts/early-childhood/
www.child-encyclopedia.com/
www.commonsensemedia.org
https://www.who.int/topics/early-child-development/en/
https://www.vroom.org/
https://parentsasteachers.org/
https://www.child-encyclopedia.com
Watch Me Grow I'm Two by Dr. Maureen O'Brien, 2001, William Morrow, New York.
The Gardener and the Carpenter by Alison Gopnik, 2016, Farrar, Straus, and Giroux, New York.

References:

62. Cliff, Dylan P, PhD; and Janssen, Xanne, PhD. "Levels of Habitual Physical Activity in Early Childhood." Encyclopedia on Early Childhood Development; Physical Activity, 2019, p.7. http://www.child-encyclopedia.com/physical-activity/complete-topic. Accessed June 8, 2021.

63. Centers for Disease Control and Prevention; Child Development; Toddlers. http://www.cdc.gov/ncbddd/childdevelopment/positiveparenting/toddlers.html. Accessed June 8, 2021.

64. Pediatrics; American Academy of Pediatrics Policy Statement. https://pediatrics.aappublications.org/content/143/5/e20190850. Accessed June 8, 2021.

65. Zero to Three; Resources & Services. "How does nutrition affect the developing brain?" https://www.zerotothree.org/resources/1372-how-does-nutrition-affect-the-developing-brain. Accessed June 8, 2021.

66. Caremans, Gregory, *"Neuroscience and Parenting."* https://www.udemy.com/course/neuroscience-and-parenting/ Section 2.7. Accessed March 29, 2021.

67. Rosenfeld, Jordan. "10 Amazing Facts About the Infant Brain." Mental Floss; The Body; October 22,2015. https://www.mentalfloss.com/article/70105/10-amazing-facts-about-infant-brain. Accessed June 8, 2021.

68. Henderson, Annette, ME; *et. al.* "The Birth of Social Intelligence." *Zero to Three Journal*, May 2008.

69. *Ibid.*

70. Thompson, Ross A. "The Psychologist in the Baby." *Zero to Three Journal*, May 2008.

71. Kandolal, Aaron. "What to know about Piaget's stages of cognitive development." *Medical News Today,* April 25, 2019. Piaget's 4 stages of development: What do they mean? (medicalnewstoday.com). Accessed June 8, 2021.

72. Lewis, Michael, PhD. "Emotions. " Encyclopedia on Early Childhood Development; 2011, p.5-7. http://www.child-encyclopedia.com/emotions/complete-topic. Accessed June 8, 2021.

73. Rothbart, Mary K, PhD. "Early Temperament and Psycholosocial Development." Encyclopedia on Early Childhood Development; Temperament; 2019, p. 9. www.child encyclopedia.com/temperament/complete-topic. Accessed June 8, 2021.

74. *Ibid.,* p 16.

75. O'Brien, Maureen, PhD. *Watch Me Grow I'm Two.* 2001, William Morrow, New York, p.9.

76. *Ibid.,* pp. 52-53.

77. *Ibid.,* p.186.

78. KidsHealth; for Parents; Toilet Training. "When are Kids Ready to Toilet Train?" Toilet Training (for Parents) - Nemours KidsHealth. Accessed June 8, 2021.

79. Newman, Andrew. Interview in *Little Humans* series https://littlehumans.com/.

80. Oxford Reference; Transductive Reasoning. Transductive reasoning - Oxford Reference. Accessed June 8, 2021.

81. Swaab, D. (2007). "Sexual differentiation of the brain and behavior." *Best Practice and Research Clinical Endocrinology & Metabolism, 21*(3), pp. 431-444.

82. Swaab, D; and Garcia-Falgueras, A. (2008). "A sex difference in the hypothalamic uncincate nucleus: Relationship to gender identity." *Brain, 131*, pp. 3132-3146.

83. Zero to Three; Resources & Services. "Nurturing Your Child's Development from 24 to 26 Months." April 15, 2003. https://www.zerotothree.org/resources/1054-nurturing-your-child-s-development-from-24-to-36-months. Accessed June 8, 2021.

84. O'Brien, pp.108 ff.

85. Rothbart, Mary K, PhD, *et.al.* "Synthesis." Encyclopedia on Early Childhood Development; Temperament, 2012, p. 5. www.child-encyclopedia.com/temperament/complete-topic. Accessed June 8, 2021.

86. Tsabary, Shefali. Interview in *Little Humans* series https://littlehumans.com/.

87. Pediatrics; Policy Statement; November 2016. "Media and Young Minds." DOI: https://doi.org/10.1542/peds.2016-2591. Accessed June 10, 2021.

88. Zero to Three; Resources & Services. "Making Good Decisions About Television and Screen Time for Young Children." Feb 29, 2016. https://www.zerotothree.org/resources/318-making-good-decisions-about-television-and-screen-time-for-young-children. Accessed June 8, 2021.

89. Zero to Three; Resources & Services. "The Influence of Media on Young Children's Development." Feb 24, 2016. https://www.zerotothree.org/resources/284-the-influence-of-media-on-young-children-s-development. Accessed June 8, 2021.

90. Barr, R. "Memory Constraints on Infant Learning from Picture Books, Television, and Touchscreens." *Child Dev Perspect.* 2013; 7(4); 205–210.

91. Courage, Mary L, PhD; and Troseth, Gerogene L, PhD. "Infants, Toddlers, and Learning from Screen Media." Encyclopedia on Early Childhood Development; 2016, pp. 6-7. http://www.child-encyclopedia.com/technology-early-childhood-education/complete-topic. Accessed June 8, 2021.

Chapter 5
Early Childhood
Years 3 to 5

"I'm not crazy . . . my reality is just different than yours!"
– the Cheshire Cat, *Alice's Adventures in Wonderland*

A Word to the "Why's"

Little Darnell

Darnell: *Mom, can Daddy and I play soccer today?*

Mom: *Not today, honey, Daddy has to go to work.*

Darnell: *Why?*

Mom: *To make money.*

Darnell: *Why?*

Mom: *So we can buy food and pay the mortgage.*

Darnell: *Why?*

Mom: *Stop asking stupid questions and eat your breakfast!*

Little Darius

Darius: *Mom, can Daddy and I play soccer today?*

Mom: *Not today, honey, Daddy has to go to work.*

Darius: *Why?*

Mom: *So he can make money.*

Darius: *Why?*

Mom: *So we can buy food and pay the mortgage.*

Darius: *Why?*

Mom: *So we can have a house to live in.*

Darius: *Why?*

Mom: *Well, do you like your bed and your room?*

Darius: *Yeah.*

Mom: *Would you rather sleep in your bed or outside in the rain?*

Darius: *In my bed. Outside I'd get all wet.*

Mom: *Yes, you would, and it would be cold, and we would have no food. Would you like that?*

Darius: *No!*

Mom: *Well, that's why Daddy has to go to work.*

Daddy: *But we can play together when I get home tonight. Would you like that?*

Darius: *Yes!*

Mom: *So let's give Daddy a big kiss so he can go to work. Then, will you help me clean up the breakfast dishes?*

Darius: *Yeah!*

Which parent are you?

The word to the "Why's" is PATIENCE. Your child's brain now understands cause and effect, so his constant question is going to be, "Why?" so he can learn the causes. Darnell's mother did not have the patience to answer his questions, so the lesson he learned was that he is stupid and annoying. That's a great way to kill curiosity! Darius' mother had the patience to answer his questions on his level, and then turned the table on him by asking him some questions of her own. If

Early Childhood

you never realized it before, the person who controls the conversation is the person who asks the questions. If your child asks too many questions, simply take control of the conversation by answering his question with a question of your own. His short attention span will follow where you lead. (By the way, this technique works on adults, too.) Darius' father also acknowledged his son's needs and offered a positive solution. His mother then moved Darius' attention to two activities he was familiar with: Kissing Daddy good-bye and cleaning up the breakfast dishes. The difference was minimal for the two mothers, but significant for the two kids.

Your child has probably now become a chatterbox, using his seemingly limitless energy to not only ask a million questions, but learning how to argue his point of view. That energy also makes it difficult for him to play quietly indoors like he used to. Find a healthy outlet for this energy, preferably with some positive structure, like early childhood martial arts, dance, or gymnastics classes. The interaction of playing with other children, even if it is on a playground, will release some of that energy and give him the social contact he craves.

His imagination will also be in high gear, so encourage make-believe play. You might even stimulate his imagination by asking questions like, "Where does the rain come from?" You'll get some interesting answers. Just be prepared for that same imagination to spook him once in a while. Listen to his fears and simply comfort or re-assure him.

As a general practice, parents of children this age should FEEL

Freeze – stop and just listen; don't try to fix everything, especially during an emotional breakdown.

Empathize – open your heart to what your child is thinking and feeling on his level.

Educate – look for teachable moments.

Let go of your guilt – you don't have to be perfect; just do your best.[92]

Major Lessons: learning to count, being able to identify likes and dislikes, dressing and undressing himself, opening jars and doors, development of executive function, and moving from not being able to distinguish make-believe from reality to understanding the difference.

Note: Please read the previous chapter(s), as all children develop at different rates and many of the advances at this age are built upon earlier developments. In case your child is a little slower in one area, or in case you missed some of the activities in the previous chapter, it is always a good practice to review where you are coming from before advancing into new territory.

It takes a Village

Children are not raised in isolation: There are relatives, neighbors, school systems, churches, and even gangs that will affect your child's growth and development. Recent research shows that where you grow up can increase or decrease your odds of success dramatically (30% increase in earnings, $300,000 in lifetime income, 30% increase in college attendance rate, 25% reduction in rate of teenage birth), but much of the effects lose significance if you move after the child reaches his 12th birthday. In one neighborhood, the rate of incarceration for black males was 45% on the date of the 2010 census, while 2 miles away the rate of incarceration for the same group was only 6% (which is still high, but much better just by moving only 2 miles.) Also, children raised in two parent homes but who live in communities with lots of single-parent households tend to have more trouble in their lives.[93]

Other research shows that the amount of greenery (trees, bushes, grass) in your neighborhood can affect the crime rate, social interaction, and health of the people who live there.[94]

What can you do about it? Move, if possible. Look up your neighborhood on https://www.opportunityatlas.org/ to see how your neighborhood is rated. If it's not so good, look for somewhere close by that has better results. Then, visit those neighborhoods and compare them for the amount of greenery. You may have to pay a little higher rent . . . or you may not. Be a good gardener by providing the best soil for your child's growth. Location is one of the environmental factors you CAN control. Moving isn't easy, but it can create life-long differences for the future of your child, and even the next generation.[93]

Early Childhood

Child Care

In the previous chapters I recommended avoiding childcare, if possible, but we have to face reality. Recent estimates indicate that nearly two out of every three children 3-to-5 years old in the U.S attend some form of regular childcare before entering kindergarten.[95] It's just a fact of modern living that parents need to work and need someone to care for their children while they are working.

Is that so bad? No, but in a NICHD study of early childcare, 56% of childcare facilities were observed to be of poor quality.[96] That's not good, but in most studies, family variables are normally better predictors of the child's development than the child care variables, so you CAN make up for it.[95]

What makes a child-care facility "higher quality?" One with qualified, well-paid, and regular care providers, reasonable adult-child ratio, and proper management[97] In the U.S. we like to think that it's a free country and you can choose any day care facility that you want, but the higher price of many higher quality centers make them unavailable to some families. Just remember you are not shopping for the most expensive; you are shopping for the most caring, best quality you can afford. Invest some time in the search before you spend your money.

Children who attend better quality childcare demonstrate modest to moderately better cognitive and social skills, especially those children from less advantaged backgrounds, and can even score higher on academic achievement tests at age 15.[98] Quality childcare can also buffer the negative influence of a depressed mother.[96] High quality early education provides a solid foundation for school readiness and academic achievement. A caring environment is especially valuable for children who have been getting insensitive care at home, improving their cognitive and language development.[97] For example, teen mothers tend to display lower levels of verbal stimulation for their children. Mothers with lower levels of education tend to read less frequently to their children, as do Hispanic and African American mothers.[99] If you are a parent in one of these categories, first of all you are different from the average of your peers just by the fact you are reading this book to improve your child's future. You can make an extra effort to read to your children and be more responsive, to give him as much an advantage as possible. If you are facing some serious life challenges that don't let you give your child the kind of attention described in the last two chapters, a high quality day care center may be just what you need to help both you and your child.

The transition to childcare is stressful for many children, so childcare providers need to intentionally form meaningful positive relationships with each child. Look for a child-care center whose staff members are responsive to the children and who stimulate them in a variety of ways. Some other things to consider when checking out day care centers is the amount of space compared to the number of children, the amount of grass compared to the amount of concrete, the kinds of snacks provided, whether your child will be protected against sunburn or cold weather, and the amount of free time and organized play (both are important.) Another consideration might be the availability of religious childcare in your neighborhood to help your child develop spiritually, but I believe the other factors are more important at this age.

Physically

His rapidly advancing gross motor skills will allow him to graduate from pedaling a tricycle to pedaling a bicycle with training wheels by the time he reaches 5, hop on one foot, and climb. Climbing trees is an especially good activity, although it involves risks of serious injury, as it has been shown to produce a 50% boost in working memory. Other safer options to achieve similar benefits include walking on a balance beam or navigating through an obstacle course.[100] Use your good judgment in choosing how much risk you are willing to accept by allowing your child to attempt any of these activities. If you have stairs, still hold his hand or at least teach him to hold the handrail. On escalators, be sure to hold his hand as he may jump.

His developing fine motor skills will allow him to draw recognizable pictures, cut with child scissors, and practice buttoning and zipping his clothes. If he insists on buckling his seat belt in the car seat, always check it.

Allow lots of free play, especially outdoors. As mentioned in the previous chapter, international guidelines are for 180 minutes (3 hours) of moderate to vigorous activity throughout the day.[101] You probably won't be able to keep up, so plan to give yourself breaks at playgrounds or on play dates by letting him run with the other children and taking turns watching closely with other parents. Let him have fun: Children who participate in "rough and tumble play" tend to be better liked by peers, demonstrate better social skills over consecutive years, and have more effective academic performance in a school setting.[102] Accept that minor injuries are part of the learning experience, but realize that asking your older children to watch their younger siblings is a risky venture, as more injuries are likely to occur than with adult supervision.

Feeding

Some generally good rules are:
- Cook one meal for the entire family.
- Your child doesn't have to eat everything on his plate.
- Stay at the table while eating, but not necessarily until everyone is done.
- Encourage him to try new food, but only one bite if he doesn't like it.
- Don't criticize how much he has or hasn't eaten.
- Offer him some control by helping to prepare, so he decides what he puts on his plate.
- Watch for choking on grapes, carrots, nuts, lollipops, and hard candies (more good reasons to avoid sugars and candies.)
- Focus on eating; turn off the TV and put away toys, and don't spoil everyone's appetite by starting family fights.
- Don't worry too much; children generally will eat when hungry.
- Offer healthy snacks throughout the day, which can be eaten on the move at this age.

Diet does not equal digestion. If your child rejects certain foods, especially proteins, it could be a digestion problem. Look into digestive enzymes as a possible solution.

The TV is more than a distraction. Children between 2 to 7 years of age see twelve food ads a day or over four thousand ads a year. The food and beverage industry spends over $1.2 Billion on marketing food and beverages to children, and consumption of an average of one hundred and sixty-seven extra calories per day was found per each hour of increased TV viewing among 11-year-old children. In addition, in a recent experiment, elementary school-aged children who saw unhealthy food advertising while watching a children's cartoon program consumed 45% more snacks than a group who watched the same show with non-food advertising.[103] Eating habits and taste preference develop early in life, so these TV ads can have a lifelong influence in health and weight control. If you don't want your child to become another sugar zombie, turn off the TV.

Potty

Many children begin potty training before their third birthday. If your child has not shown interest before now, this is a good time to arouse some. Bathroom training is often required for preschool programs. See the previous chapter for specific recommendations.

Sleeping

Your 5-year-old should get an average of 11 hours of sleep a day.

If you find you have a night owl, do something physical late in the day to tire him out or adjust his naps so he is more tired at night. If he is really resistant, encourage him to contribute in creating some bedtime rules. If he has older brothers and sisters, get him to sleep an hour before their bedtime, so he'll be out when they come to bed, especially if they share the same room.

In addition to your bedtime routine, develop a morning routine. When you wake him up, ask, "Did you have any dreams? Tell me

Early Childhood

about them." Establish that he should go to the bathroom, get dressed, have breakfast, and brush his teeth. If you have time, do a little reading together in the morning, too.

Don't forget to consult your doctor for the age-appropriate vaccinations: There are several recommended for this age group.

Activities

Work on his gross motor skills with moderately challenging activities like walking over uneven surfaces, catching a bounced ball, playing hopscotch, and climbing on playground equipment. He should be able to start practicing sports lead-up skills like throwing a ball, swinging a bat, dribbling a basketball or soccer ball, and more. He may want to participate in your home workout routine if you do yoga, Pilates, calisthenics, or not-too strenuous workout videos.

Continue to use any activities from the previous chapter that your child found either difficult or particularly enjoyed, plus add these:

Swim: Take swimming lessons as soon as local classes will admit him to prevent drowning accidents.

Get it: Throughout the day ask him to get things for you, but give two, three, or four step instructions like, "Please go to the kitchen, open the pantry door, get the broom, and bring it to Mommy." Start with two steps, then add another when he can be successful with two.

Find It: Show him any toy or object. Ask him to close his eyes while you hide it, then challenge him to find it. Explain that when you say he is getting warmer, that means he is getting closer, and when you say he is getting colder, that means he is going farther away from the object.

Animal Walk: Ask your child to act like a certain animal, making the body movements and sounds of that animal, like a monkey, a lion, an elephant, etc.

Treasure Hunt: Make a certificate good for an extra story, a back rub, or your child's favorite breakfast. Hide the slip of paper in his room, then let him look for it after he's brushed his teeth. If he's having trouble, give hints, such as, "You're getting warmer."

Easy does it: Give your child a bell and ask him to walk with it as long and far as possible (around the house) without making any noise (ringing the bell). Although it is a physical activity, it requires sustained focus, which develops executive function (see the Mental dimension later in this chapter for an explanation of what that is.)

Play Simon Says: During the third year your child should gain the ability to inhibit motion,[104] which explains why it has been difficult for him up until now to "not do" something you ask him not to do. Playing Simon Says helps him practice "not doing" something controlled by his mind, so practice as often as he finds it fun.

Music: Teach your child to play a childhood instrument; sing; dance. Practice some line dances or individual dance moves.

Art: Increase the kinds of art from crayons to paints and other media like sculpting clay or play dough.

Group Activities:

Patty-Cake: Play Patty-Cake with another child. The coordination of moving in time with a partner helps develop personality traits like being helpful and cooperative.

Balloon Bump: Play in a safe area where your kids won't bump into furniture (or play outdoors). Give each child two balloons. When you say, "Go," they must work together to keep all the balloons in the air for a set time (start with 30 seconds). For older kids you can limit which body part they are allowed to use to keep the balloons afloat.

Teamwork: Ask two children to cooperate on any activity, like drawing a picture together.

Early Childhood

The brain does not seem to recognize a division between cognitive and motor function, as the same sections of the brain are used for both, so many of the mental activities below, as long as they have some physical aspect to them, also help your child develop physically.

Mentally

Children thrive on structure. You began introducing order into your child's life by establishing a bedtime routine, a general schedule of feeding, fun, and sleeping. Now is a good time to continue that structure by organizing your child's day: morning routine, regular meal times, scheduled play time, nap time, reading time, outdoor time, play dates, very limited screen time, etc. Realize your child's attention span is not very long (about fifteen minutes), so do not be surprised if she wants to do something else after a short while. Also realize your child is not a robot. She will appreciate structure, but you cannot expect her to follow a spreadsheet of activities, locked down to the minute. Every day should have regularity, which brings security, but you must also have the flexibility to take advantage of creativity and surprises that would be fun or educational. Model for your child a reliance on structure balanced with an appreciation for novelty.

Executive functions of the brain, also called cognitive control, develop rapidly in this preschool period. These functions are the ability to control thought, behavior, and emotions with a goal in mind. They develop at this age with the ability to retain more information in the mind at one time, intentionally shift attention, and inhibit action. In the classroom, these skills show up as the ability to pay attention, follow instructions, wait your turn, and remember rules. They also predict success in early language and mathematical skills, but more importantly children who have them are easier to teach. Studies have also shown these abilities are associated with lower levels of aggression, better problem-solving skills, positive social skills, and the ability to delay gratification.[105]

So, if executive function is such a good thing, how can we improve it? Engage your child in problem-solving challenges that are (1) goal directed and motivational to the child, (2) require sustained attention, (3) require adaptation, and (4) require repetition and practice.[106] Here are two sample activities: Start with three options, and as your child gets good at the process, increase to four and then five.

<u>Sort by size:</u> Ask your child if she wants more juice (or milk, etc.) or less. When she says, "More," then show her three cups of different size and shapes, and ask her to arrange them in order from smallest to largest. Then put the juice in the smallest glass and pour it into the larger glasses to see if she was right. Re-arrange the glasses according to the results and then give her the juice. Repeat the "game" often with different kinds of containers for water, toys, or just different sized pictures and objects.

<u>Which comes first:</u> When your child wants to play a favorite game, ask, "What three things do we have to do to get ready for the game?" For example, to play with her dolls, she has to go to her room, find the dolls in her toy bin, and bring them back to the play area. The game doesn't matter, and the steps don't really matter. What matters is that she thinks of three correct steps and gets them in the right order. The reward is playing with the dolls. A more advanced version might to ask, "What if you can't find your dolls in the toy bin?" You can follow the same procedure when she wants to go to the park, and you ask her, "How are we going to get to the park?" A more advanced version might be, "How else could we get to the park?" Possible answers might be walk, ride bikes, or drive the car, or to take different streets, etc.

There is also some evidence linking pretend play with executive function.[107] Teacher directed play is an effective learning tool, but some studies indicate that the most effective type of pretend play could be child-directed, where the kids spontaneously start pretending they are characters in a situation and act out their roles.[108] You can encourage the process by first identifying an interest that all the kids involved have in common, and then suggesting, "Hey, why don't you guys play Frozen?" You can choose a movie or show they are both (or all) familiar with, but if they haven't been exposed to much screen time, they can have a pretend dinner, birthday party, a teacher in a classroom, or any other live event. Just beware of letting

Early Childhood

them practice violent situations by playing something like cowboys and Indians or cops and robbers. If your child is alone, you can encourage pretend play with stuffed animals or even imaginary friends. At 3 years of age your child's imagination seems real to her. At 5, she should be able to distinguish imagination from reality.

The active study of music also benefits brain development and cognitive performance. In one University of Wisconsin study preschool children who took piano lessons did better on a test of space-time reasoning than the children who did not take the lessons, and that kind of reasoning is important in math and science.[109]

As a martial artist, I am proud to report that Taekwondo training has been proven to improve children's executive functions (inhibition: discipline, emotion regulation; working memory: performance on a mental math task), and respectful treatment of peers.[110] Find a local martial arts school that offers a Little Dragons or Tiny Tigers program for children this age.

The most important point is that there are many ways to develop your child's brain by engaging in real-world activities rather than watching TV or playing computer games. Many of the activities listed below also develop executive function.

This is also the age where ADD/ADHD may begin to show instead of regular executive function. The increased diagnosis of ADD and ADHD may be a result of the increase of toxins in our environment as presented in Chapter 2, but it may also be over-diagnosed. Please understand that stress in your child's life can inhibit the executive functions, and the child may appear to have ADD or ADHD when the real culprit is stress or simply lack of sleep. Other research shows that simply eliminating gluten from certain children's diets can reduce or eliminate the symptoms that lead to an ADHD diagnosis.[111]

If you believe your child has it, don't think of it as a disability, but more like a super power – her brain has a race car engine with bicycle brakes. Instead of ADHD, Dr. Edward Hallowell frames it more positively as VAST: Variable Attentions Stimulus Trait. He says that untreated it can cost you 15 years of your life, but instead of treating it as a disability, learn to unwrap the gift and gain the benefits.[112] Please don't resort to drugs as your first option. Check out Dr. Hallowell's website at https://www.drhallowell.com/adhd/ or Dr. Nicole Beurkens' website at https://www.drbeurkens.com for some more positive options. Always consult your doctor, but not all doctors agree on specific treatments. Do some research and consider getting a second or even a third qualified opinion.

Activities

Continue to use any activities from the previous chapter that your child found either difficult or particularly enjoyed, plus add these:

Synonyms: Give your child a word and ask her to give you a synonym (a word that means the same thing.) For example, you say, "Big," and your child might say, "Large."

Antonyms: Give your child a word and ask her to give you an antonym (a word that means the opposite.) For example, you say, "Big," and she might say, "Small."

Homonyms: Give your child a word that has a homonym (a word that sounds the same but has a different meaning.) For example, you say, "*Here*, as in come *here*," and your child might say, "I can't *hear* you."

Past Tense: Help your child learn the past tense form of common verbs that follow different rules, for example, "Today I like you; yesterday I _____ you (liked)," or, "Today I wear shorts; yesterday I _____ shorts (wore)."

Day/Night task: Cut out two pictures or make two drawings of two things that are opposites, like the sun and the moon. Then, ask your child to say, "Sun," when she sees the moon, and, "Moon," when she sees the sun. Practice ten to twenty times in a row showing the pictures randomly, but asking her to count to 3 or sing a short song before answering. The delay before responding is what develops the executive function.

Early Childhood

<u>Match:</u> Ask your child to name two or three items that match in a particular way like, "Find two blue items in this picture book," or, "Find three round objects in this room."

<u>Name 3:</u> Ask your child to name three items of a kind in order to help her understand classifications. For example, name three kinds of animals or name three things that are red. A more advanced version might be to name three kinds of dogs (a smaller group) or to name three animals that are brown (two classifications.) An even more advanced version for an older child is to reverse the game by naming three things and asking her to name the classification.

<u>Which one is different:</u> Name three or four things and ask your child, "Which one is different?" She has to mentally identify why two are the same and therefore why the third one is different. An example would be: Shark, whale, cow. Always ask why, because in this example the cow is different because it is a land animal that has legs while the other two live in the sea and have fins, but another correct answer might be that the shark is different because the whale and the cow are both mammals and breathe air while the shark is a fish that breathes water.

<u>Tell me a story:</u> Ask your child to tell you a story – if she has difficulty, help her with a starter idea or offer ideas when she gets stuck. The first story may be short, but with practice the stories will get longer and more involved.

<u>Sequencing:</u> Ask your child to organize activities, probably not in order of importance yet, but in order of time – for example, "What do we do when we go to bed?" or, "How do we wash the dishes?" Get her used to using words like "first" and "second." Soon afterward, do the activity to verify whether she said it in the right order. As your child gets older, you can start to plan entirely new activities from her imagination rather than from her memory, like, "What would we need to pack to go fishing?" and start estimating the time each step takes.

Raising 4 Dimensional Children in a 2 Dimensional World

<u>Alphabet</u>: Teach your child the alphabet, preferably using the sing-song version.

<u>Count</u>: Teach your child to count from one to ten, then one to one hundred (as her ability permits). Then, relate the counting to counting objects like her fingers, the stairs, or her toys.

<u>Physical Arithmetic</u>: Once your child can count, use objects like apples to demonstrate addition and subtraction. For example, "Here are two apples. If I add one more, how many do we have?"

<u>Mental Arithmetic</u>: Once your child can do physical arithmetic, ask her to do mental arithmetic: For example, "How much is two plus one?"

<u>Rhymes</u>: Teach your child to make rhymes by changing the first sound in a word, like, "Bat, Cat, Fat, Hat," etc. Challenge your child to make two or three rhymes from each word you provide.

<u>Mash up</u>: Take some pictures out of a magazine or a coloring book and cut them up in a way that they can be assembled together. For example, cut different animals between the head and the body. Then, ask your child to combine them and name the new animal. For example, and elephant's body with a rhinoceros' head might be an "eliphino." As your child gets older, you can play the game without the pictures, just asking, "What would you call a giraffe's head on a poodle's body?"

<u>My list</u>: To improve your child's memory, make an imaginary grocery list. Say, "I'm going shopping for some apples." Then, it is your child's turn, and she says, "I'm going shopping for some apples and bananas." Take turns adding items to the list and see how many you can add before making a mistake. You can make lists of anything else you enjoy, like, "At the park I'm going to play on the swings."

<u>Reading</u>: When reading a story, occasionally stop and ask, "What has happened so far?" Also ask, "Why do you think (that character) did that?" "What do you think will happen next?"

Early Childhood

<u>Cause and Effect:</u> Help your child connect causes and effects by identifying one and asking for the other. For example, you could say, "I dropped a tomato," and your child could say, "So I had to mop the floor." Alternately, you could say, "I had to mop the floor because," and your child might say, "It was full of dirt." Obviously, there are hundreds of causes to each effect, so every time you play it will be different. Just be sure the two events are really connected by cause and effect.

<u>Who am I:</u> Help your child recite her name, address, and your phone number in case she gets lost. Whenever you go to places like a park or the mall, explain what to do if she can't find you. (At a park, go to a certain place and wait. At the store or mall, look for someone in uniform like a policeman or security guard, or look for a cashier who works at the store. It's also a good idea to choose a safe word, so that if anyone says you sent them to get her, she asks for the safe word before going with them.)

<u>Safe touch:</u> Review the safe-touch guidelines from last chapter: When and where it is safe to touch yourself in public or private, where it's not safe to touch others, and where it's not safe to let others touch you. Make sure your child knows it's safe to tell you if anyone else touches her, even if the person tells her not to tell you.

Group Activities

<u>Take Turns:</u> Play any board game, card game, or live game that requires taking turns, but especially those that involve counting, straight-line advancing, or shapes.

<u>Teamwork:</u> Ask two children to cooperate on any activity, like building a sandcastle or playing catch.

<u>Echo:</u> Ask one child to describe anything, and then ask the other child to repeat what she just heard to encourage careful listening. The way to "win friends and influence people" is to become a good listener.

Raising 4 Dimensional Children in a 2 Dimensional World

<u>The Alphabet Game:</u> The first child starts with the letter A and says something like, "My name is Allen, my wife's name is Ann. We come from Alabama, and we sell Apples." The second child says the same sentence, substituting names and words that begin with B. Children continue to take turns seeing if they can get all the way through the alphabet.

<u>I spy:</u> One child says, "I spy with my little eye something that is _____ (for example, green)." The other children have to take turns guessing what it is that is green. Whoever guesses it gets to spy the next object.

<u>Team Story:</u> Ask two or more children to tell a story one sentence at a time. Mary starts the story, then Susie adds the next sentence, then Mary adds the third sentence, etc.

<u>How to make a friend:</u> Teach your child how to make a friend by introducing herself and offering something nice. Practice asking one child to say to the other, "Hi. My name is _____. Can we play _____ together?" Then let the other child practice. Repeat a few times until they are comfortable but not bored with it.

Of course, when there are no other children around, you can be the other "child" and play these games with your daughter.

Emotionally

At age 3 children are beginning to show their temperament and personality more consistently, but they are still able to change and develop during their childhood and even adolescent years.[113] Obviously, the earlier you can help their plastic brain to program itself to react rationally instead of just emotionally, the more successful you will be in establishing a lifetime habit. You may also experience a second honeymoon of closeness during this time, as his need for independence changes into a desire to please you. As he enters his 4th year, he will begin to make close connections to one or two special friends and will learn a great deal from them. Both forms of closeness are a sign that his brain is advancing to a tribal mentality of "us vs.

them" and his friends may become the "us" and you may become the "them." By his 5th birthday he should be less oppositional.

Emotional intelligence can be broken down into five areas: (1) knowing your emotions, (2) managing your emotions, (3) motivating yourself, (4) recognizing emotions in others, and (5) handling relationships.[114]

Continue to talk about feelings, naming various emotions. When your child knows the words, he will know how he feels, and you will get the added advantage of passing the feelings through his thinking brain instead of letting those feelings pass directly into his body, which is the first step to get your child to manage his emotions rationally. Discuss the difference between good feelings and bad feelings and emphasize that it is better to talk about bad feelings than act on them. Whenever any problems arise, try not to focus on the problem, but rather on the positive solutions to create a positive attitude. Also remember that there is a big difference between a 3-year-old and a 5-year-old, so don't expect miraculous results too early.

As your child becomes more self-aware, introduce the idea of self-talk. If you are not familiar with the term, it is the voice inside your head that talks about yourself, saying things like, "I'm smart," or, "I'm dumb." Help him understand the difference between positive and negative self-talk, and make him comfortable sharing his self-talk with you so you know what he's thinking. You can also plant positive or negative self-talk in his mind with the things you say, so make lots of deposits into his emotional bank account with compliments and positive affirmations. Search for 100 Ways to Praise a Child on the internet on sites like http://megandredge.com/100-ways-to-praise-a-child/ and use them often. Just be aware that praising inborn talents (you're smart or you're beautiful) can create a sense of entitlement, whereas praising effort (good job or way to go) encourages dedication and hard work. These deposits will pay you a lifetime of dividends in self-confidence and self-motivation.

In the last chapter we offered several activities designed to help him recognize emotions in others. Continue play acting, practicing different facial expressions and body language expressions of emotions that he can recognize in others and himself. This knowledge will help him manage his relationships with friends and family, and may eventually translate to qualities of leadership.

The emotional aspect of effortful control, discussed in the mental dimension of this chapter, is the ability to inhibit action and shift your attention. Tests on preschool children measuring inhibitory control are closely tied to their ability to regulate their own emotions and their understanding that their thoughts are not always the same as someone else's thoughts.[115]

How can you help your child develop emotional effortful control? One of the clearest tests of this skill is the famous marshmallow test, where the experimenter tells a child, "Here is a marshmallow. You can eat it right away, but if you wait until I come back, I will give you two marshmallows." Children who are able wait and get the double benefit are high in effortful control, and later in life tend to reap the benefits of delayed gratification like studying tonight to get a good grade on the test tomorrow or staying in school to get a better education and better career. I believe effortful control is a skill that can be learned, and you can help your child at this age by practicing the test and helping him learn how to shift his attention.

First of all, I recommend you use something healthier than a marshmallow (fruit or even an enjoyable activity.) Begin with a short time, maybe a minute, and explain that your child should (1) stop looking at the prize, and (2) intentionally do something else to take his mind off of the temptation, like playing with something else. When the time is up, reward him with double the prize and praise him for having self-control. Each time you play the "game," increase the length of time and the intensity of the temptation until he can resist for fifteen minutes.

If your child has a baby brother or sister, you have a great opportunity to teach the older child about love and caring for another. Why is the baby crying? What can you do to help her stop crying? Can you make her laugh? Modeling how you care for the baby will show the older child how to care for another above himself.

Early Childhood

Emotions are contagious, and anger and resentment are the most contagious of emotions according to psychologist Steven Stosny. "If you are near a resentful or angry person, you are more prone to become resentful or angry yourself."[116] Therefore, beware of the emotions you are modeling and projecting to your child.

Also, beware of the messages you are sending with your own actions. When you criticize, the message is: You're not good enough. When you don't pay attention to your child, the message is: You're not important. When you don't show affection, the message is: You're not lovable. When you yell at mistakes, the message is: Mistakes are bad. When you do everything for them, the message is: You are incapable. Never ridicule your child in public, even as a joke. It leaves deep scars.

Many experiments have verified the "Pygmalion affect" which, based on the book, play, and movie, states that people live up to your expectations. If you expect your child is strong, smart, and caring, even if you never express it in words, your child will live up to your expectations. Unfortunately, the opposite is also true: If you expect your child to be weak, dumb, and selfish, he will live down to your expectations (called the Gollum effect). Regardless of your family history or your own successes or failures, your child is not you. He was born with certain genetic abilities, but if you have understood anything in this book so far, you must realize that his experiences can activate those abilities or not. What you believe about your child and the love and education you provide will do more to determine his future than his genetics. He can become strong or weak, smart or dumb, wealthy or poor, kind or cruel, and a saint or a sinner based on the foundation you provide, so do your best!

Discipline

If you were blessed with amazing parents, by all means, copy what they did. If not, don't be afraid to look for help. If you are not sure what to do, if you are a single parent, and/or live in a difficult neighborhood, look for local Parent Management Training programs. Some even provide home visits. You can also join local parent groups as long as there is a leader with knowledge and experience. Two separate research projects showed that parents who attended such programs were not only happier with each other, but their children showed better results than those of parents who did not attend these groups.[117] The more specific the issue you have, the more likely you will find the right group with the right answer. I would be leery of online groups as they can be a fountain of bad information. As a general rule, never take the advice of someone more screwed up than you.

Make sure both you and your spouse agree on the disciplinary procedures. Learning the rules is hard enough at 3 years old. Don't make it harder by offering different rules with different people or at different times.

You need to make the rules clear before you administer punishment of any kind. Give your child a framework and let him experiment with as little interference as possible. When he goes over the line, it's also a good idea to provide fair warning by counting to three, to give him time to realize what you are asking and then inhibit his actions. Here are three simple rules:

1. Consequences have to be clear and accepted (allow input from older children.)
2. Transgressions should always have consequences. Choose your words carefully and never make a threat you will not back up because no punishment becomes a reward. You are creating a world view that actions have consequences, which will affect decisions he makes for the rest of his life.
3. Apply the punishment calmly. Be clear that you are not angry at your child, but he cannot do what he did. The action deserves punishment, not the child.[118]

The punishment can be a short time-out, usually thirty seconds to a minute at this age, and use a timer that will sound when time is up. Remember the concept of Minimum Consequences from the previous chapter. As they approach their 5th birthday, you can increase the length of time, or you can take away an enjoyable activity. As mentioned in a previous chapter, the timeout is as much for you as for the child. If you are upset, calm yourself, then go back to the child with a quiet tone and gentle touch, and go down to his eye level to make him feel seen, felt, and heard. As described in the previous chapter, try to end the punishment with a hug and – if possible – by practicing the correct behavior.

Whenever possible, catch him doing something right and compliment it. He needs clarity, so avoid general directions like, "Clean up your room." Be specific. Realize that as his brain matures, the methods you use may have to be updated. A positive way to instruct is the PIR method, which stands for Praise, Instruct, Result. An example would be, "That was very nice when you asked Sally to play with you (praise). I think if you give her one of your toys instead of taking one of hers (instruction), she won't cry, and she will want to play with you longer (result)." Because this is a 3-part instruction, a three-year-old may not be able to grasp it all as well as a five-year-old, but the method works well for both children and adults.

He will probably want to argue about everything. Stop talking. Talking is the fuel for the power struggle. Be firm but kind (better too firm than too kind, but seek the balance.) If he is doing something he already knows is wrong, use one word in a sing-song tone to remind him of the rule, "Yell-ing?" Take a moment to understand what he needs. Why is this so important to him? This may be a Genuine Encounter Moment (a GEM) where you realize something new. Don't assume you are right and teach him that what's important to him is not important to you (and therefore he's not important.) You also may need to negotiate or at least offer him age-appropriate choices,[119] depending on the situation.

Another system that works well at this age is giving stickers for good behavior because they are concrete objects that your child can look at or hold in his hand. They are positive reinforcement. As he gets older, you may switch to a less physical version by giving him five points at the beginning of the week and taking away one point for every time he misbehaves. If he makes it a whole week without losing all five points, he gets a positive, healthy reward. Post the points on the refrigerator so he can see how many he has left, and then give him an opportunity to stop by saying something like, "If you don't _____ you're going to lose a point."

This is also the age children start to exhibit several forms of aggression with their peers: Physical Aggression, Verbal Aggression, and Relational Aggression. Aggressive children usually start with physical aggression as that is their only tool, and graduate to verbal aggression as they grow older and develop a better vocabulary. Around the age of 4 they will then move on to relational aggression, inflicting emotional harm on their target with lower risk of consequences. There is evidence that all forms of aggression are linked to certain inherited genes, plus aggression has been linked with harsh and overly controlling parenting and a lack of parental warmth. There is also strong evidence that these aggressive children tend to attribute hostile intent to others and have a lack of empathy.[120]

What can you do? Don't be that harsh or over-controlling authoritative parent. Show warmth, but be firm that aggression is not OK. Flexible and warm authoritative parenting is the most beneficial style for the child's social, intellectual, emotional, and moral growth into adolescence and adulthood.[121] Be wary of exhibiting aggression yourself by yelling and spanking. There are two sides to the spanking story: (1) If you hit them, they are only modeling you when they hit someone else, and the message they learned from you is that the bigger and stronger person wins; (2) hitting someone else takes on a whole different meaning when you get hit and understand how it hurts. Most modern psychologists advise that you can raise your children better without physical punishment – it takes a little more patience but is more effective in the long run. Children of my generation got frequent spankings and most turned out OK. My opinion (without any professional research to back it up) is that IF you are going to administer physical punishment, the time is when they are too young to understand your explanations, and the punishment fits the crime (you hit someone else, you get hit.) By the time they are 4 years old, they should understand your explanations, and you should probably move away from physical punishment.

Another area of emotional growth is Respect. Teach your child to respect all adults by not using their first name: Mr. Jones or Mrs. Smith, or if your culture permits, Uncle Bob or Aunt Maria. If you can instill in your child the use of, "Sir," and, "Ma'am" in these early

Early Childhood

years, I believe you will have fewer problems as your child grows older.

If you are having extreme trouble with discipline and need help, the earlier you start, the better the results you will get: There are several programs available to help with problem children. Parent-Child Interaction Therapy (PCIT) is a good program for oppositional or defiant children, but also for depressed children, those with separation anxiety, and victims of parental abuse or witnesses of inter-parental abuse.[122] Helping the Non-Compliant Child is a program but is also available in book form on Amazon. The Positive Parenting Program (Triple P)[123] has programs for parents and for organizations for both children and teens. The Promoting Alternative Thinking Strategies (PATHS) curriculum[124] provides weekly classroom lessons and extension activities to improve preschool children's social-emotional awareness and behavior. The Incredible Years (IY) Training Program[125] delivers teaching programs backed by over thirty years of research to prevent delinquency, drug abuse, and violence in children who have exhibited early onset conduct problems, ADHD, and autism. Look for a preschool in your area that uses one of these last two programs if you feel the need.

Another situation you may encounter is a sudden change in your child's behavior, especially after a strep infection. It has been named PANDAS for Pediatric Autoimmune Neuropsychiatric Disorder Associated with Strep infection. If you think your child might be experiencing this sudden change, research PANS and PANDAS on the Internet on sites like https://pandasnetwork.org.

Activities

Continue to use any activities from the previous chapter that your child found either difficult or particularly enjoyed, plus add these:

<u>Smile:</u> Any time of day or night smile at your child. He should immediately smile back – it is a natural reaction as smiles are contagious, but it also reminds him to smile and be happy. You can also turn it into a game, where you get points when you catch each other not smiling and give your smile to the other.

Raising 4 Dimensional Children in a 2 Dimensional World

<u>Different Strokes:</u> Ask your child to help you make a groceries list based on the different likes of each member of your family, to help him realize that different people like different things.

<u>Puppets:</u> Use at least two dolls or sock puppets and ask your child to have them act out a scene where he has to think like two separate characters to help him understand that different people feel differently in the same situation.

<u>Point of View:</u> Describe a situation that you may have seen with your child or one you would make up to illustrate a point like, "Johnny and Lee (use the real names of your child's friends) get in a fight over a game they were playing." Ask your child to take the point of view of different people by asking how he thinks Johnny feels, and why. How does Lee feel, and why? How does Mary (a child friend) feel after seeing the fight, and why? How does Lee's mother feel, and why? How do you (your child) feel, and why? What could you do about it?

<u>My Favorite Whine:</u> Read 10 sentences from a children's book into an audio recorder (on your phone?), using a pleasant voice for some and a whiny voice for others. Play them back and ask your child to raise his hand when he hears the sentences read in a nice voice. Then, have him record sentences in his silliest, whiniest, and nicest voices, and play them back for him.

<u>How I Felt:</u> Say, "I was scared when _____" and describe a recent situation where you were scared (hopefully one related to your child.) Then, let your child describe a situation when he was scared. Discuss it, then you start over with a different emotion like happy or surprised.

<u>One Up:</u> Start with a relatively neutral emotional word like, "Glad." Your child must one-up you with a gladder word like, "Happy." You must one-up your child with an even happier word like, "Joyful." See how far you can go in identifying more positive emotions.

Early Childhood

Flexibility: Ask, "How would you feel if Johnny said you were dumb?" "What would you do?" Point out that Johnny might be upset because something bad happened to him earlier that day, and then, ask, "How else could you feel?" and, "What else could you do?"

Self-Soothing: Continue to practice the Control It activities from the previous chapter like: Practice taking a few deep breaths or singing a happy song or reciting a happy nursery rhyme. When he can count, practice counting to ten when angry. Add intentionally focusing on something positive as the next step.

Self-Talk: Help your child develop confidence through positive self-talk by repeating positive affirmations like, "I'm a good person. I'm smart. I'm strong. I'm pretty/handsome. I'm kind. I care about others. I never give up." At age 3, focus on simple ideas like smart, good, and pretty. As your child gets older, switch the self-talk away from natural talents to more effort-related habits.

Negative to Positive: You say, "Sad," and your child responds with, "Happy." It is not only a vocabulary game, but a way to understand how to replace negative emotions (and negative self-talk) with positive emotions.

Problem/Opportunity: Take turns identifying a problem, and the other explains how it is an opportunity. For example, you say, "It's raining outside today," and your child says, "so I get to make Daddy a beautiful card."

Yes, I Can: Help your child become a problem solver. Ask, "What would you like to do?" Your child could answer anything like, "I would like to fly." You then answer with a problem like, "But you have no wings." He might reply, "I can make wings," to which you might reply, "But you have no feathers." The goal is to stimulate imagination but also to stimulate the winning spirit to solve every problem and overcome every challenge.

Raising 4 Dimensional Children in a 2 Dimensional World

Tell Jokes: Help your child develop a sense of humor by telling him jokes (maybe a joke of the day?) and then encouraging him to practice telling the joke back to you. Knock-knock jokes are popular at this age – look for examples on the Internet.

Store Manners: Ask your child to identify some good manners and some bad manners while shopping in a store. Give guidance where needed and explain why. Then, when you are in a store, you can remind your child what he said about good store manners.

Reading: Ask questions related to emotions like, "How do you think (that character) feels?" "Why?"

Movies and TV: Ask, "How do you think (that character) feels?" "Why?" Be especially sensitive to discuss any aggression – not just physical, but verbal and relational aggression – and how that makes the victim feel. Go one step farther by getting a commitment that he will not act like that.

Group Activities

Mother, May I: Line up the players facing you, about 10 feet away. Give commands to one child at a time, like "Joe, take one hop forward." If Joe responds, "Mother, may I?" you can say either, "Yes, you may," or, "No, you may not." If your reply is, "Yes," make sure that Joe says, "Thank you," before he goes. Anyone who forgets his manners or makes a move without permission is sent back to the starting line. Keep playing until one child reaches Mother. Give each child a chance to be Mother.

Group Project: Ask two or more children to cooperate on a short project, where they decide together what they will do, how they will do it, who does which part, and they stay on task until they finish it. It could be as simple as a drawing, or as involved as inventing a new board game.

Early Childhood

<u>The Cheer-Up Game:</u> Draw a series of faces on paper with different unhappy expressions -- sad, angry, scared, sick (at least one for every child in the game). Put the papers in a basket and ask kids to take turns choosing a face then acting out the feeling shown. It's the job of the other players to help him feel better. First, they should identify the emotion and ask questions: "Why are you sad? How can I help?" After the upset child gives an explanation like, "My friend was mean to me," the other kids can role-play solutions like giving hugs or saying, "I'm sorry."

<u>Good News and Bad News:</u> Each child will give one sentence of a story like in the <u>Team Story</u> activity, but they have to switch from positive to negative each time. For example, "One day a wizard was angry at his assistant." The next child might say, "But the assistant was happy because he discovered a magic wand." Each child would continue the story, switching from positive to negative or negative to positive each time.

Spiritually

Now that your child can speak and understand, you want to start moving her from Kohlberg's Preconventional (Punishment-Obedience) level of morality to a Conventional level of morality, where she is learning the difference between good and bad, and striving to do good not just to avoid punishment, but in order to do the right thing.

As mentioned earlier, as your child approaches 5, she should understand the relationship between cause and effect, and in your disciplinary actions you have introduced the idea of consequences. As she also can understand that other people feel differently than she feels, she can now hold all of those ideas in her mind at the same time to realize that the consequences of her actions may hurt other people, which is the foundation of morality. If you believe in God, you might explain that when she does bad things it hurts God's feelings. If you don't believe in God, you can explain the law of Karma, which states that when you do bad things, bad things will happen to you. Alternately, you can just explain the Golden Rule to "do unto others as you would have them do unto you" as a matter of fairness. If you don't want people to hurt you, then you should not hurt other people.

Explain the difference between doing good, by telling the truth, being kind, and being generous, and doing bad, by lying, being mean, and being selfish. The executive function described in the earlier sections of this chapter will allow her to link moral principles, feelings, thoughts, and actions.

Continue reading bedtime stories that teach a positive, moral message. Stories create beliefs, and a child's belief system is developed by age 6, so start creating it now. Discuss what happened in the story (or in a movie you watched together), how the hero felt, why he (or she) did what he did, and the result. Then ask, "What could you do that would be like that?" Help your child identify things she could do daily that are examples of the same principle.

Negative experiences create a negative belief system, so if your child had a negative experience during the day, it is important to repair any negative beliefs she might have formed and replace them with positive ones. Help your child integrate her day so she goes to bed comforted.

Continue bedtime prayers (or expressions, if you don't pray) of gratitude for the good things you have and appreciation for the people you love. If you do pray, start to talk to God like a real person and listen for answers, according to your religious tradition.

If you meditate, teach your child a simple meditation or at least teach her to sit still for a short period of time. Start with sitting completely motionless for thirty seconds while your child focuses on feeling her breath and/or heartbeat. Increase the amount of time thirty seconds at a time (each week?), eventually reaching five minutes or longer.

Activities:

Continue to use any activities from the previous chapter that your child found either difficult or particularly enjoyed, plus add these:

Principles: Identify three ways to be good, like: Telling the truth, being kind, and being generous. Then make up a real-life situation like, "Susie comes over to our house to play with you. You have five dolls and Susie has no dolls here. What should you do?"

Helper: Ask your child to identify three ways she can help someone tomorrow.

Amends: Give your child some challenging situations of mistakes she might make like, "If you said Mary was ugly, and she started crying, what should you do?"

Say Grace: Before dinner, say a short prayer or just express gratitude for your food and family. Occasionally, ask your child to say the grace or blessing.

Responsibility: Give your child age-appropriate responsibilities like taking care of anything. For example, she could help with caring for a pet or you might create an art or activity box with crayons, scissors, etc., and teach your child to care for the box, cleaning up after herself and putting it away when she is done using it.

Summary

Your child may be talking, but his brain is not functioning like yours, yet. He cannot follow simple logic like, "If A is greater than B, and B is greater than C, is A greater or less than C?" but he is beginning to understand the relationship between cause and effect, which prompts him to ask, "Why?" about everything. He will move from not being able to distinguish imagination from reality at 3, to clearly knowing the difference at 5. He will gain the ability to hold several thoughts in his mind at once, which will present the opportunity to choose where he focuses. He will get over the opposition of the Terrible Twos and start to value inclusiveness, getting closer to you and to "best friends." He will develop effortful control, which will help him inhibit his natural reactions so that he can learn to delay gratification. He will also begin to understand that other people are not feeling the same things he is feeling, which will help him realize that his actions can hurt others.

 This is also a good age to develop one of the most important qualities of success in life: What Angela Lee Duckworth has called "grit." Grit is a mental and emotional toughness to overcome challenge and persevere when faced with failure. In her TED Talk, Dr. Duckworth said, "So far, the best idea I've heard about building grit in kids is something called 'growth mindset.' This is an idea developed at Stanford University by Carol Dweck, and it is the belief that the ability to learn is not fixed, that it can change with your effort. Dr. Dweck has shown that when kids read and learn about the brain and how it changes and grows in response to challenge, they're much more likely to persevere when they fail, because they don't believe that failure is a permanent condition."[126] Although your child may be too young to read at this age, he can learn about grit from stories that you read together and movies that you watch together. More importantly, he can learn about grit from your example, and from your encouragement that if at first he doesn't succeed, he should try, try again.

 Some recent studies have shown that overprotective parenting in early childhood is associated with later anxiety disorders,[127] so don't be one of those "helicopter parents" who is constantly hovering over her child ready to swoop in at the slightest sign of trouble. Your child needs to have problems, face them, and overcome them. Not everything in his life is going to be easy. Give him enough space to try on his own, and if he fails, then encourage him to try a different way until he succeeds. That will help him develop grit.

Screen Time

 Consensus from educational experts is that children from 2 to 5 years old should be limited to one hour a day of sitting and watching television or other electronic media. Why? Preschoolers who spend more than two hours a day watching television have a greater likelihood of being overweight. 3-year-olds who watch more than two hours a day of television were nearly two times more likely to develop asthma by age 11. Four studies reported a positive relationship between time spent watching television under the age of 5 and lower cognitive development, academic achievement, language skills, and short-term memory one to three years later.[128] Not exactly the results you want.

As mentioned earlier, television shows tend to be too violent and have too many commercials promoting unhealthy foods. If you let your child watch TV, I strongly recommend you choose non-commercial content and watch the show with your child to engage him with questions to think about what you both have seen.

As far as educational software, little research shows very much advantage over paper books, but the software is developing rapidly, so it's hard for the research to keep up. Just be aware that ads and websites are designed to sell you on the program, and many of the claims they make are not supported by research. If your preschool center uses software as part of their curriculum, they have probably researched its effectiveness and have the ability to supplement the programming with teacher-student interaction. This situation is far different from just letting your child use a program unsupervised.

At least one study shows that some e-books that incorporate multimedia elements did enhance the understanding of verbal content better than printed storybooks, but others use of multi-media actually distracted the children and were harmful to the child's learning.[129] One place where e-books seem to be useful is in vocabulary building in children from disadvantaged homes or where English is a second language,[130] so if you are in one of those two situations, e-books could be a plus.

Note: As all children are unique and develop at different rates, I recommend you read the next chapter to prepare for your child's growth and in case your child happens to develop more quickly in one area or another, and the previous chapter in case your child happens to develop more slowly in one area or another. Specifically, some of the activities might well be continued into the older years.

Also please use your own good judgment in following any advice I offer. Research is subject to change and my advice may be based on research that has since changed or been updated since this publishing. Choose your actions based on your own beliefs, experiences, research, and judgment, especially during extenuating circumstances (like a pandemic.)

Recommended Resources:

https://littlehumans.com/
https://www.opportunityatlas.org/
https://www.drhallowell.com/adhd/
https://www.drbeurkens.com
http://megandredge.com/100-ways-to-praise-a-child/
https://www.gamesofgenius.com/
https://www.child-encyclopedia.com
https://www.who.int/topics/early-child-development/en/
https://toolsofthemind.org/
https://mindup.org/
https://www.davidlynchfoundation.org/
https://www.mindinthemaking.org/
https://www.vroom.org/
https://parentsasteachers.org/
http://www.pcit.org/
https://www.cebc4cw.org/program/helping-the-noncompliant-child/detailed
http://www.pathstraining.com/main/
http://www.incredibleyears.com/
https://pandasnetwork.org

References:

92. Jain, Renee. Interview in *Little Humans* series, https://youtu.be/xULoiPFBAcY.

93. Chetty, Raj. Interview on *Hidden Brain*, November 12, 2018. https://www.npr.org/templates/transcript/transcript.php?storyId=666993130. Accessed June 11, 2021.

94. Kuo, Ming. Interview on *Hidden Brain*, September 10, 2018. https://www.npr.org/transcripts/646413667. Accessed June 11, 2021.

95. Peisner-Feinberg, Ellen S, PhD. "Child Care and Its Impact on Young Children's Development." Encyclopedia on Early Childhood Development; updated February, 2021, p.64. http://www.child-encyclopedia.com/child-care-early-childhood-education-and-care/complete-topic. Accessed June 11, 2021.

Early Childhood

96. McCartney, Kathleen, PhD. "Current Research on Child Care Effects." Encyclopedia on Early Childhood Development; updated February, 2021, p. 43. http://www.child-encyclopedia.com/child-care-early-childhood-education-and-care/complete-topic. Accessed June 11, 2021.

97. Ahnert, Lieselotte, PhD; and Lamb, Michael E, PhD. "Child Care and Its Impact on Young Children." Encyclopedia on Early Childhood Development; updated February, 2021, p.14. http://www.child-encyclopedia.com/child-care-early-childhood-education-and-care/complete-topic. Accessed June 11, 2021.

98. Belsky, Jay, PhD. "Child Care and Its Impact on Young Children." Encyclopedia on Early Childhood Development; updated February, 2021, p. 38. http://www.child-encyclopedia.com/child-care-early-childhood-education-and-care/complete-topic. Accessed June 11, 2021.

99. Tamis-LeMonda, Catherine S, PhD; and Rodriguez, Eileen T, PhD. "Parents' Role in Fostering Young Children's Learning and Language Development." Encyclopedia on Early Childhood Development; updated September 2015, p. 32. http://www.child-encyclopedia.com/parenting-skills/complete-topic. Accessed June 11, 2021.

100. Caremans, Gregory. *"Neuroscience and Parenting,"* https://www.udemy.com/course/neuroscience-and-parenting/ Section 2.6. Accessed May 29, 2021.

101. Cliff, Dylan P, PhD; and Janssen, Xanne, PhD. "Levels of Habitual Physical Activity in Early Childhood." Encyclopedia on Early Childhood Development; updated June, 2020, pp. 7-8. http://www.child-encyclopedia.com/physical-activity/complete-topic. Accessed June 11, 2021.

102. Pellis, Sergio M, PhD; and Pellis, Vivien C, PhD. "Play-Fighting During Early Childhood and its Role in Preventing Later Chronic Aggression." Encyclopedia on Early Childhood Development; updated April, 2012, p.36. http://www.child-encyclopedia.com/aggression/complete-topic. Accessed June 11, 2021.

103. Arcan, Chrisa, PhD; Bruening, Meg, Mph, RD; and Story, Mary, PhD. "Television (TV) and TV Advertisement Influences on Children's Eating Behavior." Encyclopedia on Early Childhood Development; updated September, 2013, pp. 33-35. http://www.child-encyclopedia.com/child-nutrition/complete-topic. Accessed June 11, 2021.

104. Eisenberg, Nancy, PhD. "Temperamental Effortful Control (Self-Regulation)." Encyclopedia on Early Childhood Development; updated June 2012, p. 16. www.child-encyclopedia.com/temperament/complete-topic. Accessed June 11, 2021.

105. Zelazo, Philip David, PhD. "Reflections on the Development of Executive Function: Commentary on Knapp and Morton, Muakata *et al.*, Rueda and Paz-Alonso, Benson and Sabbagh, Hook *et al.*, and Blair." Encyclopedia on Early Childhood Development; Executive Functions; updated January, 2013, pp. 27-29. http://www.child-encyclopedia.com/executive-functions/complete-topic. Accessed June 11, 2021.

106. *Ibid,* p. 45.

107. Berk, Laura E, PhD. "The Role of Make-Believe Play in Development of Self-Regulation." Encyclopedia of Early Childhood Development; Play-based Learning; updated February 2018, pp. 13-14. http://www.child-encyclopedia.com/play-based-learning/complete-topic. Accessed June 12, 2021.

108. Daniels, Erica, MEd; Pyle, Angela, PhD. "Defining Play-based Learning." Encyclopedia of Early Childhood Development; Play-based Learning; updated February, 2018, p. 8. http://www.child-encyclopedia.com/play-based-learning/complete-topic. Accessed July 12, 2021.

109. Rauscher, FH; Shaw, GL; Levine, LJ; *et al.* "Music Training Causes Long-term Enhancement of Preschool Children's Spatial-temporal Reasoning." *Neurological Research* (February 1997), pp. 2-8.

110. Lakes, Kimberly D; and Hoyt, William T. "Promoting Self-Regulation through School-Based Martial Arts Training." *Applied Developmental Psychology*, 2004, vol 25, pp. 283-302.

111. Niederhofer, Helmut; and Pittschieler, Klaus. "A preliminary investigation of ADHD symptoms in persons with celiac disease." *Journal of Attention Disorders* 10.2 (2006): 200-204.

112. Hallowell, Edward, MD, interview in *Little Humans* series, https://youtu.be/xULoiPFBAcY.

113. Rothbart, Mary K, PhD. "Synthesis." Encyclopedia of Early Childhood Development; Temperament; 2012, pp.4-5. www.child-encyclopedia.com/temperament/complete-topic. Accessed June 13, 2021.

114. Richburg, Melanie; and Fletcher, Teresa. "Emotional Intelligence: directing a child's emotional education." p. 1. http://citeseerx.ist.psu.edu/viewdoc/download?doi=10.1.1.542.8733&rep=rep1&type=pdf. Accessed June 13, 2021.

Early Childhood

115. Benson, Jeannette, MA; and Sabbagh, Mark A, PhD. "The Relation between Executive Functioning and Social Cognition." Encyclopedia of Early Childhood Development; Executive Functions; updated January, 2013, pp.18-19. http://www.child-encyclopedia.com/executive-functions/complete-topic. Accessed June 13, 2021.

116. Restak, Richard, MD. *The New Brain – How the Modern Age is Rewiring Your Mind.* Rodale and St. Martin's Press, 2003, p.37.

117. Cowan, Philip A, PhD; and Pape Cowan, Carolyn, PhD. "The Role of Parents in Children's School Transition." Encyclopedia of Early Childhood Development; Parenting Skills; updated September, 2015, p. 39. http://www.child-encyclopedia.com/parenting-skills/complete-topic. Accessed June 13, 2021.

118. Caremans, Gregory. *"Neuroscience and Parenting."* https://www.udemy.com/course/neuroscience-and-parenting/ Section 4.20. Accessed May 29, 2021.

119. Schriever-Levy, Avital. Interview in *Little Humans* series, https://youtu.be/mXjrxbsfbfg.

120. Brendgen, Mara, PhD. "Development of Indirect Aggression Before School Entry," Université du Québec à Montréal, Canada. February 2012.

121. Bornstein, Lea, BA; and Bornstein, Marc H, PhD. "Parenting Styles and Child Social Development." Encyclopedia of Early Childhood Development; Parenting Skills; updated September, 2015, pp. 23-24. http://www.child-encyclopedia.com/parenting-skills/complete-topic. Accessed June 13, 2021.

122. http://www.pcit.org/.

123. https://www.cebc4cw.org/program/helping-the-noncompliant-child/detailed

124. http://www.pathstraining.com/main/.

125. http://www.incredibleyears.com/.

126. Duckworth, Angela Lee. "Grit: The power of passion and perseverance." Ted Talks, transcript. https://www.ted.com/talks/angela_lee_duckworth_grit_the_power_of_passion_and_perseverance/transcript. Accessed June 13, 2021.

127. Hudson, Jennifer L, PhD. "Parent-Child Relationships in Early Childhood and Development of Anxiety and Depression." Encyclopedia of Early Childhood Development; Parenting Skills; updated September, 2015, p. 50. http://www.child-encyclopedia.com/parenting-skills/complete-topic. Accessed June 13, 2021.

128. Okely, Anthony D, EdD; and Jones, Rachel A, PhD. "Sedentary Behaviour Recommendations for Early Childhood." Encyclopedia of Early Childhood Development; Physical Activity; updated June, 2020, p.22. http://www.child-encyclopedia.com/physical-activity/complete-topic. Accessed June 13, 2021.

129. Korat, Ofra, PhD; and Segal-Drori, Ora, PhD. "Electronic(E)-Books as a Support for Your Children's Language and Early Literacy." Encyclopedia of Early Childhood Development; Technology in early childhood education; updated April, 2021, p. 20. http://www.child-encyclopedia.com/technology-early-childhood-education/complete-topic. Accessed June 13, 2021.

130. Wong, Kevin M, PhD Student; and Newman, Susan B, PhD. "Educational Media Supports for Preschool-Aged English Language Learners." Encyclopedia of Early Childhood Development; Technology in early childhood education; updated April, 2021, p. 29. http://www.child-encyclopedia.com/technology-early-childhood-education/complete-topic. Accessed June 13, 2021.

Chapter 6
Childhood
Years 5 to 7

"Whether you think you can, or you think you can't . . . you're right."
– Henry Ford

Making the Grade

Little Margarita

Mama: *How was school today?*

Margarita: *Not so good.*

Mama: *Why, my darling?*

Margarita: *We had a math test and I failed. I'm sorry, Mama.*

Mama: *Ay, pobrecita Margarita. I was never very good at math, either. That's why I never finished high school. The women in our family are great cooks, but we just can't do math. You are a beautiful girl and I still love you. You'll have to try a little harder, but don't worry too much about those silly math tests. You'll be fine.*

Little Maria

Mama: *How was school today?*

Maria: *Not so good.*

Raising 4 Dimensional Children in a 2 Dimensional World

Mama: *Why, my darling?*

Maria: *We had a math test today and I failed. I am sorry, Mama.*

Mama: *Ay, pobrecita Maria. I used to have trouble with math, too, but then I found out if I practice the problems over and over, I know how to do them. Let me see the test. What are you working on?*

Maria: *Subtraction. I just don't understand it.*

Mama: *OK, let's see the first one you got wrong. What is twelve minus seven?*

Maria: *Seven?*

Mama: *Why do you say that?*

Maria: *I don't know . . . I just don't understand.*

Mama: *Well, lets see. . . . What do we have twelve of? Aha! Beans. Here are twelve beans. If I take away seven, how many do I have left?*

Maria: *One, two, three, four, five. You have five left.*

Mama: *So, what is twelve minus seven?*

Maria: *Five!*

Mama: *That's subtraction. It's not really that hard, is it?*

Maria: *No . . .*

Mama: *OK. Let's try another one, but this time with money!*

Which parent are you?

Margarita's mother had negative beliefs about herself that she projected on her daughter, influencing her to limit her potential. Maria's mother had similar difficulties with math but found a way to overcome any self-imposed limitations. Instead of limiting her daughter, she projected a growth mindset, challenging her to learn from her mistakes and continue to grow.

Childhood

The early childhood years are generally spent responding to the child's needs. Beginning at age 5 is the time to foster independence. From the child's point of view, she spent the first years of her life learning to control her body and her senses, and at about age 6 she will transition to focusing on her feelings. If you have been reading the previous chapters and using the emotional activities, your child will have a head start in this department, but one of the most important feelings to develop is the feeling that she is capable.

Your child will probably now be attending school, so the school will take on more responsibility for developing her mental dimension, but as illustrated in the two stories above, you still play a big role. In order to learn, your child must believe she can learn, and that making mistakes is part of the process of learning. Now that she is in school, you will most likely have less time together. It is important to prioritize the time you do have together to be as high-quality as possible. Of course, you are juggling a lot of responsibilities, but some responsibilities are like rubber, and some are like glass. Your family and your health are like glass in that if you let them slip, you can cause serious damage. Some other responsibilities like spending time with friends or posting on Facebook are like rubber, and will bounce back if you drop them now and then.

If at all possible, get involved with the school. The more contact you have with administrators, teachers, counselors, and coaches, the more feedback you will get on your child, and the better you will understand how to help her. In addition, you can create "family capital" with your school by donating time and/or money or otherwise supporting it in the Parent-Teacher Association, fundraising activities, chaperoning, or other volunteer work. Your investment in family capital can pay huge dividends if your child experiences trouble at school.

Major Lessons: Going to school and getting grades; losing baby teeth; preferring playing with friends to playing with adults; becoming aware of unsafe activities and environments; developing habits and focusing (sometimes obsessing) on favorite activities, and learning rules.

Note: Please read the previous chapter(s), as all children develop at different rates and many of the advances at this age are built upon earlier developments. In case your child is a little slower in one area, or in case you missed some of the activities in the previous chapter, it is always a good practice to review where you are coming from before advancing into new territory.

The Birth Order Effect

Many parents are surprised that their children can be so different when they believe that they raised each of them the same way. Research supports what many other parents have observed: There is a birth order effect that causes you to treat each child differently based on who was born when, and how many other children are competing for your attention.

Of course, not every family fits the mold, but here are the generalizations:[131]

The First Born gets more attention, and therefore tends to be more reliable, conscientious, structured, cautious, controlling, and a higher achiever. They often are perfectionists with a competitive mindset.

The Middle Child gets less attention, as you have at least one other child to attend to, and you are a little more confident that you know what you are doing. They tend to be people pleasers, somewhat rebellious, thrive on friendship, large social circles, and to be peacemakers. Sometimes the First Girl can get the extra attention to give her more firstborn characteristics.

Childhood

The Last Born (the baby) tends to be more free spirited, as the parents have loosened the discipline. They are generally fun-loving, uncomplicated, manipulative, outgoing, attention-seekers, and self-centered.

If you have an **Only Child,** she has no competition, so she gets all the attention all the time. They tend to be super firstborns, more mature than other kids their age, and leaders.

Of course, blended families, adoptions, and large age differences upset the "norms" and create exceptions.[131]

Physically

Somewhere during his sixth year, your child may lose his first baby tooth, usually beginning in the front. This process will continue, tooth by tooth, until about 10 years of age.

This is a good age to discover your child's talents and interests. What sports or physical activities does he enjoy? Of course, you can offer the sports and physical activities you enjoy, but remember that your child is not you, and you cannot re-live your own life (and regrets) through him. Be a gardener not a carpenter. Try lots of things to see what he likes.

What are his talents? Can he run? Is he strong? Is he flexible? Does he have a better body for Football? Basketball? Gymnastics? Martial Arts? Dance? What teams and classes are available in your area? Help him learn what his strengths are, and develop them, and learn what his weaknesses are, and augment them. Instill in him the belief that skills can be developed through practice, and those who excel are the ones who practice more and practice better. Also consider the risks of danger in each activity (like concussions) and help him to make wise choices.

What is his level of desire? Olympic athletes and world-class musicians tend to start early in order to get enough practice hours in before they reach their prime, but imposing that level of discipline on a child is not healthy. Let him try different things, practice what he loves, and if he loves practice and competition, give him the opportunity. If he has the desire to become a world-class performer, he will know it and push himself. If he doesn't, don't push him . . . let him have fun and just be happy.

Feeding

Continue to model good table manners and good eating habits at home. Going to school and having lunch in the cafeteria with other children will likely introduce your child to a smorgasbord of sugary treats and semi-food products that the other children will be eating. The foundation of healthy food taste you (hopefully) built over the previous 5 years should mitigate some of the attraction, but be patient in explaining why you don't buy those kinds of foods and you don't recommend eating them. If you can, pack a healthy lunch for your child to take to school. If you can't, at least recommend which part of the cafeteria lunches are healthy and not-so-healthy.

If your child is too heavy, adjust his diet (without saying anything) by the foods you keep in your home and the meals you cook. Being a "fat kid" is not only physically unhealthy, but it can also cause damage to his self-image. On the other hand, don't impose your own weight-loss guidelines on a child who is not overweight. Kids need carbs. They burn lots of energy. Just do your best to provide healthy carbs instead of empty sugars.

At this age your child should be able to sit at the table for the entire meal, and if he finishes early, simply enjoy the conversation and family time without getting up and leaving.

Sleeping

Be sure your child is getting to bed early enough to get a full night's sleep before he has to get up for school in the morning. What time should he go to bed? If he doesn't want to get up in the morning, he is going to bed too late – easy enough?

I recommend adding one more item to his morning routine: Making his bed. This simple activity is a way to start the day on a positive note with an easy accomplishment that brings order to his day and instills responsibility.

Childhood

Activities

Continue to use any activities from the previous chapter that your child found either difficult or particularly enjoyed, plus add these:

Run: Let your child play tag and other running games with friends whenever safe outdoors.

Swim: Take swimming lessons and "drown proof" your child if you haven't already done so.

Bike: Teach your child to ride a bicycle without training wheels if you can buy or borrow one.

Climb: Take advantage of trees, monkey bars, and other equipment on the playground, but always be aware of the danger of falling and use your good judgment.

Jump Rope: Practice coordination by learning to jump rope.

Hula Hoop: Practice rhythm and coordination with hula hoops.

Skate: Learn to roller skate or skateboard in the summer and ice skate in the winter. Wear protective gear where needed.

Ski: Learn to safely ride a sled, ski, or snowboard.

Dance: Teach your child simple dance moves. You can learn line dances, individual moves, or aerobic dance movements. The Internet is full of examples and knowing how to dance will help him in social situations.

Practice Sports Lead-up Skills: Continue exploring different sports and practice component skills like dribbling and shooting a basketball, kicking a soccer ball, swinging a bat or golf club, throwing and catching a baseball or football, skating, skiing, etc. Search the Internet for drills and skill-builders.

Workout: If you do Yoga, Pilates, or other programs at home, let your child share your workouts with you if he is interested. If you can motivate him to develop his strength with calisthenics like push-ups, sit-ups, and squat jumps, that's wonderful, but his body is entirely too young to start weightlifting.

Fine motor skills: Develop fine motor skills not only in sports lead-up skills, but also in drawing, sculpting, knitting, sewing, playing a musical instrument, practicing magic (sleight of hand), juggling, origami, and other manual skills.

Note: Use your good judgment in these and any physical recommendation I make. Take whatever precautions you think necessary for your child in your unique situation (like a pandemic) to keep your child and everyone else safe.

Mentally

Your child's neo limbic brain is developing, and this is the part of the brain that is associated with memory and performs routine actions with little or no conscious attention. Now is a good time to start forming habits. Research has shown that highly successful people are not the ones who have the discipline to resist lots of temptations, but rather the ones who have reduced the number of temptations in their lives and created habits that occur literally without thinking. According to Dr. Wendy Wood, a professor of psychology and business at USC, "Habits are cognitive associations. They're mental associations that we form when we repeat an action over and over again in a given context and then get a reward."[132] Help your child form good habits and learn how to form habits by doing the same good things over and over. Dr. Wood has found that about 43% of everyday activities are done repeatedly, almost every day in the same context.[132] The two keys are to make it easy and make it fun. Have a morning routine, a routine for after school that incorporates outdoor play and homework time, an after-dinner routine, and a bedtime routine. As I recommended previously, children love structure, so help them structure their day with positive habits. However, help them understand that they should take advantage of fun and exciting opportunities and not become slaves to a schedule. If 43% of activities are done repeatedly, that leaves over half of our daily activities to be different and unique. Help your child develop a sense of balance.

You may have heard discussions about right brain and left brain functions. Traditionally, left brain function was more logical and right brain function was more artistic and emotional. Recent research by Iain McGilchrist published in his book *The Master and His Emissary* has updated this understanding (through studies of brains damaged on either the left side, right side, or in the connecting tissue of the *corpus callosum*)[133] to show that the right hemisphere sees the whole of a situation, while the left hemisphere focuses on the details. It is a survival mechanism that, in animals, allows a bird to focus on eating with its left brain (specifically how to pick up a seed with its beak), while not *being* eaten as the right brain scans the area for predators. In humans, we see the interplay when we try to play a piece of music on the piano: The left brain focuses on which keys to play in which order for each note, while the right brain focuses on how the notes fit together to create a rhythm or melody.

For your child's development, her left brain deals with reading, writing, and grasping, while her right brain deals with the structure of reality. The left brain is more black and white, while the right brain sees many shades of gray. The left brain focuses on results while the right brain appreciates intent. The left brain is the seat of anger, while the right brain tends to be more emotionally literate and appreciates humor and art.[133]

McGilchrist believes our modern society prioritizes the details and facts of the left brain over the wisdom and judgment of the right brain,[133] but we obviously want to develop both sides of the brain in our children, which involves different kinds of training.

Musical training is one activity that improves both halves of the brain and the communication between them. German scientists found that the *corpus callosum* (the bundle of fibers that passes messages between the two sides of the brain) is 10 to 15 percent thicker in musicians who started training before the age of seven than in non-musicians. They think that rapid communication between the hemispheres – needed, for example, when playing a difficult piano piece – may explain the increase.[134]

    Your child will probably be receiving grades in school, so it is important to create a healthy attitude towards them. Grades are a measure of success and accomplishment, and therefore important, but please remember that your child can control her effort but not the result. Treat each test and each grading period as a learning opportunity. The grades are feedback, not a judgment. Not all children can get straight As, but most can make the A-B Honor Roll with the right amount of effort. It is up to you to help your child determine and then provide that amount of effort. Children live up to our expectations, so we should expect them to work hard and do well. We cannot expect them to be perfect. Help them establish the habits that result in good grades like daily homework and study time.

    Another piece of input you may receive from the school is the result of an IQ or Achievement test. Generally, these tests are administered to measure (1) your child's ability and (2) your child's accumulated knowledge. If your child places very high on an IQ test, she may be recommended to an advanced or gifted program. If your child places very low on the IQ test, she may be recommended for special education classes. If there is a stark difference between your child's IQ and Achievement scores, your school counselor should make specific recommendations. These test results are not meant to be lifelong sentences. If you don't like the results you are given, discuss with your counselor ways to improve any deficient areas. These tests have some cultural bias, and studies based on identical twins raised in different environments show that about half of measured intelligence is inherited and the other half is determined by environmental factors (like parental input and educational opportunities.)[135] There is also very little correlation to IQ scores and success in life, so don't place too much emphasis on them.

    If your child is like most children and falls in the middle range, help her understand that there are lots of different children in her class with lots of different abilities. In the average classroom, about 1/3 of the class will learn at the pace that the teacher teaches, about 1/3 will be a little bored because the teacher is moving too slowly, and about

Childhood

1/3 will be behind because the teacher is moving too fast. Help your child determine which 1/3 she is in, and what to do about it. If she is in the top 1/3, she can help some of her friends and do extra reading on her own. If she is in the bottom 1/3, she needs to study and practice more at home to keep up.

Communication

Generally, ask for more detail in communications to improve your child's vocabulary and speaking ability. When your child says something was "fun," ask, "Why was it fun? Tell me more about exactly what you did. How did it make you feel?" You can even suggest some better words to use during the conversation to describe the experience or the feeling.

I would like to re-emphasize something I mentioned in the previous chapter, because vocabulary instruction may be missing in your child's academic classroom. Children who grow up in poverty and children whose families do not speak English in the home tend to get better benefits from E-books than middle-class and upper-class children. The multi-media approach in many of these educational programs, especially in bi-lingual programs, helps these children improve their English literacy and vocabulary. The benefits increase when the children watch the video more than once, and when used at home in conjunction with instruction at school.[136] If your family is in one of these categories, take advantage of your ability to access these online and downloadable educational games and programs.

Activities

Continue to use any activities from the previous chapter that your child found either difficult or particularly enjoyed, plus add these:

<u>Mazes:</u> Buy a book of mazes (or find some online) and ask your child to find her way through the maze.

Raising 4 Dimensional Children in a 2 Dimensional World

<u>Discuss School</u>: Ask, "What did you learn at school today?" then show how that knowledge is important in your child's daily life or in the future.

<u>Homework:</u> Be present while your child is doing school homework to help – don't provide the answers, but rather provide the direction as to how she can solve the problem herself. You want her to feel the sense of accomplishment when she solves a difficult problem to create a love of learning and confidence in her ability to overcome challenges. Depending on your own level of education, especially if you are not strong in English, math, or whatever else your child is learning, homework time presents a great opportunity for you to learn while spending quality time with your child. You can improve your vocabulary, grammar, spelling, math, and many other skills you may have missed in your own school years or simply forgot.
An excellent practice is to ask your child to teach you whatever she is working on. Teaching takes a higher level of understanding and therefore makes your child learn the material more thoroughly. If she can't teach it, she doesn't understand it well enough, yet.

<u>Memory:</u> Play memory games where you challenge your child to remember sequences of numbers, words, or the words to songs and nursery rhymes. A visual version of the game is to show 3 playing cards one at a time, then ask your child to name the 3 cards, in order of appearance, then in reverse order. Increase to 4, 5, 6 or more cards as your child's ability allows. A non-visual version would be to say five numbers and ask your child to repeat them back to you. If she is successful, try six, then seven. You can also continue to play the <u>My List</u> activity from Chapter 5.

<u>Concentration</u>: Place a group of cards face down in a pattern like a square (five rows of five cards). Take turns turning over two cards trying to find a match. When you find a match, you keep those two cards. If you don't find a match, you turn your cards back over and it's the other person's turn. Whoever has the most cards at the end, wins the game.

Childhood

<u>War</u>: To reinforce the value of numbers (which number is larger than which), divide a deck of cards in two, and then each player "plays" the top card in the stack by turning it over. Whoever has the higher card wins by collecting the two cards and putting them in their winning stack. Continue playing until one player gets all the cards. When your child can add, upgrade the game by each player turning over two cards and adding them together to see who has the higher total (all face cards are worth 10).

<u>Discuss Art</u>: When your child creates something, whether it is a drawing, painting, sculpture, or any other media, ask questions about the details like, "Why did you do this?" or focus on one section and say, "Tell me about this ____."

<u>Same or Different</u>: Name two things, then ask your child to identify some way they are the same. Then ask her to identify some way they are different. When your child gets good at this game, ask for two or three ways they are the same or different.

<u>Analogies</u>: Challenge your child to complete an analogy and then challenge you with an analogy of her own. For example, you might say, "Kitten is to Cat as Puppy is to _____." The obvious answer is "Dog," but if your child gives a different answer, ask her to explain it. She may see a different relationship than the one you saw. If her explanation is not accurate, explain the relationship and move on.

<u>Similes</u>: A simile is a comparison using "like" or "as." You can start the game by saying something like, "When I look up to the sky, the clouds look like _____" and challenge your child to complete the comparison. Once again, if you don't see the comparison, ask her to explain it. Then, ask her to challenge you with a simile.

<u>Metaphors</u>: A metaphor is a comparison without using the words "like" or "as," making it an implied comparison by transferring the characteristics of one thing to the other. Instead of saying, "Her hair fell over her shoulders like a waterfall," (a simile), you might say, "Her hair was a golden waterfall glistening in the sun," and then ask

your child what two things you are comparing and how they are similar.

Puns: Explain that puns are the same word with two meanings, or two words that sound the same but mean something different, like, "Why don't you make like a tree and leave?" or "The main ingredient in dog biscuits is Collie flour." Help your child develop her vocabulary and sense of humor by finding puns in everyday conversations and activities.

True or False: Teach your child to examine each part of a statement to decide if it's true or false. For example, "Cats are four legged animals with sharp claws, sharp teeth, feathers, and a tail." Although most of the sentence is true, cats do not have feathers. Take turns making up example sentences and deciding if they are true or false, and why.

Fact or Opinion: Teach your child the difference between fact and opinion: A fact can be proven, but an opinion can't be verified. For example, "The New York Yankees won 57 games this year," is a fact if it is true – they either won 57 games or they did not. "The New York Yankees are the best team in baseball," is an opinion that can't be proven. What does it mean to be the best? How can you prove it? Then take turns making statements and asking each other to identify it as fact or opinion, and why.

Expanding Sentences: Start with a short sentence like, "I saw a dog." Challenge your child to expand the sentence like, "I saw a dog bark." Then you follow with something like, "I saw a dog bark at the mailman." See how many times you can go back and forth but still be in one sentence.

Storytelling: Continue asking your child to tell stories or take turns with you developing a story where each of you gets to add one sentence to the story. Add some similes, metaphors, and puns to your stories.

Musical Feelings: Give your child some drawing materials (paper, markers, crayons) and then play a selection of music and ask your child to draw something based on the feeling of the music. When she is finished, ask her to explain the drawing and how it shows the feeling she got from the music.

Safe Touch: Reinforce safe touch practices and what to do if anyone touches her in a private place.

Safety: Reinforce that your child knows her name, address, and your phone number. Review what to do if she gets lost in the park or at the store. Teach her how to answer the home phone (if you have one) without giving information ("My father can't come to the phone right now. May I take a message?") and not to open the door for anyone or answer questions ("My father can't come to the door right now. Please come back later or leave the package outside.") Practice phone calls and doorbell rings until you are confident she knows what to do, even if the other person is pushy.

Group Activities

These are some activities you might use in the car during a carpool, at home on rainy days, or even at a restaurant if the kids get a little restless. Of course, you can use some of the individual activities above with one child taking your (the adult) part, or you might use these group activities with your child alone, with you taking the part of the first child.

Count on Me: The children take turns counting by 2s (2, 4, 6, etc.). If that is easy, count by 3s or 5s or 10s. If that is easy, start with a number and add a specific number, for example: Start with 5 and add 3 (8, 11, 14, etc.) If that is too easy, try multiplying by 2 or 3 or even a larger number.

A to Z: The first child thinks of a word that begins with the first letter of the alphabet like, "Apple," and the next child must think of a word that begins with the next letter of the alphabet like, "Box." Can they make it all the way through the alphabet? As they get older, turn it into a classification exercise by limiting words to one group, like only animals or only foods. If this becomes too easy, challenge them to play the game backwards from Z to A.

Gestures: The first child will show a common gesture. The second child must identify what the gesture means, then the second child will show a common gesture.

Quick Math: Two children stand back-to-back, hold out one or two hands with a specific number of fingers, then they both say, "One, two, three, Turn!" They turn around to see who can add up the total number of fingers correctly first.

Be Specific: One child describes how to do something while the other child does exactly what the first child says, to illustrate that choosing the right word is important.

Emotionally

Your child is learning to become self-conscious and may become aware that his internal feelings and his external expression are not necessarily the same. As he does, he will try to present a public persona, trying to appear "cool" with his peers. This knowledge also allows for intervention strategies that can separate a feeling from expressing an emotional reaction.

It seems logical that in recent decades, neurophysiological research related to learning and education has focused on the brain, but other recent research has shown that the brain is not the sole captain of the ship. Neurological and hormonal signals flowing to the brain from various organs and systems not only play a role in regulating the body, but also influence higher brain centers involved in perception and emotion. The heart actually sends more messages to the brain than the brain sends to the heart. Heart rate variability can signal the brain to go into sympathetic mode (flight, fight, or freeze) or parasympathetic mode (rest and digest),[137] so the heart controls the brain in some ways, and the brain controls the heart in others.

Childhood

During anger, frustration, anxiety, and emotional stress, the heart sends a desynchronized signal to the brain, limiting our ability to think clearly, remember information, and causing us to make careless mistakes. During positive feeling states like appreciation, love, and compassion, the heart transmits an ordered, coherent signal to the brain, often resulting in better focus, memory, comprehension, and creativity.[138]

The HeartMath Institute has developed tools to help people of all ages regulate their emotions, and I recommend the one called The Freeze-Fame Tool for children this age. When your child (1) realizes he is having a stressful or disturbing feeling, he should (2) freeze it like freezing the frame in a movie or video, (3) shift his focus to the area of the heart, (4) imagine he is breathing in through the heart and out through the *solar plexus*, and (5) intentionally generate a positive feeling like appreciation or care to replace the negative one. This simple five step exercise should help your child calm down and shift from sympathetic response to parasympathetic response.[138]

One specific area of negative emotion your child will deal with are the emotions associated with failure, and one of the best ways to help him deal with failure is to create a Growth Mindset. According to Dr. Carol Dweck, a Fixed Mindset is one that believes people are born smart or dumb and can't change. It focuses on results and avoids risks. A Growth Mindset believes people can improve in any area. It focuses on the process and encourages experimentation. Help your child understand that failure is not the opposite of success, but a path to success. As we discussed earlier when talking about grades at school, failure is not a permanent result, it is just feedback. It is part of the learning process. Help your child follow the OLD Method: Own your mistakes, Learn from them, and Don't repeat them. If one way didn't work, try another way until you find one that does work. Winners never quit, and quitters never win.

Your relationship and your approval of your child should not focus on results, but on effort. Your child cannot control the results, but he can control his effort. When you focus on results, you create extrinsic motivation, which changes depending upon whom you are trying to impress. It can create approval junkies and workaholic personalities. When you focus on effort, you encourage intrinsic motivation, where your child creates his own internal reward based on his goals. Encourage the inner voice that eventually becomes his conscience.[139]

Also be aware that children at this age can develop fixations or even obsessions. It's part of the process of developing habits, so encourage a good healthy habit like music, a sport, or a physical activity over a two-dimensional activity like video games. Children like to share activities with their family members and tend to try the favorite activities of older siblings, but they also have their own unique interests. If your child shows signs of having an addictive personality or your family has a history of alcohol or drug addiction, he is better off getting addicted to something like basketball or martial arts that might last into his teen and adult years, than not providing a healthy outlet for his obsessive personality and opening the door to drugs or alcohol addiction later in life.

Discipline

Put connection before control. When your child disobeys or acts out emotionally, ask yourself, "What is he trying to express?" Is he tired? Hungry? Frightened? What is the underlying cause of the surface behavior? Listen first before you react. Show you are on his side. If he seems to be in "Flight" mode, give him options or even crack a joke. If he seems to be in "Fight" mode, don't fight back. Share in his outrage by saying, "I understand you are angry because . . ." and then help him calm down. If he is in "Freeze" mode, just be there to support him. Offer a hug. If he is too angry for a hug now, just assure him it will be available later.[140]

On the other hand, if he is simply testing his boundaries, you need to reinforce the boundary. Be positive whenever you can, using the PIR Method from the previous chapter. If there is a deeper problem, solve the deeper problem and the behavior will solve itself. Over time, teach him to stop the negative emotion himself by shifting his attention into his brain (by counting to ten) or changing his heart

Childhood

with the Freeze-Frame Method. With practice, these techniques will become habits.

    Continue to demand respectful treatment for yourself, your spouse, teachers, coaches, religious leaders, and really all adults. Habits are easier to maintain than to establish, so maintain treating others with respect from an early age.

    You may have heard this story before, but I will tell it anyway for its application: When an elephant is a baby, trainers tie a rope around its leg and attach it to a stake in the ground to keep it from running away. No matter how hard it tries, the baby elephant doesn't have enough strength to pull up the stake, so it eventually stops trying. Years later when it definitely has enough strength to pull up the stake or break the rope, the full-grown elephant just doesn't try because it remembers the lesson learned long ago.

    I believe if you can establish a healthy level of fear in your child at this age, it will stay with him for many years to come. I am not recommending beating your child: Intense disapproval with a loud voice might impress upon him now, while punishment and reward are his level of moral understanding, that he is not to disobey you. You don't need to do it regularly – perhaps just once if you make a significant emotional memory – but I have heard teens say, "My father would kill me if he found out I _____." Of course, the death penalty was not a realistic consequence, but the fear of disobedience (on a very childlike level) was effective in preventing the bad or even dangerous behavior later in life. Think about it.

Activities

    Continue to use any activities from the previous chapter that your child found either difficult or particularly enjoyed, plus add these:

<u>Wait</u>: When you see your child experiencing difficulty in any activity, just watch and wait. Don't help right away. Let him try and maybe succeed. When he asks for help, give the minimum amount for him to figure it out. If he still needs help, show him how to solve the problem. When you jump in too quickly, the message is, "You are not capable."

Raising 4 Dimensional Children in a 2 Dimensional World

<u>Simon Says:</u> Continue to play Simon Says to develop the ability to inhibit reactions.

<u>I'm Gonna Be:</u> Help your child learn to change his emotional state by practicing saying things like, "I feel afraid, but I'm gonna be brave. I feel sad, but I'm gonna be happy. I'm worried, but I'm gonna be all right." Then, when your child seems upset, ask, "How do you feel?" and when he answers, prompt, "but I'm gonna be . . ." and allow him to answer.

<u>Discuss Friends:</u> Ask what his friends did and said during the day and comment on it. You are trying to establish that you will listen to what he has to say and care about him and his friends to establish trust, so that when he grows older, these questions and discussions will be normal and not viewed as an invasion of privacy. Establish the trust and connection now, so that when he has questions about relationships in the future, he will be more comfortable discussing them with you.

<u>Emotional Scripts:</u> Discuss social situations that you have observed between your child and his friends, that he has encountered at school, or that you might imagine he will encounter. Discuss how your child did (or will) feel in the situation, but then discuss how others in the situation might be feeling. Discuss what was said and what else could have been said instead. The goal is to help your child not only understand other people's feelings, but also understand common emotional scripts of expected behavior, including what to say and what not to say.

<u>When I Grow Up:</u> Start asking your child what he would like to be when he grows up. It's a way of introducing the idea of long-term goal setting as well as a way to participate in the choice of his childhood obsession. Teach about goal setting by establishing together that if X is the long-term goal, what are some short-term goals he must set and achieve to reach X.

<u>What Else Could You Do:</u> Whenever your child comes to you with a

disappointment or a complaint, ask, "Why do you think that happened? What did you do about it? What else could you do?"

<u>Sunday Transparency Talks:</u> Meet with the entire family, perhaps over a meal, and each one gets to share a challenge they have had during the past week. Everyone else should acknowledge the feeling, not take it as a personal accusation, and discuss it honestly to come up with a solution. This is a great way not only to heal emotional wounds, but to learn how to deal with hurt emotions and treat other people more compassionately.

<u>Pay it forward:</u> Just before bed, either during prayers or while reviewing the day's activities, ask your child, "What could you do tomorrow to be more compassionate? Whom do you know that needs help?" See if he can identify an act of kindness or one person to help. Help him realize that just because you can't do everything, you can still do something. The next night follow up on whether he was able to complete his "assignment."

<u>Martial Arts:</u> Beginning at age 5 the study and practice of the martial arts provides an exceptional balance of physical, mental, and emotional benefits for both boys and girls. In addition to getting great exercise while learning exciting skills, your child will learn self-discipline, respect, and gain self-confidence. The belt ranking system provides experience at setting short-term goals, achieving them, and setting new goals along the way to achieving long-term goals. Some programs will even pick up your child at his elementary school and bring him to the martial arts school so that you can pick him up on your way home from work. Plus, you will provide a ready group of positive friends who provide good peer pressure. I highly recommend it for both boys and girls.

Spiritually

Now that your child is attending school, you face a new challenge: Public schools have been hit by lawsuits from various groups to remove religion from the curriculum, basically leaving them to teach what amounts to an atheistic way of life. They even have a difficult time teaching what used to be called "character" without upsetting someone, so most schools have accepted the role of providing your child's academic (mental) education, but have intentionally steered away from her spiritual education. You, on the other hand, may choose a religious school if you can afford the tuition or get a scholarship, a charter school that addresses your needs, can homeschool your child, or you can just take advantage of the religious education classes offered by your church, temple, or mosque.

At this age, she will believe that resources should be distributed equally, without regard for need. In her mind, she wants everyone to get an equal amount to insure she gets her fair share.[141] Her morality is self-centered.

This age is a good time to introduce rules at home that incorporate universal principles, to move your child up to what Kohlberg calls the Law-and-Order level of moral development. Kids this age like to know the rules. However, a child at this age will still have trouble applying a universal principle to a concrete example in her life. In other words, she will be learning the rules, but not quite ready to apply them to herself. It is still a good foundation to teach the rules. You can use rules from your religious tradition like the 10 Commandments, or you can compile some more secular rules like:

- When you promise, you deliver.
- If you want something, you earn it.
- If you value it, take care of it.
- If you make a mess, clean it up.
- Count your blessings, not your problems.
- Be a giver, not a taker.
- Just because you can, doesn't mean you should.
- Lessons are repeated until they are learned. Never stop learning.
- Love is expansive and inclusive; hate is constricting and exclusive.

Continue to read together, especially stories of heroes and

Childhood

saints that portray high ethical values. Use some of your limited screen time to watch PG movies about historical figures or even inspirational imaginary heroes, and then discuss why they decided to do what they did, what challenges they faced when trying to do what is right, and how they overcame those challenges.

Activities

Continue to use any activities from the previous chapter that your child found either difficult or particularly enjoyed, plus add these:

Positive Reinforcement: Catch your child being kind, generous, honest, etc., point it out and ask, "How did that feel?" so that she knows what it feels like to be kind and realizes that it feels good.

What's the Intent: Discuss situations based on the intent not the result. For example, "Which is worse: Mary steals Susie's doll to make her cry, or Mary accidentally drops a book on Susie's foot, and she starts to cry." Susie cries in both cases, but the first case is morally worse because Mary intentionally hurt Susie, and in the second case it was an accident. Look for examples in your child's life, in reading, or in movies, and discuss how the intent is important.

How to Share: Discuss with your child different ways to share. For example, if you have two toys, it's easy to lend one to your friend. How do you share a tablet or game controller? How do you share one box of crayons among four people? How can three children share a seesaw?

Meditation: In addition to keeping still for a set length of time, help your child become aware of her thoughts – where they come from and practice how to stop thinking for a while by focusing her attention somewhere.

Principles: Upgrade the activity from last chapter by not only identifying three ways to be good, like: Telling the truth, being kind, and being generous; but then making up a real-life situation like,

"Susie comes over to our house to play with you. You have five dolls and Susie has no dolls here. What should you do?" This time, add the question, "Which principle are you following?"

Summary

As your child continues to grow, I hope you continue to grow as a parent. Your child's brain has still not developed to think like an adult, so you must continue to reach him on his own level. In many cases, that means listening more than telling, experiential learning where the whole world becomes your classroom, and getting support from the village, providing as many positive role models as possible through family, friends, teachers, coaches, and religious leaders. Help him choose positive friends by enrolling him in activities where he will meet them.

Attending school may be something completely new or may be just an extension of the day care routine you have already established. Exposure to a new group of children and a more organized learning environment will bring some interesting opportunities and challenges. Spend as much quality time as you can when you are together.

Your child's personality should start to become consistent, but you still can help him grow. Now is a good time to establish positive habits through various routines at different times of the day. He may start trying to be "cool" for his friends, and may find something that sparks his interest to the point that it seems like an obsession. As long as it is a healthy (or at least not an unhealthy) activity, roll with it. Who knows, he may become a world champion one day, or he may grow tired of it in a few weeks. At least he will gain practice at working on something consistently, and the focus and dedication will be useful skills later in life.

Introduce your child to Hebrew School, Bible Study, or other religious educational programs available and appropriate for you. The school system has (somewhat) taken over the mental dimension of his education, but you still need to provide for the other three dimensions. Just the fact that you are reading this book shows you are trying your best, so use the activities and suggestions to round out his education and develop a well-balanced child.

Screen Time

It may take a village to raise a child, but the modern village includes the Internet, video games, and marketers. Advertisements are telling our children that they are not worthy, and they need _____ (whatever the marketer is selling) to be happy. Your child's brain isn't yet sophisticated enough to ignore these messages, so try to avoid even PG or educational TV programs that have commercials. You are better off with subscription-based programming without the advertising.

According to Professor Brad Bushman of Iowa State University "The correlation between violent media and aggression is larger than the correlation between exposure to lead and decreased I.Q. levels in kids. . . . It's larger than the effects of exposure to asbestos. It's larger than the effect of secondhand smoke on cancer."[141] That's pretty big.

There are over 1,000 other studies that support the conclusion that when children watch violent media, they become more aggressive. On the other hand, aggression can be decreased by as much as 25% simply by decreasing the amount of television and movie violence the child sees. Pediatricians and psychiatrists explain that while most adults can distinguish media images from real images, due to left hemisphere immaturity and lack of life experiences, a child's brain can't put the images into context.[142]

There are three effects on children who view violence on television:
1. They may become desensitized to the pain and suffering of others,
2. They may become more fearful of the world around them, and
3. They may be more likely to behave in aggressive or harmful ways towards others.[142]

In long-term studies from New York, heavy TV watchers were more likely to act in aggressive ways, and in separate studies scientists got similar results when they studied the effects of violent video games or songs with violent lyrics.[143] It all goes back to the simple idea of building blocks: You get out what you put in. If you view a steady diet of violence, you accept violence in thought and possibly in action. Do the best you can to guard the images and behaviors that go into the building blocks of your child's mind.

As far as telephone usage at this age, the question I would ask is, "Why?" Why does a 6-year-old child need a phone? To keep up with Joneses? Because all his friends have phones? Childhood is a precious time and does not last long. Please encourage your child to run and play in the four dimensional world and postpone the two dimensional world for later. He will have plenty of time and opportunity in the years to come to become fully technologically literate. Raise a 4 Dimensional child.

Bullying:

Now that your child is attending school, bullying can become a common problem. Most schools have anti-bullying programs, and most schools have bullies. In an elementary school a sixth grader is much bigger, stronger, and smarter (his brain is more developed) than your kindergartner or first-grader. Your child will probably not be able to avoid the bullies completely, so you should invest some time in Bully Avoidance and Anti-bully Programs. Your school or your community center may offer one, and there are many such programs online, and many books available with simple, sound tactics. Once again, I strongly recommend martial arts training – not for the physical self-defense (we don't want to encourage fighting), but for the Stop the Bully programs they offer or incorporate in their regular classes. When you visit the martial arts school, ask about their Stop the Bully programs. If they talk about physical self-defense, look for another school that teaches verbal, mental, and emotional self-defense along with the physical techniques. We want to teach children how to deescalate potentially violent situations with knowledge and humor, in order to stop the bully without fighting.

Note: As all children are unique and develop at different rates, I recommend you read the next chapter to prepare for your child's growth and in case your child happens to develop more quickly in one area or another, and the previous chapter in case your child happens to develop more slowly in one area or another. Specifically, some of the activities might well be continued into the older years.

Also please use your own good judgment in following any advice I offer. Research is subject to change and my advice may be based on research that has since changed or been updated since this publishing. Choose your actions based on your own beliefs, experiences, research, and judgment, especially during extenuating circumstances (like a pandemic.)

Recommended Resources:

https://littlehumans.com/
https://www.drhallowell.com/adhd/
https://www.gamesofgenius.com/
https://www.child-encyclopedia.com
https://www.who.int/topics/early-child-development/en/
https://toolsofthemind.org/
https://mindup.org/
https://www.davidlynchfoundation.org/
https://www.mindinthemaking.org/
https://www.vroom.org/
https://parentsasteachers.org/

References:

131. Caremans, Gregory. *"Neuroscience and Parenting."* https://www.udemy.com/course/neuroscience-and-parenting/ Section 6.34. Accessed May 29, 2021.

132. Wood, Wendy. "Creatures of Habit: How Habits Shape Who We Are – and Who We Become." NPR; *Hidden Brain*; December 30, 2019. https://www.npr.org/transcripts/787160734. Accessed June 15, 2021.

133. McGilchrist, Iain. "One Head, Two Brains: How the Brain's Hemispheres Shape the World We See." NPR; Hidden Brain; February 4, 2019. https://www.npr.org/templates/transcript/transcript.php?storyId=690656459. Accessed June 15, 2021.

134. Schlaug, G; *et al.* "Increased Corpus Callosum Size in Musicians." *Neuropsychologia,* August, 1995, pp. 1047-1055.

135. Oswalt Morelli, Angela, MSW. "Causes of Intelligence." Helen Farabee Centers; Child Development Theory: Middle Childhood (8-11). https://www.helenfarabee.org/poc/view_doc.php?type=doc&id=37684&cn=1272. Accessed June 15, 2021.

136. Wong, Kevin M, PhD Student; and Newman, Susan B, PhD. "Educational Media Supports for Preschool-Aged English Language Learners." Encyclopedia on Early Childhood Development; Technology in early childhood education; updated April, 2021, pp. 29-30. http://www.child-encyclopedia.com/technology-early-childhood-education/complete-topic. Accessed June 15, 2021.

137. HeartMath Institute; Scientific Foundation of the HeartMath Institute. https://www.heartmath.org/science/. Accessed June 15, 2021.

138. Arguelles, Lourdes; McCraty, Rollin; and Rees, Robert A. "The Heart in Holistic Education." HeartMath Institute; Assets; Uploads; 2015. https://www.heartmath.org/assets/uploads/2015/01/heart-in-education.pdf. Accessed June 15, 2021.

139. Munakata, Yuko, PhD; et al. "Executive Functioning During Infancy and Childhood." Encyclopedia on Early Childhood Development; Executive Functions; updated January, 2013. http://www.child-encyclopedia.com/executive-functions/complete-topic. Accessed June 15, 2021.

140. Caremans, Gregory. *Neuroscience and Parenting.* https://www.udemy.com/course/neuroscience-and-parenting/ Section 2.4. Accessed May 29, 2021.

141. Oswalt Morelli, Angela, MSW. "Kolberg's Stages Continued." Encyclopedia on Early Chldhood Development. https://www.helenfarabee.org/poc/view_doc.php?type=doc&id=37693&cn=1272. Accessed June 15, 2021.

142. Restak, Richard, MD. *The New Brain – How the Modern Age is Rewiring Your Mind.* Rodale and St. Martin's Press, 2003, p. 85-86.

143. *Ibid,* pp. 99-100.

Chapter 7
Middle Childhood
Years 7 to 10

"I think the reward for conformity is that everyone likes you except yourself." – Rita Mae Brown

Something in the Air

Smokin' Joe

Mom: *What's that smell? Have you been smoking?*

Joe: *No.*

Mom: *I better not catch you smoking.*

Joe: *Dad smokes.*

Mom: *He's an adult.*

Joe: *I'm not a kid any more!*

Mom: *You're not an adult, either. If I catch you smoking, I'm going to tan your hide!*

Joe: *You won't.*

Vapin' Vic

Mom: *What's that smell? Have you been smoking?*

Vic: *No.*

Mom: *Come here, let me smell your clothes and your hair. . . . it's not tobacco. What is it?*

Vic: *It's not dangerous. I tried vaping.*

Raising 4 Dimensional Children in a 2 Dimensional World

Mom: *How did you do that?*

Vic: *Willie's borrowed his brother's JUUL.*

Mom: *Well, was it fun?*

Vic: *Well . . . kind of.*

Mom: *What was fun about it?*

Vic: *It tasted good – like fruit, and it was cool to share it with the guys.*

Mom: *And what made you think it's not dangerous?*

Vic: *Willie's brother does it all the time and he's OK. He said it's not dangerous at all.*

Mom: *Well, let's do a little research. Come here to the computer. This is the CDC site, that's the Centers for Disease Control, and they say that 99% of e-cigarettes DO contain nicotine and other harmful products, and nicotine is not only addictive, but it can also harm your brain, which is still growing. It changes the way your brain works and can increase the chance that you might do other drugs. Plus, there are other chemicals that can harm your lungs and even cause cancer. Lately there have even been a few cases in the news of kids who have died from vaping . . . . let's do a quick search . . . . 47 people have died from vaping. Does that sound like it's not dangerous?*

Vic: *No . . .*

Mom: *Look, I know that you want to do what your friends do, but do you really think this is something you want your friends to do?*

Vic: *I guess not . . .*

Mom: *Then I think you should be a leader. Next time they want to vape, you should tell them how they are hurting themselves, and maybe search online with them like we just did. What do you think?*

Vic: *I could try.*

Mom: *Please do. Friends take care of friends. If you can't convince them, then at least they will understand why you won't do it. Do you want to do it again?*

Vic: *Not really . . . I didn't know it was so dangerous.*

Mom: *If they insist you vape or not be their friend, then they are not really good friends, are they?*

Vic: *They wouldn't do that.*

Mom: *Well, let me know how it goes. Fortunately, nobody got hurt yet. It's also illegal for kids your age, so you don't want to get in trouble with the police, do you?*

Vic: *No.*

Mom: *Talk with your friends and help them out, and let me know how it goes.*

Which parent made a bigger impact?

Joe's mom didn't ask enough questions. She never found out if he was lying, smoking, or vaping. Her answer was a threat, and the only commitment she got was that she wouldn't catch him – not that he wouldn't do it. Vic's mom asked questions to find out exactly what was going on, engaged her son in a search for evidence, and asked his opinion. She did not threaten, but instead made a positive suggestion and asked for a commitment, and then asked to keep the lines of communication open.

Middle Childhood

Your child is getting smarter, but don't overestimate her yet. At about age 7 she will be entering the "age of reason," or what Piaget called the Concrete Operational Stage, where she is not yet capable of abstract or hypothetical thinking, but she can appreciate logic. Specifically, she will make generalizations from specific instances like, "If my neighbor's dog bites, then all dogs bite," but not yet be able to apply a general rule to a specific situation, like knowing that stealing is bad, but maybe not connecting taking a candy bar from the store as stealing. She will try to live up to your expectations, but don't be too surprised if common sense is not common at the beginning of this age group.

She should be able to accept more responsibility at home in the form of chores, and begin to start organizing and managing her time better to achieve her own goals. She may also develop some interest in what she wants to be when she grows up, or begin modeling herself and her interests after an older sibling.

As she spends more time at school and away from the family, she will become more independent. She may walk or bike to school, or ride a bus, which bring about more safety concerns for you. She will think less about herself and have more concern for others, while developing her self-concept in relation to her peers. She may join extra-curricular activities at school, the community center, or your church, and consider a teacher or coach as a role model, which will open her to different points of view. She will want to spend more time with her friends, and probably be ready to have her own phone to talk with them. Before giving her a phone, ask her to explain to you why she needs one, and more importantly, how she is going to be responsible for not losing it, not breaking it, and using it properly.

It is an exciting time, sometimes considered "the golden age of childhood," where she is learning at a tremendous rate, enjoying physical activities with excellent coordination, yet has none of the anxieties and responsibilities of adolescence.

Major Lessons: learning to read and succeed in school; learning to get along with peers; learning the rules of society in preparation for adolescence; developing a self-image; moving from a self-based to an other-based understanding of morality.

Note: Please read the previous chapter(s), as all children develop at different rates and many of the advances at this age are built upon earlier developments. In case your child is a little slower in one area, or in case you missed some of the activities in the previous chapter, it is always a good practice to review where you are coming from before advancing into new territory.

Middle Childhood

Family Changes

Divorce rates began rising in the US in the 1970s and peaked in the early 1980s, causing a lot of concern over its effect on children. Divorce affects different children differently, depending on the degree of conflict between the parents before the divorce, the amount of financial hardship after the divorce, and the attitudes of the parents, especially the custodial parent.[144]

If your family has gone through a divorce (or a death of any family member, for that matter), expect that the children will grieve over losing daily contact with missing family member(s). They may also have to adjust to a reduced standard of living, possibly move and enter another school, and may have long-term anxieties about their own future relationships.

Although most early research on divorce focused on the problems of the children, more recent studies have found that most children of divorce lead happy, well-adjusted lives. Communication with the custodial parent often improves, and families tend to become more democratic, allowing children greater participation in decision-making.[144]

If your family has gone through a divorce, first, take care of your own mental health as a parent. Find positive friends and/or support groups. Cultivate a healthy, conflict-free relationship with your ex for the sake of the children – cooperation is better than conflict. Finally, establish a healthy, positive, and comfortable environment for the kids. If you are the wealthier partner, do your best to make sure the children don't lack financially.

When you begin dating, keep it away from the kids. Don't bring a parade of boyfriends or girlfriends into your child's life. Only introduce a potential new partner after you have had time to get to know each other and believe it might work. Don't expect instant love from the kids. Take time to earn each other's respect and affection.

If you decide to try a blended family, be patient. Love is not all you need (but it sure helps). It can take up to seven years to iron things out. Respect past loyalties and never say anything about an ex that you might later regret. There will be conflicting expectations, shifting loyalties, and some intense emotions.[144] Research some successful strategies before you try it, like those provided by Summer Felix-Mulder and her husband Mike in the *Little Humans* series,[145] and refer back to them when you encounter the inevitable challenges. It won't be easy, but with work, it can be worthwhile.

Physically

Your child will probably have lost all his front baby teeth and replaced them with permanent ones by now. During the middle childhood years, the back teeth (molars) will fall out and also be replaced. Because the increase in schoolwork can cause eye strain, eye exams are a good idea if your child hasn't had one.

Generally, children gain about 2 inches in height and five to seven pounds of weight each year during middle childhood. Their bodies tend to slim down, gain muscle, and increase lung capacity. They may experience "growing pains" if the growth of their bones exceeds the growth of their tendons and muscles, but these are usually temporary and harmless. Boys are usually taller at the beginning of middle childhood, but because girls start their growth spurts earlier, the girls may be taller than the boys just before puberty.[146] However, since each child will start his growth spurt at a different age, there can be some big differences in size among children of the same age or in the same classroom, which can cause some emotional duress.

During middle childhood, your child's fine motor skills (those that require eye-hand coordination) will improve dramatically, as can be seen in his ability to draw (now using 3D elements), to write using both printed and cursive letters, and his manual dexterity in handling a cell phone or a gaming controller. This is a good age to learn how to touch-type on a keyboard. Many boys take up model assembly at this age while girls may try beading or bedazzling.

You may also notice rapid improvement in sports-related skills as your child's balance, coordination, reflexes, strength, agility, speed, and flexibility increase. If your child is interested in sports, be sure to impress upon him that, yes, some kids are bigger or stronger, but practice is the biggest difference in ability. Change his thinking from being either "good or not good" at the sport, to being either "trained or untrained." He who trains (practices), becomes good.

Feeding

According to the CDC, the obesity rate for children ages 6 to 11 is 18.4% (and even higher for Hispanic and black children),[147] compared to only 4% in 1974.[148] That's a big change. If your child is starting to show signs of obesity, the earlier you try to correct it, the healthier your child will be, as diabetes tends to follow obesity. Control the portions you serve at each meal, but especially control the amount of sugary and processed food you buy and have available in the house. If you were careful in your food choices earlier in your child's life, he should not have much of a taste for super-sweet treats, but one can be acquired quickly at any age. Fortunately, sugar addictions are not permanent, so a week or two without sweets can reduce the cravings to almost zero. Don't make it a big thing that might lead to an eating disorder – it's mostly a matter of availability and habit. You do the grocery shopping, so you control most of the availability.

The other half of the equation is physical exercise. Get your child outdoors for at least one hour of vigorous activity in the neighborhood (if it's safe), the park, the YMCA, or enroll him in sports teams, classes, or other activity programs. A body in motion tends to stay in motion, so start the habit early.

Sleeping

Your child will need between nine- and twelve-hours sleep, with most averaging about ten. As I said in the previous chapter, if your child has difficulty waking up in the morning, he needs to go to bed earlier. Studies have shown direct links between sleep and academic performance, focus, memory, anxiety, depression, and aggression.[149]

Raising 4 Dimensional Children in a 2 Dimensional World

Activities

Continue to use any activities from the previous chapter that your child found either difficult or particularly enjoyed, plus add these:

Personal Hygiene: Discuss with your child some daily personal hygiene habits and why they are important. At this age he may be more conscious of his appearance (and smell), so now is a good time to re-impress upon him some of the habits you established years ago.

Calisthenics: Teach your child proper form for push-ups, sit-ups, mountain climbers, and more. Count how many he can do with proper form, record it, and practice every day to increase one repetition every couple of days or so.

Stretch: Teach your child basic stretches to increase flexibility. If you can teach properly and safely, set a goal of achieving front splits and side splits before his body tightens up.

Balance: Have your child lift one knee up to waist height, establish his balance, then make small circles with the raised foot. Count how many circles he can do without losing balance, then try it with the other foot.

Posture: Place a book or a pillow on top of your child's head and challenge him to walk around the house without the book or pillow falling off. (Pillows are easier to balance than books). Also, be aware that a falling book or pillow may break something, so pick a safe pathway.

V-Sit: Have your child sit on the floor with his legs straight out in front of him. He should grab each calf muscle with the same side hand, lean back and balance on his bottom, with both his back and his legs off the floor. How long can he hold his balance?

Twist Stand: Have your child stand with his feet shoulder width apart and his arms crossed. Ask him to twist around 180° so that his legs are crossed. Ask him to sit down. Then, ask him to stand up and return to

Middle Childhood

his starting position without uncrossing his arms.

<u>Bent Knee Hop</u>: Have your child balance on one leg, bend down, then jump up and land on the same leg. Try the other leg. How many repetitions can he do with one leg? By switching legs each time?

<u>Jump Twists:</u> Have your child squat down, jump up and twist in the air to turn 180° before landing. If he can turn half-way, challenge him to turn ¾ of the way around (270°), and then all the way in a complete circle (360°).

<u>Step Through</u>: Have your child clasp his hands interlocking his fingers. Challenge him to step through his hands without releasing his grip (practice on a soft surface in case he falls.)

<u>Straight-Line Balance</u>: If you have a 2 x 4 piece of wood, lay it on the ground and ask your child to walk across the board without falling off. If you don't have wood, use a string or piece of tape.

<u>Juggling</u>: Teach your child to juggle three balls or other soft objects. Look online for videos if you don't know how.

<u>Basic Gymnastics</u>: Teach your child to do a handstand or a head stand. Be sure to practice on a soft surface in case he falls, and be a good "spotter" by holding his legs up until he gets his balance, and catching his legs if he falls. I recommend you have him practice against a wall, so that he cannot fall backwards, only frontwards, but be careful not to be kicked by him.
Practice doing a cartwheel on a soft surface.
Practice a round-off. Again, look for videos online for instruction.

<u>Dance</u>: Continue to teach your child simple dance moves. You can learn line dances, individual moves, or aerobic dance movements. The Internet is full of examples, and knowing how to dance will help him in social situations.

<u>Practice Sports Lead-up Skills:</u> Continue exploring different sports and

practice component skills like dribbling and shooting a basketball, kicking a soccer ball, swinging a bat or golf club, throwing and catching a baseball or football, skating, skiing, etc.

Group Activities

Thumb Wrestling: Two players face each other, interlock their fingers of the same hand, and raise their thumbs. The object of the game is to use your thumb to pin down your partner's thumb to his hand. Both partners say, "1, 2, 3, Go!" and begin to wrestle. If a player twists his wrist in any way, he loses.

Slap Fights: Child A places both palms up in front of his chest. Child B places both palms down, resting on Child A's palms while facing him. The goal is for Child A to bring his hands around and above Child B's hands and slap them downward. If Child A can make contact, he wins and tries again. If child B can remove his hands before getting slapped, he wins, and they switch roles (he places his hands palms up.) If Child B moves his hands from the top without child A actually making a slap attempt, Child A gets a free slap on Child B's hands and keeps the bottom position.

Arm Wrestle: Teach your child and a friend to arm wrestle. If you have a group, create a tournament pairing evenly matched children against each other, then winners against winners and alternates against alternates.

Chinese Pull-up: Sit two children facing each other with their knees straight out in front so that their heels and toes touch. They then grasp each other's hands and pull each other up to a standing position. Their hands and feet must continuously touch, but they may need to turn their feet sideways or possibly open their legs to be able to grasp hands.

Tug-o-War: Get a strong rope and set an equal number of children on each side. Mark the center of the rope with a anything (a piece of tape or tie a napkin) and mark a center line on the ground. When you say,

"Go!" each side tries to pull the other side across the center line. Be sure no one wraps the rope around his hand, wrist, or arm to prevent significant injury.

Wheelbarrow Races: Create a starting line and a finish line. Two children form a team. One goes into push-up position while the other holds his ankles off the floor. When you say, "Go!" the bottom player walks on his hands while the standing player follows behind as if he were pushing a wheelbarrow.

Crab Races: Create a starting line and a finish line. All children place their feet and their palms on the floor with their belly facing upwards behind the starting line. When you say, "Go!" they lift their bottoms off the floor and race like crabs to see who can cross the finish line first.

Leap Frog: Two or more children squat down on the floor in a line. The child in the back of the line must jump over each child in front of him (he can use his hands on their shoulders if necessary) until he reaches the front of the line where he squats down again, and then it is the turn of the child who is now in the back to jump over everyone.

Group Juggle: Teach at least two children to juggle three or four balls.

Note: Use your good judgment in these and any physical recommendation I make. Take whatever precautions you think necessary for your child in your unique situation (like a pandemic) to keep your child and everyone else safe.

Mentally

Although the brain reaches its full adult size at about age seven, it does not reach its full development for many years to come. Your child should be getting better at planning, controlling emotional outbursts, and coordinating both left and right hemispheres of the brain. As the prefrontal cortex matures, she will become better at focusing her attention over longer periods of time, and as the myelin continues to develop, her speed of reaction will improve.[150]

Raising 4 Dimensional Children in a 2 Dimensional World

Her brain should now be in what Piaget called the Concrete Operational Stage, which means she can understand the physical (concrete) world by classifying objects, recognizing that they retain their identity even if they are modified (a scrambled egg is still an egg), and can reverse a set of numbers or set of steps. She will also be able to imagine the consequences of an action that hasn't really happened yet, like if she leaves the door open, the dog will get out. This same ability will allow her to do math "in her head" without writing the numbers down or counting physical objects.[151]

One of the best ways for parents, teachers, and older children to help a child this age learn is to prompt her with questions that reveal problem-solving techniques when the child can't discover the answer by herself. For example, if your child can't read a new word, instead of just telling her the word, ask, "What is the first letter? What sound does that make? Now what is the second letter? What sound does it make?" to help her learn how to figure out other unfamiliar words in the future. The more problem-solving strategies you provide instead of just offering the answer, the more she will increase her problem-solving ability and her meta-cognitive ability (the ability to judge whether she is successfully solving the problem or needs to try another strategy.)

She also is gaining more memory capacity. According to Information Processing Theory, her brain has three different kinds of memory: Sensory Memory, Working Memory, and Long-term Memory. Sensory memory comes from the senses (seeing, hearing, feeling, smelling, tasting, and touching) and is fleeting – it is either dismissed immediately as irrelevant or passed on to Working Memory. Learning what is relevant and irrelevant is one of the accomplishments of childhood. Short-term or Working Memory is limited to a maximum of eleven bits of information at a time, and must be rehearsed (repeated) or lost, or it can be passed on to Long-term Memory, where it can be accessed when needed. Schoolwork should be stored in Long-term Memory as a knowledge base, but it must be stored in a meaningful way.[150] Mnemonic devices (ways to remember) and study tips will help your child improve her memory for recall on tests at school and for use in everyday life.

Middle Childhood

It is fortunate that her brain is developing because school is getting harder. Two great resources for helping your child "learn how to learn" are https://jimkwik.com/ and https://kwiklearning.com/. Jim Kwik offers some great advice like being a FAST learner:

Focus – Focus on one thing at a time.

Active – Be Active: Learn by doing. Think it, feel it, do it.

State – You learn best in an emotional state, one where you are curious.

Teach – Teach it back to someone: Have your child teach you the lesson.[152]

This advice also illustrates the mnemonic device of using a single word whose letters remind you of the key words you are trying to remember. A similar version of this device is to construct a sentence where the words begin with the letters in question. For example, the sentence, "Every Good Boy Deserves Favor" is often used to teach the notes on the musical scale: EGBDF. Another mnemonic device you might teach your child to help memorize lists of words is to create a picture of each word in a location like a room in your house or a place on your body. It's fairly easy to remember 10 or more items in a list, in order, if you picture each item on a certain part of your body from top to bottom like your hair, eyes, ears, mouth, etc.

Emphasize to your child that cramming is not an effective way to learn. You learn better when you learn often, so even if she doesn't have a specific homework assignment, she should study by reading from her books or practicing her math problems, reviewing them, and then reviewing them again for a short time each school night (no longer than 25 minutes without a break). Your child will remember her lessons better and longer.[152]

She should be able to tell time and count money at this age, so it is a good idea to begin some financial education: What each coin and denomination mean, and how to add them up or subtract them, so that she can calculate her change when she buys something. You can set up an allowance to teach her to budget, and teach her the cardinal rule of money management: Spend less than you make. It doesn't matter if you make $5.00 a week or $10,000 a week, if you spend more than you make, you will always be broke and feel financial stress. When you spend less than you make, you eliminate one of life's biggest headaches.

Communication

Your child's vocabulary should be growing at a rate of about 20 words a day, so that by fifth grade she will understand about 40,000 words. She will be learning the rules of grammar and speak more properly.[153] She will be learning to emphasize certain words to change their meaning in context, and learn to use more sophisticated constructions like passive voice and infinitive phrases.[154] If your child has been growing up bi-lingual, the middle childhood years are the best time to be taught the rules of grammar for both languages.[153]

Talk About Drugs

Look for opportunities to talk with your child about the dangers of alcohol, drugs, and tobacco, like seeing some kids smoking or drinking (if not in real life, perhaps in a movie). The basis for them being lumped together is that they are all unhealthy. Why risk lung cancer, liver disease, brain damage, sickness, and early death? They are also all addicting, so why would you give away control of your life to something else? Plus, if your child is money conscious, point out that these habits are very expensive.

You can look at information together about tobacco at https://www.cdc.gov/tobacco/basic_information/youth/information-sheet/index.htm,[155] about alcohol at https://www.cdc.gov/alcohol/fact-sheets/underage-drinking.htm,[156] and about drugs at https://www.drugabuse.gov/drug-topics/adolescent-brain.[157] Your child may claim that vaping isn't dangerous, but you can find counter evidence at https://www.cdc.gov/tobacco/basic_information/e-cigarettes/Quick-Facts-on-the-Risks-of-E-cigarettes-for-Kids-Teens-and-Young-Adults.html.[158]

Now, if you smoke, drink, or do drugs yourself, it will be a hard argument to make. Your kids will do as you do, not as you say. You may need to look in the mirror first to prepare your arguments, or maybe make a change yourself. However, there is a significant

Middle Childhood

difference between adults and children. Your child's brain is still developing, so alcohol and drugs (and even tobacco) can alter her brain development.[157] Of course, they are also illegal, so underage use could cause arrest, imprisonment, or at least a difficult record to overcome when applying to college or for a job.

If alcoholism or drug addiction run in your family, you must emphasize that the addiction is probably in her blood or in her brain, and your child is not like her friends who can choose to drink or not on a given day. Strongly emphasize that if you are predisposed to have alcoholism or drug addiction, you really can't take even the first drink or the first toke. The odds are so far against you that the only way to win that game is not to play.

When having the discussion, first make a plan and research what to say and do[159] on sites like https://www.drugabuse.gov/publications/family-checkup/communication. Next, find out what your child knows (or thinks she knows). Make your rules clear. Explain that your first interest is to keep her safe. Explain that she is not to vape, smoke, drink alcohol, or do any form of drugs not prescribed by her doctor, and what will happen if she does. Allow questions, listen carefully, and answer them honestly. If she breaks the rules, enforce them – the sooner, the better.

One further step I recommend is rehearsing how to say, "No." Create an imaginary situation where your child is with Susie, Kanesha, and Maria (name three of her real friends), and one lights up a cigarette. You play the role of Susie and say, "Try it – it's cool." Help your child practice saying, "No, thanks, not for me." Push her, tease her, plead with her, insult her, and do everything you can imagine the other kids will say. The more aggressive and more uncomfortable you make your child feel, the more effective it will be. It's easy to resist in a cold emotional state, but people act entirely differently in a hot emotional state,[160] so if you can get her to practice in a hot state (like feeling peer pressure), it may be more effective. If she doesn't know what to say or how to answer, help her figure it out, and keep practicing until you are both confident in the result.

Raising 4 Dimensional Children in a 2 Dimensional World

Talk About Sex

You probably want to wait to have the puberty discussion until your child's body begins to change, but some children (more likely girls) will start to change before their 10th birthday. Look for that information in the next chapter if your child is an early bloomer.

Even if your child hasn't physically started to change, our culture will most likely have aroused her curiosity about sex, so it's good to have a basic talk to straighten out any misinformation and prevent surprises. First, talk with your spouse about what you will say, and what sort of sexual values you want to communicate. You don't want to send mixed messages, so you should agree with each other, and then communicate afterwards what was actually said during the conversation with your child. This first conversation may be uncomfortable, but don't put it off. Talk with each other and then talk with your child younger than you think you should, and definitely BEFORE your child is tempted to experiment on her own.

When you talk to your child, be as calm and matter of fact as you can. If you show discomfort with the conversation, that may signal that you don't like talking about it, and your child will be hesitant to talk about sex with you in the future when she has questions. Start off by asking what she already knows (or think she knows) about sex and making babies. Help her understand the actual process, what happens, the danger of sexually transmitted diseases, and the likely result of pregnancy. Remind her of the safe touch and not-safe touch conversations you have had, and what is permissible in public, in private, and with other people. Understand that your child's cognitive immaturity leads to a lack of good judgment, meaning she likely doesn't think things through to the end, so emphasize the negative consequences. Give her a quick preview of the changes to come when she begins to enter puberty, and also help her understand that although it is not likely, it is possible for a girl to get pregnant before her first menstruation.[161]

Remember to listen at least as much as you talk, and finish up the conversation asking if she has any other questions. At this age, it is

Middle Childhood

just a preliminary preventative talk, not a full-blown discussion of sexual health and habits. You are just trying to prevent problems in response to what she may be seeing from our culture and hearing from her friends – you are probably not dealing with hormonal desires, yet. Make sure she feels comfortable coming to you with questions when she has them or when she learns something from her friends or the Internet that she is curious about. Paint yourself as a trusted resource rather than a prosecutor, judge, and jury.

Talk About the Law

If your child hasn't had a run-in with the police yet, good for you! Sooner or later, it will happen. Teach your child to treat police officers with respect. They have a dangerous job, where bad guys sometimes try to kill them, so they have to be extremely cautious. Police officers don't know that your precious baby is not going to hurt them, so she must behave in a way that shows she is cooperating. Imprint on her mind that when you disrespect a police officer or refuse to cooperate in any way, you are asking for trouble.

If your child is a member of a minority that might experience bigoted behavior, prepare her to be extra careful not to endanger her own life by being disrespectful or uncooperative. If the officer is racially profiling or treating her unfairly, she should cooperate the best she can, remember the officer's name and badge number, and then report the incident to the officer's superiors. Emphasize that your child cannot control anyone else's behavior, especially not that of a police officer, but she can control her own behavior, so she should NEVER do anything that will turn a routine police stop into a dangerous or even deadly situation. It may not seem fair at the time, but it's just self-preservation.

Activities

Continue to use any activities from the previous chapter that your child found either difficult or particularly enjoyed, plus add these:

Raising 4 Dimensional Children in a 2 Dimensional World

Descriptive Words: Pick a common noun like, "Car," and take turns with your child describing the word with adjectives like, "Fast car," "Red car," "Ugly car," etc.

Imagine It: Ask your child to imagine and act out different scenarios: Swimming in a pool; putting on skates and roller skating; climbing a high mountain; running in a pool of honey; flying like an eagle; swimming like a dolphin; etc.

Brain Stretcher: Ask your child to name as many different members of a classification as she can, like, "Name as many different kinds of dogs as you can." You can also do this exercise with situations, like, "What sounds could you recognize without seeing what made the noise?"

A Type of: Help your child understand classifications by asking her to identify a classification for different words. For example, baseball is a type of _____ (sport). A greyhound is a type of _____ (animal, mammal, dog, transportation, bus company).

Narrow the Category: Start with a broad class of things like "animals" and ask your child to narrow the category by naming a sub-category like "zoo animals" and then another sub-category like "zoo animals from Africa." See how many sub-categories she can name.

Brain Teasers: Ask questions that misdirect your child's attention to improve her listening and thinking skills like, "Mary's mother, Mrs. Jones, has four children. She named the oldest boy North, the next oldest, a girl, South, the third, a boy, she named East. The youngest child is another girl. What do you think her name is?" The answer is Mary, the first word in the question. You can find more brain teasers like this by Googling "brain teasers" or looking on a site like https://icebreakerideas.com/brain-teasers/.

20 Questions: When your child learns the parts of speech, play the game using nouns or verbs. For nouns, say, "I'm thinking of something that is _____ (any vague descriptive word.) Your child has 20 chances to ask a Yes or No question to figure out what the word is. (Is it a

Middle Childhood

person? A place? A thing?) It's a little harder for verbs, but you might say, "I'm thinking of something to do." Your child has 20 chances to ask a Yes or No question to figure out what the action word is (Would I do it Inside? Outside? Alone? With someone else?)

Circular Thinking: Ask your child to draw twenty circles on a large sheet of paper (four rows of five). Challenge her to draw twenty different pictures using the circle as the main focus of the drawing (for example, a face, a jack-o-lantern, etc.)

Imagination Drawing: Draw some simple shapes on a piece of paper (two lines, a circle, and a squiggly line), and then challenge your child to draw something specific from the shapes you provided (for example, a dog.)

Map It: Ask her to draw a map of her neighborhood, complete with appropriate landmarks and relative distances between locations.

Art Show: Ask your child to create a piece of art (draw, paint, sculpt) and then explain it as if she were in an art show, to practice her presentation skills.

Journal/Diary: As your child becomes more comfortable with writing, suggest she keep a diary or a journal to record her thoughts and feelings – to clarify them to herself and for future reference.

Phone Messages: Teach your child to get five pieces of information when she answers the house phone (if you have one): 1. Who is calling? 2. for Whom? If that person is not home or unavailable, take a message: 3. What do they want? 4. Why do they want it? and 5. What is their phone number? Give your child a simple script, like, "Hello, _____ residence, how may I help you?" Re-affirm the information from the previous chapter that she should never give out any information like her name, age, or where her parents are. Simply say that her parents cannot come to the phone and ask the questions, write down the message, and hang up with a polite, "Thank you."

Raising 4 Dimensional Children in a 2 Dimensional World

Group Activities

These are some activities you might use in the car during a carpool, at home on rainy days, or even at a restaurant if the kids get a little restless. Of course, you can use some of the individual activities above with one child taking your (the adult) part, or you might use these group activities with your child alone, with you taking the part of the first child.

Word to Word: The first child says and spells a word like, "Cat: C-A-T." The next child says a different word by changing only one letter like, "Bat: B-A-T." The next child says a different word by changing only one letter like, "Bam: B-A-M." The more letters in the word, the more challenging it becomes.

First to Last: The first child will pick a word like, "Dog." The next child must pick a word that begins with the last letter of the word just said, for example, "Garage." The next child must pick a word that begins with "e." To make it harder, you can limit the words to nouns, verbs, or adjectives, or limit it further to animals, sports, titles of songs, etc.

ABC Story: Ask two or more children to cooperate on creating a story. Each one gets to add one sentence to the story, but each sentence must begin with a successive letter of the alphabet. The first sentence begins with A, the second with B, etc.

Rhyming Words: The first child must think of two words that rhyme, like "funny bunny" and then think of two synonyms to give as a clue like, "A comical rabbit." The second partner must then guess what the two rhyming words are. Then the second child gets to give the clues for the next rhyming words.

Short for What: The first child chooses a short word that is an abbreviation for a longer word like "gas." The second child must then identify the longer word "gasoline" before she can choose her own short word.

Middle Childhood

Tic-tact-toe: Teach two children to play Tic-tact-toe and give them enough paper, pencils, or crayons to play.

Hang Man: Teach two children to play Hang Man and give them enough paper, pencils, or crayons to play.

Draw by Description: Give two children a piece of paper each and ask them to draw any simple design using geometric shapes like circles, triangles, squares, etc. Keep them far enough apart that they cannot see what the other draws. Bring the two children together and have Child A turn over his paper, describe what he has drawn, and have Child B try to draw it from the description. Compare the two drawings, to see how close they are. Switch roles.

Tag-Team Art: Give two children a pencil each and one piece of paper for the pair. The first child draws a line or shape on the paper and passes it to the second child, who adds a line or shape and passes it back. The two children may not talk. They continue to pass the paper back and forth until they jointly create a design or picture that they both believe is complete.

My Favorite Food: Ask each child to prepare a one-minute speech about her favorite food to practice organizing her thoughts and public speaking. Give each child a chance to make her presentation. You can change the activity to "My Favorite Sport" or "My Favorite Animal" or any other topic your children are interested in.

Emotionally

One of the most important developments for middle childhood is the self-concept. Your child is trying to balance establishing his independence and individuality while still trying to keep a connection with the family. Now that he is in school, you will find that the children have (to some extent) established their own society with a different language, set of rules, behaviors, and roles for each other. On one hand it is a great laboratory for learning social skills like communication, negotiation, and problem-solving,[162] but on the other hand you no longer have the control you did a few years ago. He can still be proud of his family . . . or embarrassed by it, depending on your social status.

Your child's developing identity is becoming more complex. His description of himself should move from physical attributes ("I'm a boy") to include his beliefs about his personality and emotions ("I like to help people.") As he begins to understand how he feels about others and how other people feel about him, he will understand that he has many different attributes – some strengths and some weaknesses – and sees many shades of gray instead of seeing himself in simple black and white terms.[163] Every day he is learning how to be a more authentic version of himself.

According to Dr. Brian Little there are three kinds of authenticity in people: Biogenic authenticity, where we do the things that come naturally according to our genetics; Socio-eugenic authenticity, where we do things that matter to our culture; and Idiogenic authenticity, where we do things based on our personal choices, which may be in conflict with the other two.[164] At this age it is probably more of a juggling act than a balancing act, so be ready to help him pick up the pieces after some mistakes and guide him in the right direction.

As he establishes his identity and personality, he will go through what the psychologist Erik Erikson calls the time of industry vs. inferiority, where he directs his considerable energy to gain useful skills that bring recognition from his peers and the adults in his life. He will base his self-concept and therefore his self-esteem in three separate areas: Academic, social, and body image.[162]

Parents and teachers usually value the academic achievements, and there are two main ways you can help your child achieve academic success: (1) Make sure he is in the right "track" or class at school according to his ability, and (2) Schedule time for homework and home study, and be available to offer guidance. If your child is earning good grades, keep up the good work. If he is not, help him learn and practice better study and memory skills like those in the Mental section of this chapter.

Peers usually value social skills and body image, and, again, you can help. In the previous chapters we've been practicing activities to improve your child's emotional skills. He should know how to introduce himself, how to listen, how to express himself, and how to read other's emotions. You can enroll him on athletic teams or in classes to create a potential group of friends, and you can help him practice the skills to become a valuable member of the group.

As far as body image, your child is growing taller, leaning out, and gaining muscle during these years. I've offered broad dietary and exercise advice to prevent your child from being the "fat kid," and you can motivate your child to pursue various exercises and activities to increase strength, speed, endurance, flexibility, and skill. The good news is that at this age it is easy to become an admired athlete because most of the other kids don't know how to practice and don't have the discipline to do it. Simply by being "trained" can make your child one of the better athletes.

As your child becomes more aware of his appearance, I recommend you spend some time and energy on grooming tips. Although most children still want to emulate the same-sex parent, you may find that your child wants a different haircut or different clothes than you like. You can discuss it and come to a reasonable conclusion. You might look in magazines or on websites for models who show possible hairstyles and clothing styles, and maybe invest in a stylish haircut. For girls, discuss makeup, appropriate amounts and kinds of makeup for her age, and for what kinds of events she might wear more makeup, etc. Use your grown-up knowledge and experience to keep your child from being a nerd, and to help him look cool to his friends. However, make it clear that the haircuts, clothing, and makeup appropriate for a music video are not appropriate for school or everyday wear. Thinking back to Erickson's theory of industry vs. inferiority, and if your child starts comparing himself to the images he sees on television shows, commercials, magazines, movies, and the Internet, the potential for feelings of inferiority are pretty high. Bring him back to reality by looking at his peers, not at unachievable commercial images.

Also help him realize that the natural tendency is to want what he doesn't have, and that is not healthy. Girls with straight hair spend hours trying to curl their hair; girls with curly hair spend hours trying to straighten theirs. Whether your child is white, black, or Asian, has dark or light hair, is tall or short, or has curly or straight hair, help him appreciate what he has and not waste his emotions wishing he could change things he cannot change. Cultivate an attitude of gratitude. Happiness is not getting all you want, but wanting all you've got.

Along with becoming aware of his appearance, your child will start to show an interest in the opposite sex, perhaps begin behaving differently when in their company, and might even develop a crush on someone in particular. Because of the constant bombardment of sexuality in our culture, your child may want to explore how romantic relationships are different than friendships. Be on the lookout for evidence that he is prematurely acting out sexually, but more likely, you will see some stereotypical behavior in an attempt to be more adult-like: Your son may start embracing macho qualities while your daughter may start practicing her feminine wiles on an elementary level. I strongly recommend you not only monitor but guide these developments. I think boys who believe "real men" hide their feelings and never talk about them are setting themselves up for emotional problems now and later in life. If you can start talking to your son about his feelings at an early age, it will make it easier to continue these discussions as he becomes a tween and an adolescent, and make it easier for him when it comes time to express his feelings to a girl.

Likewise, a young girl who embraces extreme femininity may think she needs to act like a sex object to get attention, or at least seek to have others do things for her instead of learning how to do them for herself. Self-reliance is a powerful virtue for both men and women, boys and girls. As I said in a previous chapter, I don't believe anyone should be 100% male or 100% female like some cartoon character. A balanced individual is probably closer to 60/40 in male vs. female characteristics, especially because many of those characteristics vary from culture to culture. There is also research to support that children who develop more flexible attitudes toward gender-appropriate behavior are ultimately better prepared to cope with the stresses throughout childhood and into adulthood.[165]

Your child should by now have made considerable improvement in his ability to recognize emotions in himself and in others, to control his emotions, and to communicate his emotions verbally and non-verbally. Instead of needing you to help him regulate strong emotions as he would have a few years ago, he should now have some skills at regulating them himself. By learning the culture both at home and at school, he should have a pretty good grasp on acceptable behavior and non-acceptable behavior in each context, and how those rules might be different for different people. Of course, these are never-ending lessons, and he still needs your guidance.

He is also becoming wise enough to realize that if he has a wide range of abilities and emotions, and many shades of gray, so do other people. He can begin to understand why someone might say one thing when they feel something entirely different. He will see both admirable qualities and flaws in teachers, coaches, friends, and even you. He will start to choose his friends not only on their availability (for he has more choices now), but more on an appreciation of their personality traits, their shared interests and beliefs, and their support for to each other. He will also start to understand sarcasm and begin to feel empathy.[166]

Negative Beliefs

As part of the process of ranking himself compared to his peers and establishing himself on the industry vs. inferiority scale, he may establish some erroneous beliefs that can carry on through the rest of his life. One or two moments of rejection can be combined to the belief that, "Nobody likes me," or "I am not worthy of love." The middle childhood years are an important time to continue the message that you love your child, and he is worthy of love. Have discussions whenever you see your child upset. Ask what happened at school, with friends, or even with you that caused this feeling. Try to discover if your child is making a negative belief about himself like, "I'm stupid," and counter that belief with your love and your belief in the opposite, and supply ample evidence to convince him. In addition, point out that everyone has strengths and weaknesses and there are many ways to be happy and successful in life.

Here is a technique called Attitude Breathing to help him shift his mood, feeling, or belief: When he identifies that he has an undesirable feeling, he should shift his attention to the area of his heart. He should then ask himself, "What would be a better attitude?" If the negative belief was, "I'm stupid," he would counter it with the better belief, "No, I'm smart!" He would then focus on breathing the new attitude, feeling, or belief as if it were coming in through the heart and out through the *solar plexus* until his feelings have stabilized.[167]

Ideally, you want to help your child through these doubts enough times that he learns how to internalize the process, so that when he sees a negative belief pop into his head, he knows how to refute it both logically and emotionally. Point out that you can't please everyone, so if you seek your approval from others, you will constantly be disappointed. Instead, help him realize HE has control over his self-esteem by developing his own moral compass, so that he learns how to like himself and provide his own guidelines for self-approval. Instead of comparing himself to others and trying to meet their conflicting expectations, he should compare himself only to himself in the past, and meet his own expectations by continuing to be better today than he was yesterday.

Sibling Rivalry

If you have more than one child, sibling rivalry is a normal result of the competitive attitude of children to achieve your recognition and an essential process in the development of healthy self-esteem. At first, the younger child will try to be like the older one, but during middle childhood he will need to establish his own identity. They will flip flop from being best friends to mortal enemies and back to best friends again. Usually, no matter how frustrated they are with each other, they will unite against an outside threat.

One thing you can do to reduce the rivalry is NOT compare them. When you say something like, "Why don't you behave like your brother?" you fan the flames of discontent and even inspire jealousy. It will be tempting, but try to remember that each child is a unique individual, so love them all, praise them for their own virtues, and if you want to motivate them to change, don't compare them to anyone, but especially not a sibling.

Middle Childhood

Discipline

Continue to follow the guidelines laid out in the previous chapters. Because your child is starting to judge others and judge himself, it might be a good time to take advantage of his new ability by asking him for input on the consequences for his behavior. Obviously, you have to consider whether he is in a hot state or cold state when you have this discussion. You can't expect him to offer a fair consequence when he is in the middle of a hot state: When you catch him doing something wrong and he is angry and self-righteous. Instead, when he is cool, calm, and collected, discuss that you think he should have more input into his disciplinary procedures and ask what he thinks would be a fair punishment for certain infractions. You may find he is tougher on himself than you would be, but he may also be too lenient. Each of you should get a fair opportunity to offer your opinion, and why, and you might do a little negotiating if you need to. For example, if you disagree on the consequences of two different infractions, you might hold firm on a harsher penalty for the more dangerous behavior and give in to his suggestion on the less dangerous one. It is still your responsibility as the adult to make the final decisions, but giving him input will help when it comes time to enforce the rules by saying, "You agreed that . . . ." Setting up the understanding that he agreed to the consequences is also important in the long run, where you won't be there to discipline him later in life, and he must make his own decisions on what to do based on self-discipline and his internal compass.

Once again, continue to demand respectful treatment of all others, but especially adults and authority figures. Part of his attempts to appear more "macho" may be to show a disrespectful attitude. Stop it early, before it gains traction in his personality, by utilizing his newfound understanding of how other people feel. Emphasize that he wouldn't like to be treated disrespectfully, so he shouldn't treat others that way.

Activities

Continue to use any activities from the previous chapter that your child found either difficult or particularly enjoyed, plus add these:

Raising 4 Dimensional Children in a 2 Dimensional World

<u>Read:</u> Reading fiction helps students "get into the minds" of other people to experience the world differently than they do as themselves. There is evidence that the more fiction people read, the more empathetic they become.[168]

<u>Character Analysis:</u> Exercise your child's empathy muscles by discussing books and movies to help identify what the characters are feeling – what emotions? Do you understand why they would feel that way? Have you ever felt that way? How do you feel about the way they feel?

<u>Tone of Voice:</u> Practice repeating the same sentence with your child emphasizing a different word (by speaking louder) each time and discussing the different emotional meaning: WHAT are you doing? What ARE you doing? What are YOU doing? What are you DOING?

<u>People Watching:</u> When in public places like a park, the mall, or a restaurant, point out other people, see how they behave, and discuss them as if they were a character in a movie. What do their clothes say about them? Their haircut? Tattoos? Piercings? Help your child form an opinion of the look he wants to portray and the person he wants to become. At this age and in these discussions, you may help your child develop a dislike for tattoos and piercings, if you choose.

<u>What to Wear:</u> Point out to your child that a bathing suit is appropriate to wear to the pool or beach, but not appropriate for church. Then, begin a discussion about what kind of clothes are appropriate to wear to different places.

<u>Emotional Brain Stretcher:</u> Ask your child to name as many different ways as possible that he might know something emotionally, like, "How would you know that you hurt someone's feelings?" or, "What are some signs that someone is angry at you?"

<u>Show you Care:</u> Ask your child what he would say in some emotional situations like, "Your best friend's dog got run over by a car." What should he say or do? What should he not say or do? Identify other

Middle Childhood

situations that may have already happened to him or that you might imagine will happen to him, and go over the proper ways to respond.

Good and Bad: Ask your child to name something he likes about school. Discuss it. Then ask him to name something he doesn't like about school. Discuss it. You can ask another round about school, or you can ask about the good and bad for teachers, friends, family, church, or anything else you would like to discuss with him. These discussions might also be a good way to set up and then begin a later conversation about smoking, drinking, drugs, sex, or the police.

Changes: Ask your child to name something about himself that has changed in the past year, the past month, the past week, and since yesterday. Discuss each change, sometimes probing for an emotional change ("I used to like _____" or, "I used to think _____") over a physical change like, "I changed my clothes."

Stop and Feel: Whenever you have an emotional incident, check with your child – is he feeling the same emotion? Help him identify what he is feeling and what to do about it.

Practice Arguing: Give your child two sides of an issue, and let him choose which side to argue, while you take the other side. You can even pretend it's a mock trial, using someone else as the judge or jury. Teach sound reasoning skills, appealing to emotion, and other argumentative techniques. Another time, have him argue for the side he doesn't like. This activity teaches him to discuss without becoming angry at the person on the other side of the argument, and to see the world from a differing point of view.

Joy Spy: Look for items that bring joy. Transform I Spy to naming things that bring us joy, like, "I spy, with my little eye, a little yellow butterfly." Play the game in different locations – not just the park, but in your bedroom, in the car, etc. As your child gets good at it, you can play it in your imagination, looking for items of joy in some place where you are not currently present, like, "I spy with my little eye, in my classroom at school, Betty Lou's pigtails."

Raising 4 Dimensional Children in a 2 Dimensional World

Take this activity one step farther by creating things that give joy. Create art projects for a certain person. Create gifts instead of buying them. Put bright, happy colors on your walls, ceilings, and refrigerator.

Compassion: We tend to judge others by their actions, while we judge ourselves by our intent. If your child has a bully or someone he doesn't like, or you can even choose a "bad guy" from a book or movie, ask your child to picture that person as a mother or father, sister or brother, being nice to someone and showing love. The object of the activity is to learn to look past the surface and circumstance to see the good in everyone, even those who seem like enemies.

Group Activities

These are some activities you might use in the car during a carpool, at home on rainy days, or even at a restaurant to make better use of the time. Of course, you can use some of the individual activities above with one child taking your (the adult) part, or you might use these group activities with your child alone, with you taking the part of the first child.

Telephone: Place all the children in a line and the first child whispers a sentence into the ear of the second child. That child then whispers the same sentence to the third child, who whispers it to the next child. No one is allowed to repeat the sentence. The last child will say the sentence out loud and then the first child will say the original sentence. Chances are they will be quite different, which should initiate a discussion on how stories (and gossip) get distorted the more they are told.

Like and Dislike: Ask children to identify what they like about other people and what they don't like. Specify that they can think of another person when they are thinking of something they like or don't like, but they should not say that person's name. The goal is to come up with a list of good and bad personality traits and then discuss how to develop the good ones and stop doing the bad ones.

Middle Childhood

Self-Improvement: Identify something about yourself that you would like to improve, and then offer ideas on how you might improve it. The other children can offer feedback on whether or not they agree that you need to improve it, and make additional suggestions on how to improve.

True Friends: Ask each child, "What makes a true friend?" and allow anyone else to discuss the answer before asking the next child the same question.

Heart of Gold: Explain what it means to have a heart of gold, and then ask each child, "What could you do to feel like you have a heart of gold?" Allow discussion of each child's answer before asking the next child the same question.

I'm Lonely: Ask each child to describe an occasion when he felt lonely and how bad it felt, and allow discussion of each child's answer before asking the next child the same questions. Follow up by asking if each child knows someone who seems to be lonely (someone at school?) and what they could do to help that person feel less lonely.

Violent Discussion: Ask the group, "What are the good things and bad things about playing video games that have violence in them?" Encourage each child to express his opinion, and if there are not enough bad things, ask some questions yourself that reveal some of the bad things.

Spiritually

Middle childhood is a significant age for the spiritual development of a child, and you will find important rituals in several religions to mark this milestone. Your child's participation in these rituals is very important as they relate to her on a level she can understand, and give her a sense of spiritual identity. Continue to bring her to religious education classes at your church, synagogue, or mosque.

Raising 4 Dimensional Children in a 2 Dimensional World

The psychologist Lawrence Kolberg created a series of stages of moral development based on Piaget's research. Up until about the age of 7, your child would probably be in the Preconventional Stage, where moral decision-making was based on reward or punishment. If you recall from the previous chapter, Preconventional children believe that all resources should be distributed equally. Hopefully, she has reached the point where she is no longer just acting on impulse, but rather taking a moment to think about her actions, weighing the possible consequences, and making a moral decision. For example, if a friend says something mean, which is an emotional stimulus, instead of having a purely emotional response, she may take a moment to think and offer a rational response, or she may even think, "No, that would be wrong," and offer a moral response in line with her spiritual beliefs.

At about age 7 your child should enter the Conventional Stage, where moral reasoning becomes based on the opinions of others. She will believe something is right or wrong because you, her religious leader, teacher, coach, or even her friends say it is. Her desire to gain approval takes over and rules her morality, which means that it is still self-centered. She will believe that distribution should be based on merit, so that when Susie gets and A on her project and Lee gets a B, she will accept it as fair if Susie worked harder and had a better project than Lee.[169] She will no longer assume that the teacher likes Susie better than Lee.

Toward the end of middle childhood, about age 10, she will be ready for the Post-Conventional Stage, where she will begin to see a morality of cooperation and, because she values her membership in a group, will view the good of others over her own personal benefits. Her beliefs about fairness may take *need* into consideration at about age 8, so that if mom and dad can only afford one pair of shoes, the child with the oldest and worst shoes should get the new pair.[170] As your child matures, attempt to bring her up to this stage of understanding whenever she is ready by discussing principles and how they apply to different situations.

A simple way of communicating her responsibility is to teach her the difference between dumb and stupid: Dumb is when you don't know any better; Stupid is when you know better and do it anyway.

Middle Childhood

This little memorable explanation provides a basis for moral discussions on decisions she makes for years to come.

Continue evening prayers or expressions of gratitude as described in earlier chapters.

Activities

Continue to use any activities from the previous chapter that your child found either difficult or particularly enjoyed, plus add these:

Rituals: Ask your child her understanding of the religious rituals she participates in and offer guidance if she has a misconception. Help her look forward to other rituals that will become available when she gets older.

Meditation: If you meditate yourself or have already instituted a practice of meditation with your child, continue it. If not, you may consider it as a way to help your child focus, become calmer, and more spiritually aware.

Manners: Discuss different situations by describing (or acting out) how someone with bad manners might behave, followed by how someone with good manners might behave in the same situation.

Ask Permission: Discuss with your child appropriate times to ask for permission to do something and times when it is unnecessary. Discuss how the rules are different with people and situations outside the house/family.

Professions: Discuss with your child some different professions and whether or not she might like to pursue that profession, and especially why.

Gifts: Ask your child, "What are some things you can give someone that don't cost any money?" Emphasize gifts of time, interest, help, affection, and ways to give them to specific people in her life.

Raising 4 Dimensional Children in a 2 Dimensional World

Dilemmas: Start discussing dilemmas that your child has encountered or might encounter in her daily life, where the answer is not black or white, but a shade of gray. For example, "Your best friend _____ asks you to give her answers on a test at school." Probe a little deeper: What if you knew you wouldn't get caught? What if she just wanted the answers to a homework assignment instead of a test?

Thank Spy: Look for items to be thankful for. Transform I Spy and Joy Spy into a game of gratitude where you take turns naming things that you are thankful for, like, "I spy, with my little eye, my beautiful daughter, whom I am thankful for."

Moral Response: Discuss situations your child has encountered or might encounter that might generate an emotional response, and ask for the proper moral response. For example, "If Isabel wants to fight with you and pushes you, what should you do?" The emotional response might be to push back, a more rational response might be to ask her what she is so angry about, and a moral response would include reasoning that fighting is wrong, and how could she disarm Isabel by showing concern and compassion?

Summary

Middle childhood is often referred to as the golden age of childhood because it is a great time to be a child: It is a time of seemingly limitless energy, close friendships, possibly an innocent romantic crush, and very little responsibility. It is the time to run and play and have fun!!

Their bodies are growing taller, leaning out, gaining strength, coordination, and balance. It is a great time to develop physical skills in sports, martial arts, gymnastics, dance, or whatever interests them. Boys tend to be taller than girls at seven, but then everyone will begin a growth spurt at their own timing, so many of the girls will be taller than the boys by age ten.

Their brains are getting better at focusing and their memories are increasing, which come in handy because schoolwork is getting more challenging. It is a time to learn how to learn and how to study to become better at reading, writing, arithmetic, and at test taking. In the previous chapter I recommended how to help your child do homework, even if you did not do well in school yourself, or you simply forgot. Please review that information and help your child be successful in school.

Emotionally, children start to solidify their self-image by comparing themselves to others. It is a time of industry vs. inferiority, where they develop talents and skills that others find valuable. The membership in a group becomes important, as do the opinions of that group. They understand that they have many attributes, and so do other people, so they begin to understand that people are complex, and good in some ways and not-so-good in others. The radical difference in growth spurts creates an awareness of body image and a curiosity about the opposite sex, so they will appreciate your help in making them attractive. In addition, our society bombards them with sexual messages, so they will need your guidance to handle their curiosity about sex, romance, and the possible offers of alcohol, drugs, and tobacco. You also need to be on the lookout for erroneous beliefs like, "I am stupid," that they may form based on one or two pieces of evidence that they generalize into a self-fulfilling prophesy.

Spiritually, they will reach the age of consent to accept certain rituals, and they will have the mental capacity to embrace those rituals. They will move from punishment/reward morality to a rule-based understanding, where authority figures deliver decrees that are not questioned. The desire for approval becomes the guiding principle. As they get more involved with peer groups, they may get conflicting rules and start to question which authority they should believe. Toward the end of this period, their regard for group membership will help them transform from self-centered morality to a group-centered morality, where the good of the many outweighs their own personal needs.

Once again, I would like to recommend enrolling your child in a high-quality martial arts program, either in an afterschool program where they transport your child from the elementary school to the martial arts school, or as an activity several times a week. There is no better program to provide a balance of physical, mental, emotional, and even spiritual growth, plus it is a place to find positive role models (especially if you are a single mom) and positive friends. It is an investment in self-discipline and self-confidence that will pay dividends for many years to come.

Screen Time

We have now reached the age where screen time is not only valuable, but almost unavoidable. Your child may have his own phone, may be doing schoolwork and/or homework on a computer or tablet, and all his friends will be gaming. I am not recommending you throw in the towel, because the evidence presented in the previous chapter still holds true: Violence on TV, in video games, and in song lyrics make children more likely to act out in aggressive ways.[142,143] Instead, I recommend you develop a Family Media Plan. Here are some recommendations:[171]

1. Establish some screen-free zones, like the kitchen, dining room, and your child's bedroom, where no incoming messages can interrupt her sleep.
2. Charge ALL devices (including yours) overnight in a specific place away from the bedrooms.
3. Do not use devices:
   when crossing the street,
   at school,
   during homework,
   in the car (except on long trips),
   at mealtimes,
   during designated family times,
   1/2 hour before bed (blue light from the screen interferes with sound sleep),
4. Install a security code on all devices to prevent unauthorized downloading of apps and making of purchases.
   Activate parental control functions.
   Turn on the GPS locator, primarily to find a lost phone, but also to find a lost child.

Middle Childhood

5. Establish co-viewing, co-playing, or at least parent present times with:
   Acceptable apps, games, and lessons,
   Acceptable shows,
   Limited video chats or calls with friends and relatives,
   NEVER chat or game with strangers online – only people you know in person.
6. Clearly identify Cyberbullying and the consequences if your child does it.
   Identify how to report Cyberbullying if your child receives it or witnesses it.
   For physical bullying, see the recommendations in the previous chapter.

Please understand that tech giants spend millions of dollars making their programs and apps more and more addicting. Some psychologists have even called social media a drug because of the way technology companies have engineered their services to take advantage of subconscious human weaknesses to achieve their own corporate goals of keeping your attention. I highly recommend keeping your child off social media until at least high school. You will probably get a lot of complaints because all his friends will be on social media, but there are real risks to young, not-yet-developed minds. It is a good idea to establish rules and limitations now, when your child first gets a phone, instead of later. It is always harder to take away something that has been allowed, than to live without something you have never had.

Note: As all children are unique and develop at different rates, I recommend you read the next chapter to prepare for your child's growth and in case your child happens to develop more quickly in one area or another, and the previous chapter in case your child happens to develop more slowly in one area or another. Specifically, some of the activities might well be continued into the older years.

Also please use your own good judgment in following any advice I offer. Research is subject to change and my advice may be based on research that has since changed or been updated since this publishing.

Raising 4 Dimensional Children in a 2 Dimensional World

Choose your actions based on your own beliefs, experiences, research, and judgment, especially during extenuating circumstances (like a pandemic.)

Recommended Resources:

https://littlehumans.com/
https://www.drhallowell.com/adhd/
https://www.gamesofgenius.com/
https://www.child-encyclopedia.com
https://mindup.org/
https://www.davidlynchfoundation.org/
https://www.mindinthemaking.org/
https://www.cdc.gov/ncbddd/childdevelopment/positiveparenting/middle.html
https://www.healthychildren.org
https://health.gov
https://www.helenfarabee.org/
https://www.commonsensemedia.org/
https://www.cdc.gov/tobacco/basic_information/youth/information-sheet/index.htm
https://www.cdc.gov/tobacco/basic_information/e-cigarettes/Quick-Facts-on-the-Risks-of-E-cigarettes-for-Kids-Teens-and-Young-Adults.html
https://pubs.niaaa.nih.gov/publications/MakeADiff_HTML/makediff.htm#Talkingwith
https://teens.drugabuse.gov/teens/drug-facts
https://www.drugabuse.gov/drug-topics/adolescent-brain
https://www.drugabuse.gov/publications/family-checkup/communication
Me, Myself and Us by Dr. Brian Little
Raising Cain by Dan Kindlon, PhD, and Michael Thompson, PhD, Ballentine Books, 2000.
The Social Dilemma, a documentary film on Netflix, 2020.

References:

144. Overstreet, Laura. "Middle Childhood." Lumen Learning; Developmental Psychology. https://courses.lumenlearning.com/suny-hccc-ss-152-1/chapter/lecture-middle-childhood/. Accessed June 17, 2021.

145. Felix-Mulder, Summer; and Mulder, Mike. Interview in *Little Humans* series, https://youtu.be/Hwex4eKXW-k.

Middle Childhood

146. Oswalt Morelli, Angela, MSW. "Importance of Healthy Lifestyles." Gracepoint; Child Development Theory: Middle Childhood (8-11). https://www.gracepointwellness.org/1272-child-development-theory-middle-childhood-8-11/article/37675-importance-of-healthy-lifestyles. Accessed June 17, 2021.

147. Centers for Disease Control and Prevention; Overweight and Obesity; Childhood Obesity Facts. "Prevalence of Childhood Obesity in the United States." https://www.cdc.gov/obesity/data/childhood.html#:~:text=The%20prevalence%20of%20obesity%20was%2018.5%25%20and%20affected,obesity%20is%20also%20more%20common%20among%20certain%20populations. Accessed June 17, 2021.

148. Iannelli, Vincent, MD. "The Facts about Childhood Obesity." Verywell Health; Kids' Health; Childhood Obesity & Overweight Kids. https://www.verywellhealth.com/childhood-obesity-child-obesity-statistics-2633989. Accessed June 17, 2021.

149. Caremans, Gregory. *"Neuroscience and Parenting."* https://www.udemy.com/course/neuroscience-and-parenting/ Section 2.8. Accessed May 29, 2021.

150. Lumen Lifespan Development; Module 6: Middle Childhood. "Physical Development in Middle Childhood." https://courses.lumenlearning.com/wmopen-lifespandevelopment/chapter/physical-development-in-middle-childhood/. Accessed June 17, 2021.

151. Oswalt Morelli, Angela, MSW. "Cognitive Development: Piaget's Concrete Operations." Helen Farabee Centers; Child Development Theory: Middle Childhood (8-11). https://www.helenfarabee.org/poc/view_doc.php?type=doc&id=37677&cn=1272. Accessed June 17, 2021.

152. Kwick, Jim. "Accelerating Your Child's Learning." Interview in *Little Humans* series. https://littlehumans.com/.

153. Lumen Lifespan Development; Module 6: Middle Childhood. "Cognitive Development in Middle Childhood." https://courses.lumenlearning.com/wmopen-lifespandevelopment/chapter/cognitive-development-in-middle-childhood/. Accessed June 17, 2021.

154. Oswalt Morelli, Angela, MSW. "Language Development." Helen Farabee Centers; Child Development Theory: Middle Childhood (8-11). https://www.helenfarabee.org/poc/view_doc.php?type=doc&id=37682&cn=1272. Accessed June 17, 2021.

155. Centers for Disease Control and Prevention; Smoking and Tobacco Use; You(th) and Tobacco; "What You(th) Should Know About Tobacco." https://www.cdc.gov/tobacco/basic_information/youth/information-sheet/index.htm. Accessed June 17, 2021.

156. Centers for Disease Control and Prevention; Alcohol and Public Health; Underage Drinking. Underage Drinking | CDC. Accessed June 17, 2021.

157. National Institute on Drug Abuse; Drug Topics; "Adolescent Brain." https://www.drugabuse.gov/drug-topics/adolescent-brain. Accessed June 17, 2021.

158. Centers for Disease Control and Prevention; Basic Information; Electronic Cigarettes; "Quick Facts on the Risks of E-cigarettes for Kids, Teens, and Young Adults." https://www.cdc.gov/tobacco/basic_information/e-cigarettes/Quick-Facts-on-the-Risks-of-E-cigarettes-for-Kids-Teens-and-Young-Adults.html. Accessed June 17, 2021.

159. National Institute on Drug Abuse; Family Checkup; "Family Checkup Communication." https://www.drugabuse.gov/publications/family-checkup/communication. Accessed June 17, 2021.

160. Lowenstein, George. "In the Heat of the Moment: How Intense Emotions Transform Us." NPR; *Hidden Brain*; December 2, 2019. https://www.npr.org/transcripts/783495595. Accessed June 17, 2021.

161. Oswalt Morelli, Angela, MSW. "Primary Physical Changes Associated with Puberty." Helen Farabee Centers; Child & Adolescent Development: Puberty. https://www.helenfarabee.org/poc/view_doc.php?type=doc&id=38406&cn=1276. Accessed June 17, 2021.

162. ChildHealth Explanation; "Psychosocial Development of Middle Childhood." https://www.childhealth-explanation.com/psychosocial-development.html. Accessed June 17, 2021.

163. Oswalt Morelli, Angela, MSW. "Identity and Self-Esteem." Helen Farabee Centers; Child Development Theory: Middle Childhood (8-11). https://www.helenfarabee.org/poc/view_doc.php?type=doc&id=37688&cn=1272. Accessed June 17, 2021.

164. Little, Brian, PhD. "Brian Little: Are Human Personalities Hardwired?" NPR; *Ted Radio Hour;* August 25, 2017. https://www.npr.org/2017/08/25/545093051/brian-little-are-human-personalities-hardwired. Accessed June 17, 2021.

165. Oswalt Morelli, Angela, MSW. "Gender Identity and Sexual Development." Helen Farabee Centers; Child Development Theory: Middle Childhood (8-11). https://www.helenfarabee.org/poc/view_doc.php?type=doc&id=37696&cn=1272. Accessed June 17, 2021.

166. Oswalt Morelli, Angela, MSW. "Emotional and Social Development." Helen Farabee Centers; Child Development Theory: Middle Childhood (8-11). https://www.helenfarabee.org/poc/view_doc.php?type=doc&id=37687&cn=1272. Accessed June 17, 2021.

167. Arguelles, Lourdes; McCraty, Rollin; and Rees, Robert A. "The Heart in Holistic Education." Heart Math; Assets; Uploads; 2015. https://www.heartmath.org/assets/uploads/2015/01/heart-in-education.pdf. Accessed June 17, 2021.

168. Zaki, Jamil. "You 2.0: The Empathy Gym." NPR; *Hidden Brain*; July 29, 2019. https://www.npr.org/transcripts/744195502. Accessed June 17, 2021.

169. Oswalt Morelli, Angela, MSW. "Kohlberg's Stages of Moral Development." Helen Farabee Centers; Child Development Theory: Middle Childhood (8-11). https://www.helenfarabee.org/poc/view_doc.php?type=doc&id=37692&cn=1272. Accessed June 18, 2021.

170. Oswalt Morelli, Angela, MSW. "Kohlberg's Stages Continued." Helen Farabee Centers; Child Development Theory: Middle Childhood (8-11). https://www.helenfarabee.org/poc/view_doc.php?type=doc&id=37693&cn=1272. Accessed June 18, 2021.

171. Healthy Children; Create Your Family Media Plan. https://www.healthychildren.org/English/media/Pages/default.aspx#wizard. Accessed June 18, 2021.

Chapter 8
Preteens
Years 10 to 13

"The secret of change is to focus all of your energy not on fighting the old, but on building the new." – Socrates

Fighting over Principles with the Principal

Young Ray

Mrs. Johnson: *Thank you for coming in to see me. I guess you know by now that Ray got into another fight. This is the second fight in three weeks.*

Mrs. Robinson: *You may not know it, but his father walked out on us about a month ago.*

Mrs. Johnson: *I'm sorry to hear that, but we have to be united in telling him that fighting is not the way to express his anger.*

Mrs. Robinson: *You sayin' I'm a bad parent?*

Mrs. Johnson: *No, ma'am, I'm just trying to help.*

Mrs. Robinson: *Well, we don't need your help.*

Mrs. Johnson: *Three weeks ago I would have agreed with you, but now, I think you might.*

Mrs. Robinson: *Well, I can handle my son and my problems. And if you keep calling me out of work, I'm gonna lose my job. Leave me alone!* (She gets up to leave)

Mrs. Johnson: *Mrs. Robinson, Ray is suspended for a week for fighting, and if he gets in one more fight we will have to expel him. We don't want that so we are here to help any way we can.*

Mrs. Robinson: *If you want to help, stop pickin' on my son! He's a good boy!*

Young Tommy

Mrs. Johnson: *Thank you for coming in to see me. I guess you know by now that Tommy got into another fight. This is the second fight in three weeks.*

Mrs. Jones: *You may not know it, but his father walked out on us about a month ago.*

Mrs. Johnson: *I'm sorry to hear that, but we have to be united in telling him that fighting is not the way to express his anger.*

Mrs. Jones: *You're right, but he's been a handful lately. He says he's old enough to make up his own mind, but he makes one bad choice after another.*

Mrs. Johnson: *That's normal for kids his age. They think they are as smart as any adult, but their brain hasn't fully developed yet and, unfortunately, it's not developed enough to realize it.*

Mrs. Jones: *I just don't know what to do. His father doesn't want him.*

Mrs. Johnson: *First of all, talk with Tommy about his feelings. Admit to him that you are angry, or scared, or whatever you feel, and bring his suppressed feelings out where he can see them and begin to deal with them. Touch his heart and his desire to help and protect you.*

Mrs. Jones: *It's been a while since we talked like that, but I can try.*

Mrs. Johnson: *Second, I recommend getting a positive male role model. What activities does he like? Any sports he plays with his friends?*

Mrs. Jones: *Lately, he's been hanging out with some rough looking kids. I'm afraid he might be joining some kind of gang.*

Mrs. Johnson: *All the more reason to find a better group of friends. We're looking for an activity where he can get his anger out safely. Does he like football?*

Mrs. Jones: *He loves Kung-Fu movies and video games with fighting.*

Mrs. Johnson: *OK, let's work with that. How about martial arts classes? I know a couple of good schools in the area.*

Mrs. Jones: *With his father gone, I can't afford lessons.*

Mrs. Johnson: *The YMCA has an excellent and affordable program, and I know Master Lee in the school about a mile from here offers scholarships to students who need help. What do you think?*

Mrs. Jones: *He's already gotten into two fights. Won't martial arts make him fight more?*

Mrs. Johnson: *A good program will teach him not to fight. I strongly recommend it for the self-discipline and the positive male role models.*

Mrs. Jones: *OK, if you think so.*

Mrs. Johnson: *Great! I still have to suspend him for fighting, but if we work together, I believe we can turn him around before it's too late.*

Mrs. Jones: *Thank you, Mrs. Johnson. Do you recommend the YMCA or that Master Lee fella?*

Which Parent is more like you?

Mrs. Robinson was defensive. She was hurt, having trouble with her son, and probably feeling a little guilty about the mounting problems in her life. Instead of asking for help or even accepting it when it was offered, she withdrew. Her principle was that she didn't need help. She didn't want to admit her problems, which usually makes them worse. Chances are good Ray would get in another fight, be expelled from school, and have dug a deep hole for himself to climb out of.

Mrs. Jones was in the same situation, but her principle was that she wanted the best for Tommy and was open to getting help. She listened to Mrs. Johnson and took her advice seriously. We don't know what will happen, but Tommy has a good chance to recover from a bad month because his mother is trying to improve her parenting and give him better opportunities.

Preteens

The preteen years are sometimes call the tween years, the years between childhood and adolescence. The major development will be the onset of puberty, with the physical changes, the raging hormones, and the resulting attitudes. Many of the themes of middle childhood (like the desire to gain approval from both peers and significant adults) continue. In addition, preteens become capable of making more serious spiritual commitments.

Major Lessons: Adapting to a changing body, changing hormonal impulses, peer pressure, and spiritual growth.

Note: Please read the previous chapter(s), as all children develop at different rates and many of the advances at this age are built upon earlier developments. In case your child is a little slower in one area, or in case you missed some of the activities in the previous chapter, it is always a good practice to review where you are coming from before advancing into new territory.

Parental Needs

At this stage of your life, you are probably neck deep in responsibilities: You are at or near the prime of your career, you are balancing a budget of income vs. rising expenses, you have been raising at least one child (maybe more) for over 10 years, and it may feel like you are about to be overtaken and drown.

If you are still in a relationship, congratulations! Even if it's your second or third relationship, make it a priority. Your child needs to feel secure. Your child needs to see unity. Your child needs positive role models to see how to make a relationship work. It's not selfish to take some time for yourself. Plan weekly date nights according to your budget – even if it's a picnic or a walk in the park. You need "us time." Communicate with each other often, but especially at the end of the day. The images you see and the feelings you have right before you sleep will set the tone for tomorrow, so make them good ones – whether you just cuddle or do more. Eat dinner together, schedule family time, and/or family meetings regularly to keep a strong relationship with the whole family. Don't hide problems from each other; help each other solve them.

Physically

Hopefully, your child has chosen one or more sports or other physical activities to pursue, so continue to support his training and practice. If your child has chosen gaming or another two-dimensional sedentary activity, do your best to schedule some kind of physical activity, whether that means joining school or community center teams, taking classes, or just biking with the family. We don't want to discourage him from becoming a world champion gamer, but we do want to encourage him to grow in all four dimensions. He should get at least sixty minutes of physical activity every day and an average of nine hours of sleep a night.[172]

Consult your doctor for the latest schedule of vaccinations, but especially the HPV vaccination for girls, which can prevent cervical cancer. The same vaccination is generally recommended for boys, too, but consult your doctor for more specific advice.

Puberty

The biggest physical changes at this age will be the onset of puberty, which happens according to its own timeline, not yours, so you will have to deal with it when it comes. It is different for boys and girls, so I will talk about them separately. However, both sexes will have to adjust to fluctuating levels of hormones, which tend to create mood swings. In addition, these hormonal swings will affect sleep patterns (circadian rhythms), and the irregular sleep will intensify moodiness. Add to the mix an immature brain that does not yet have

Preteens

good judgment,[173] and it's time to fasten your seat belts because you're in for a bumpy ride.

One of the issues you will address with both sexes, partially due to the fluctuating hormones, will be acne. There are many causes of skin problems, and hormones are only one. Some others are largely under your child's control like diet and cleanliness. If your child starts to break out in acne, try eliminating all refined sugars (cookies, cakes, candies, etc.), eliminating fast foods (especially greasy ones), and eating as naturally as possible. Also emphasize cleanliness, especially if your child is an athlete who sweats a lot. If these natural solutions aren't enough, consult your doctor or research some products specifically designed to combat acne like Proactiv. The tween years are hard enough emotionally without having a face full of zits.

As your child matures, the sweat glands under the arm pits will change and start to emit more powerful odors. No need to start early, but when you notice the change in fragrance, introduce the use of deodorants. I personally don't like antiperspirants because of their aluminum content, but you can make your own decision.

Boys
The most obvious changes for boys will the enlargement of the penis and testes, and the development of the internal supporting parts. He will start to grow pubic hair, hair under his arms, thicker, darker body hair, and soon facial hair. He will begin his growth spurt toward adult size and his voice will begin to crack and eventually get deeper. You may want to explain the difference between circumcised and uncircumcised penises and why your child's is the way it is.

Probably the most emotional event will be the first ejaculation, which normally will occur in a wet dream. Prepare your child for this event by explaining about erections (he may have already had one) and the different function of the penis when pointing up or pointing down. It's a good idea to teach your child how to do his own laundry, using cold water to keep the semen stains from setting, and perhaps either an enzyme cleaner or hydrogen peroxide on light colored fabrics to pre-treat the stains, so that he can clean up his own mess when it happens. I will not give any advice on masturbation, as that is a matter of your own faith and morality, but I strongly recommend you discuss it with your son and give him advice.

In addition to being aroused by girls, he will also experience spontaneous erections and will need to know how to deal with them. Explain that he can sit down to make it less obvious, cover the area with a jacket or book, or think unpleasant thoughts until the arousal goes away.[174] If someone points it out in an attempt to embarrass him, assure him that it is natural and offer something to say to the accuser like, "You're just jealous because you've never had one." (OK, you may want to be a little nicer than that . . .)

Girls

The most obvious changes for girls will be the onset of menstruation (the period) and the development of the internal supporting parts. She will start to grow pubic hair, hair under her arms, thicker, darker hair on her legs, perhaps some facial hair, her breasts will begin to bud, and her hips will begin to widen. She also may begin a growth spurt toward adult size, and she may reach her full height younger than her male counterparts, especially if she will not be tall. Makeup can increase problems with acne, so use as little as possible and be sure to remove it every day.

The menstrual blood is not really bleeding (there is no open wound), but rather a shedding of bloody tissue lining the uterus. Many girls have a light or spotty period the first few times, and irregular intervals until their bodies get into a rhythm.[175] However, the range is enormous as each body is unique.

It is normal for breasts to grow asymmetrically, so don't be alarmed. If there is still a noticeable difference once they have reached their full size, consult a doctor, but don't worry unnecessarily.[176] Discuss wearing a bra with your daughter and perhaps take her bra shopping.

You will need to prepare your daughter on how to deal with the first blood. It may occur at night, but it may occur anywhere, at any time, including at school. Explain the difference between a tampon and a pad, and which you recommend, and why. Practice using one so that she will be mentally and emotionally prepared, and when it happens, she can just go into action. Tell her where to find (or keep) a tampon or pad, and how to excuse herself in order to apply it. If it occurs at night, just like with a boy, teach her to pre-treat the stain (with cold water and OxyClean) and wash her own sheets; likewise, if she stains her clothes, knowing how to launder them gives her some privacy.

You should also educate her on the different requirements during the cycle, and which products are best, in your experience, for each time of the cycle and with different kinds of clothing. Also give guidance on how often to change the products (every 4 hours?) and how to dispose of them properly. Other topics that are important are cramps, moodiness, toxic shock syndrome, vaginal infections, and foul odors.[177] If you are a single dad, you will either have to do a LOT of research on a site like https://www.helenfarabee.org/, or find a female relative or friend who has the experience you lack in using them.

Generally, the same sex parent is the preferred choice for having these discussions, and I will go into more depth on what to say later in the Mental section of this chapter.

Activities

Continue to use any activities from the previous chapter that your child found either difficult or particularly enjoyed, plus add these:

Discuss Foods: Discuss with your child what foods are healthy and unhealthy, and why it is not a good idea to eat the unhealthy foods, especially if he is experiencing acne.

Food Groups: Help your child understand the different classifications of foods: Meats, poultry, fish, dairy, eggs, grains, beans, nuts, vegetables, and fruits. Name foods and ask your child to identify which food group they belong to. Alternately, you can identify proteins, fats, carbs, and sugars, and then name foods and ask your child to identify which of those groups the food belongs to as a simplified way to discuss diets and healthy eating.

Laundry: Teach your child how to do laundry by using the washing machine and dryer. This skill can come in especially handy now that your child has reached puberty. Also teach him how to fold the clothes when they come out of the dryer.

Ironing: Teach your child how to iron his own clothes, even if he doesn't need to do it on a regular basis. The skill will come in handy sooner or later.

Dishes: Teach your child how to properly set a dinner table: What size and shape of plate is used for what kind of food, where the plates and glasses are set, and where the utensils are set. Explain that formal settings like having guests may require more plates and utensils than a family or an individual meal. Also teach him how to wash dishes, how to stack and turn on the dishwasher, and where to place clean dishes, utensils, and cookware in the closets.

Cleaning: Teach your child how to vacuum, sweep, mop, wipe, and dust. If you have a lawn or pool, you can also teach him how to mow, edge, sweep, and balance the chemicals. You may assign him daily or weekly chores, or connect chores to his allowance to help him understand that you have to work for your money.

Jump Rope: If your child hasn't learned to jump rope, introduce the activity and then make it more challenging with advanced techniques like changing feet, jumping continuously on one foot, spinning the rope twice for each jump, crossing your arms, etc. Look on YouTube for examples and tutorials.

Hula Hoop: The hula hoop is a simple device that can challenge a child to practice for hours. Buy a hoop and look on YouTube for videos that show different ways to learn and some more advanced skills.

Sports and Activities: Continue to practice valuable skills for his favorite sports or physical activities and some of the strength, coordination, and balance activities from the previous chapter.

Group Activities

In addition to the fitness activities from the previous chapter, some of these activities might be fun for parties or boy/girl groups.

Preteens

Jump Rope: Jumping rope is more challenging with several children. Two children face each other and spin a long rope while the third child steps into the space, jumps several times, and then jumps out. A much more challenging version is to have the two spinners spin two ropes at the same time by alternating them in different directions. The third, or maybe even a fourth child attempts to step in and jump "Double Dutch" with two ropes spinning. Again, look on YouTube for examples and tutorials.

Leg Support: Child A lies down on a soft surface on his back, slowly raises both legs together and brings his knees in towards the body until his upper legs are against his chest and his lower legs are straight up and down with his back still flat on the floor. Child B stands over Child A facing the opposite direction, with his back toward Child A. Slowly, Child B sits down so that his bottom comes to rest on Child A's feet. To help support Child B, Child A should take hold of each of Child B's feet to help steady them. How long can they stay in that position? Switch roles. To make it a competition, which pair can hold the position longest?

Arm and Leg Support: Child A lies down on a soft surface and raises both legs just like the previous exercise. Child B stands over the Child A facing his feet. Slowly, Child B leans over and places his hands on Child A's feet. Next, Child B places each foot onto Child A's hands. Child A then pushes up with his hands so that Child B has his arms, his legs, and his back straight. How long can they stay in that position? Switch roles and repeat. To make it a competition, which pair can hold the position longest?

Limbo: Two children hold a broomstick or other straight rod about that size at face level and challenge the other children to pass under the stick by bending backwards. When each one has passed under the stick, the two lower the stick and everyone tries again. Those who don't make it are out as they keep lowering the stick until only one person can successfully pass under it.

Follow the Dancing Leader: Play some dance music, arrange all the children in a circle, and each child gets a chance to step into the circle and lead the group with a couple of dance steps for about 30 seconds.

Dance Through: Play some dance music, arrange all the children in two lines facing each other (boys in one line, girls in the other), and each child gets a chance to dance through the lines (between the partners) from his position at one end of a line to the other end of the same line. An alternate version is for the two children on the end to dance through together as a couple.

Freeze Dance: Play some dance music and everybody begins dancing. When the music stops, everyone must freeze exactly in the position they are and maintain balance until the music starts again. To make it a competition, anyone who loses balance sits out until there is only one dancer left.

Balloon Dance: Play some dance music and pair up children, one boy and one girl. They have to dance holding a balloon between them with their heads or chests. To make it a competition, anyone whose balloon touches the floor is out until there is only one couple remaining

Interpretive Dance: Play some different kinds of music that illustrate an emotion, and then ask an individual child to dance to that music expressing that emotion. The next child may try the same music with the same emotion, the same music with a different emotion, or different music.

Lip Sync: Each child gets to lip sync a favorite song, acting out the emotions of the performance. Choose the music carefully to avoid bad language and violent lyrics.

Note: Use your good judgment in these and any physical recommendation I make. Take whatever precautions you think necessary for your child in your unique situation (like a pandemic) to keep your child and everyone else safe.

Mentally

As I said in the previous chapter, the brain has reached its adult size and is no longer growing larger. The pre-frontal cortex is not fully formed, the myelin sheaths are not fully developed, so communication within the brain is slow and inhibitions are even slower. The gray matter will grow some in preadolescence, but then decrease in adolescence. The myelin continues to grow throughout the teen years, which increases the speed of communication within the brain. In early adolescence the myelin in the fibers of the *corpus callosum* is growing rapidly, connecting the major speech producing areas of the left side of the brain to the right.[178]

At about age 12 your child may enter into Piaget's Formal Operational Stage, where she can improve her deductive reasoning (from general to specific) so that she can better apply the principle to her specific action. She can solve verbal logical problems, employ "what if" thinking, and entertain possible futures. She will understand ideals like love and values, and develop her meta-cognition (thinking about thinking.) Not all children move to this stage at 12, with some arriving later, and some cultures around the world may never need to advance to this stage.[179]

The brain also begins pruning. The formation of new neurons slows down, and the brain starts economizing for the long life ahead. If a connection is useful, it becomes permanent; if it's not, it's simply eliminated.[180] As much as one-third of connections may be lost. For this reason, it is important for children this age to be active in school, sports, music, hobbies, and social relationships. They are literally hard wiring their brains for the remainder of their lives, so we want them to be wired for accomplishment, not for lying on the couch and watching TV.[181]

Once the pruning is complete, the brain loses some of its capabilities. For example, by 13 the language centers are completely developed so learning a new language after that becomes harder (but not impossible).

Raising 4 Dimensional Children in a 2 Dimensional World

Communication

If you have been communicating with your child about her experiences and feelings as recommended in previous chapters, you should be able to build on that trust and communication when dealing with these more difficult subjects. If you have not (perhaps you just got this information recently), it's time to begin some meaningful discussions. Review some of the background research and activities in previous chapters and begin where you think your child is ready to meet you. The very fact that you are reading this book shows you are interested in reaching out and doing what it takes to succeed. Start the process at whatever level you can and work your way up to the present. You will get there!

Talk about Dress

When your 5-year-old wants to dress like a Disney princess, it's cute. When your 11-year-old wants to dress like her favorite singer in a music video, it's not so cute. Try to impress upon her the difference between stage costumes and school clothes. She wouldn't wear the Disney princess costume to school, so why would she want to wear the music video costume to school?

Talk About Sex

Please read the "Talk About Sex" section of the previous chapter for some guidelines on how to begin the conversation with your partner and with your child. At this age you are no longer talking about some changes to come in the future. The future is here, so you now need to have the full-blown discussion about puberty, hormones, sex, and love. If you can think back to your own preteen years, what you didn't know and the confusion you felt about things, try to help your child avoid all that chaos with some solid information and a shoulder to lean on. Also please note that although I am referring to your daughter throughout this section of the chapter, most of the same advice applies to your son, but I will separate out information specific to boys where I indicate.

Preteens

Assume the role of trusted advisor and educate your child on these topics:

1. what puberty is and what changes to expect,
2. how to care for your body,
3. how to understand sexual feelings and attraction,
4. the difference between sex and love,
5. how to deal with peer pressure and unwanted sexual advances, and
6. the potential consequences of sexual activity.[182]

Do your best to be relaxed and matter of fact. If you do feel uncomfortable, admit it to your child, but assure her that you need to and want to talk about it now and anytime in the future that she has questions. It's usually best for the same-sex parent to have the talk, but if that's not practical, do what you have to do. Set aside some time where you won't be interrupted and perhaps even give your child fair warning, so she doesn't feel ambushed.

The first point to make is that this is a normal process. Your child, her older siblings, all her friends, you, and even her teachers, coaches, and religious leaders had similar experiences at her age. It's new to her, but she's not the only one to ever go through it. At the same time, acknowledge that is will be an emotional time for her, and you understand that. It's normal, but not trivial. It's important, her feelings are important to you, and you want to help her with information and experience.

If you had the talk recommended in the previous chapter, you have some idea what she knows. Even so, ask her what she has heard at school or from her friends about puberty and sex. It's best to find out what she knows, correct any misinformation, and then build on the truth. As I said in that chapter, have the talk *before* you think it's necessary. You don't want your child to find out after she is pregnant or have her think something is wrong with her because she is growing hair or bleeding.

Raising 4 Dimensional Children in a 2 Dimensional World

In the Physical section of this chapter, I went over most of the physical changes to expect. You can use that as a resource or find more on the Internet. I also briefly covered how to take care of her body, but you certainly need more than a few paragraphs. You will need to provide more information on caring for menstruation, shaving and hair removal, and more. Just remember that your child is still a child and doesn't need to know everything – just enough for her age.

As far as sexual feelings, there is a wide range of possibilities. Some have intense desires, and some have hardly any, especially at this age. Your child may have inherited your tendencies, but not necessarily. This is exactly the kind of situation to ask questions. "What do you think of sex?" It may help start the conversation if you share some of your own experience when you were her age. "Do you feel any desire?" "What do your friends say?" Especially for boys, but for girls, too, you should offer some guidelines about masturbation – I just ask you not to set an unattainable standard, but it is ultimately a matter of your personal morals and religious faith.

There will no doubt be some confusion between sex and love. I strongly recommend you make clear the difference. You can love someone without having sex, and you can have sex without being in love. The confusion usually happens when one person loves the other, and the other person just wants sex, so he says he loves her. One clear statement you can make is that if someone loves you, he will never pressure you to do something you don't want to do. Your child is not accustomed to the intensity of these emotions and may truly believe she is in love (and she may well be), but if she believes love lasts forever (as most romantics do), she can wait until she is older to experience the sexual part of love. After all, if love lasts forever, she and her beau will still be in love when they become adults, won't they? So, they will have plenty of time then.

When it comes to peer pressure, we are again in a situation to ask questions. What do her friends think? Is kissing OK? Is oral sex really sex? What about manual sex? One kind of peer pressure will come from the same sex friends. Girls will encourage other girls to take the next step, even if they wouldn't do it themselves. Boys will be ashamed to admit their virginity. Then there is the peer pressure from the opposite sex. Boyfriends say, "If you love me, you would do it," and if a boy declines to have sex for religious reasons, he might even be called "gay." Prepare your child to handle these situations.

And speaking of gay, what if your child feels she is gay? Will you stop loving her? I cited some evidence in the Mental section of Chapter 4 that recent research shows that sexual preference may not be a choice. Read those articles and consult several qualified psychologists for a better understanding if you find yourself in this situation.

In the previous chapter I recommended role-playing as a way to prepare for peer pressure about smoking, drinking, and drugs. I also recommend role playing about sex. Set clear guidelines about what are acceptable activities for your child and what are not. Explain why: (1) Your religious beliefs, and (2) health reasons. Explain which specific diseases are transmitted through kissing, oral sex, and vaginal sex, and what happens when you get one of those diseases. Discuss contraception so she has no "contraception misconceptions." Understand that people are different in a hot state and a cold state.[160] She might know all the facts, have rehearsed all the responses to pressure, and be a model of morality in a cold, logical state, but act differently when in a hot state. When she gets excited, she doesn't think the same way. Especially for boys, when they get excited, they will say things and do things that will surprise even themselves the next day. Try to get your child in a hot state by embarrassing her and making her uncomfortable, and then rehearsing what to say.

Another area of practice, especially with daughters, is how to deal with unwanted advances. There are simple, non-violent self-defense techniques that can be used to gently but firmly push a date away. I also recommend some more serious rape-prevention self-defense instruction from a local martial arts school. Physical training in a self-defense clinic or class is also closer to hot state practice. When it comes to self-defense, it's better to know it and not need it, than to need it and not know it.

Also impress upon your son that "No means No." Despite what his friends say, it's not OK to touch anyone else without permission. There is a fine line: The male is supposed to be the initiator, but if his amorous attempts are met with resistance, that should be the end of the matter. He should never pressure anyone he cares for to do something she is uncomfortable doing. It's not just a matter of respect – it's called sexual assault.

One final area of unwanted sexual advances is the Internet. Explain what a sexual predator is, how they operate, and why your child should never reveal any personal information about herself or arrange to meet anyone in person that she met online, because it's safest to assume people will lie on the Internet. Also impress upon her that anything posted on the Internet may never go away. Pictures, messages, and comments can be shared without your consent and may be recorded on some server so that they appear again later when you least expect it – like during a job application, college admissions application, or even a political campaign.

Finish up the discussion with the unwanted results of sexual activity: Pregnancy, STDs, and broken hearts are all real possibilities, and I believe a healthy dose of childhood fear may be the appropriate prescription. You certainly don't want to lie, but emphasizing the negative outcomes should discourage mild curiosity. I don't believe any 12-year-old wants to be pregnant or get someone pregnant, and STDs are nasty and hard to get rid of – especially HIV/AIDS. Also point out that whenever you let someone get close enough to you emotionally to engage in any level of sexual activity, you risk getting hurt emotionally, so you want to be very careful whom you allow to get that close . . . really at any age. Let your child get her first broken heart without the complications of sex.

Remember, this is a puberty discussion, so you want to tailor the information you provide to the needs of your child at this age. You don't need to be the Wikipedia of Sex in one conversation. For example, you might want to reserve discussions about condoms and other birth control methods to a later time. As she grows older her outlook and situation will change. Her desires may change. She may feel she is in love. She may feel "everybody's doing it." Of course, if she approaches you with questions, be available. If she does not, probe every once in a while when you notice changes in friends, demeanor, or behavior to start a conversation. The Talk about Sex should not be

Preteens

"one and done," but broken up into "bite sized pieces" that are easy to digest, and revisited every so often. Open lines of communication are the basis of any good relationship.

You may also want to provide a resource with appropriate illustrations to give to your child, like the one called "Growing Up OK" at https://www.gov.mb.ca/healthychild/mcad/growingupok.pdf. You can download and provide it as an electronic file or print it as a booklet. I recommend you read it yourself to help with your discussion and to be sure you are comfortable providing it, plus there is an accompanying pamphlet for parents at https://www.gov.mb.ca/healthychild/mcad/helpgrowingupok.pdf. Another powerful resource is https://health.gov/myhealthfinder/topics/everyday-healthy-living/sexual-health/talk-your-kids-about-sex with links to additional, more detailed resources for you about specific issues.

Activities

Continue to use any activities from the previous chapter that your child found either difficult or particularly enjoyed, plus add these:

Brain Teasers: Continue to use brain teasers like in the previous chapter, but look for more difficult ones, like those on https://parade.com/1025639/marynliles/brain-teasers/.

Fine Print: Teach your child to read the "fine print" in ads whenever you see an ad on TV, in a magazine, or on a mailer. For example, listen carefully to the warnings during popular drug ads, or try to read the fine print in car sale ads, credit card offers, etc.

Sell Me: Help your child develop her persuasive skills by choosing any object (something handy or any common object not present that you can name) and trying to sell it to you by praising its virtues. When she is done, challenge her to try to dissuade you from buying the same object by pointing out all of its dangers and problems. Identify what she did well and offer constructive criticism of other arguments that might have been more persuasive.

Jingle: Explain that a jingle is a short song, about 30 seconds or so, designed to sell a product in an advertisement. Ask your child to write a jingle about one of her favorite products.

Advertise: Ask your child to create an advertisement for a made-up product. She first must "invent" the product, and then she can create a paper ad, a live presentation, record a radio ad, or a video commercial.

Free Association: You say any word and ask your child to say any word that pops into her head. For example, you might say, "Cat," and she might say, "Dog." You can switch roles giving her a chance to pick a new word or you can simply respond to, "Dog," with your own word. Although it is free association, don't be afraid to challenge each other on what the association is – there are no wrong answers, just different ways of thinking about or associating ideas.

What was the Question: Give your child an answer, like, "A good friend," and ask your child to ask the question like, "Who is Mary?" or, "What would I hate to lose?" Then, your child provides an answer, and you provide the question.

What Else Could It Be: Take a familiar object, like a spoon, and ask, "What else could it be?" Take turns with your child offering different uses to develop her imagination, like: A garden tool, very long earrings, a weapon, a screwdriver, etc.

Invent a Game: Especially on a rainy day, but really anytime, find three or four household objects that won't break and ask your child to invent a game using these objects. Play the game together.

Group Activities

Pictionary: It's a real game you can buy, or you can approximate it by providing two or more children with some paper and pencils. With a large group, you can make two teams. The first child picks a word and has two minutes to draw pictures to get the other child/team member to say the word. She cannot write letters or numbers. If the other child/team member guesses the word, she gets one point. If he/they cannot, no points are scored. Then, the next child picks a word and has two minutes.

Invisible Show and Tell: Each child needs a few minutes to decide what she will show and tell, and then present it to the entire group. However, she doesn't need to really show anything – she simply describes what she is showing and how to use it, and the other children get to guess what she is describing.

Number Pattern: The first child gives a set of numbers following a pattern, like "2, 4, 6, 8." The next child has to identify the pattern. If she is successful, she offers a pattern of her own. An alternate version is for the second child to give the next number in the pattern to show she knows it.

Body Parts: The first child names an object that has "body parts" like a clock, which has a face and two hands. The second child must name the body parts. Then the second child gets to name another object, like a potato, which has skin and eyes. Continue to take turns.

Location 20 Questions: Take the game of 20 Questions from the previous chapter to a higher level with locations. The first child selects a location and gives a clue like "I'm in a location that's cold." The other children get 20 chances to ask a Yes or No question to figure out where the first child is (in her imagination). Another "higher level" of the game is for the first child to imagine she is a specific person, and the others have 20 questions to determine who the first child imagines she is.

One Word Stories: Take the Group Story activity difficulty up a notch by getting two or more children to create a story providing one word at a time. When a child wants to end the sentence, she says, "Period," and then provides the first word of the next sentence.

<u>Famous People</u>: The first child gives the name of a famous person. The second child must identify who that person is. If she can't, the first person explains who that person is, and then it is the second person's turn to name someone famous. For example, "Who is Adam Driver?" "He is an actor who has played many roles, including Kylo Ren in the *Star Wars* movies."

Emotionally

The preteen years will be a time of further establishing your child's identity, preparing for the teen years when he will be biologically programmed to break away. Expect him to test his boundaries with clothing, behavior, and activities. Preteen girls will often try express their unique identity by spelling their name differently. Your job is to offer positive ways to express an unique identity rather than negative ones.

Understand that your child's brain is not yet fully developed, but it doesn't realize that. He thinks he is just as smart as any adult, and his opinions are just as good as anyone else's. Although the principle may be true on one level: That all people are created equal (in the eyes of the law), on another level it is not: People are not all equal in learning, experience, and accomplishment, so some opinions ARE better than others. In the next chapter I will identify some adolescent myths that are commonly believed, but for now, just realize your preteen's attempts to establish a unique identity are not about you – they are just part of the normal and natural developmental process of showing the world and himself that he is growing up.

If you have open lines of communication as recommended in the previous chapters, continuing discussions should not be difficult. If you haven't had the chance and are just beginning the process now, just as I recommended in the Talk About Sex section, go back a few chapters, and find a place to start. Begin with some of the easier and non-threatening emotional activities to build trust and a relationship that includes talking about feelings, and work your way up to the present. It may take a little longer, but you can get there.

Preteens

    I strongly recommend you pick your battles rather than fight about everything, and start sooner rather than later. When your preteen's overriding principle is to establish his unique identity, keep the fights on safer subjects. For example, to keep his rebellion focused on a hairstyle or some clothing is better than to ignore the appearance discussions and wait to start the fights when his rebellion progress to smoking, drinking, or doing drugs. In my opinion, if you can keep the rebellion in the safe zones, it may never progress to the dangerous ones.

    On a more positive note, if you can provide positive options where your child can establish a unique identity in a sport or other physical activity, in music, or in academics, the whole rebellious thing may be unnecessary for a couple of years. You also have some control of your child's friends. There is an old saying, "Show me who your friends are, and I will show you who you are." By enrolling him on sports teams, in religious activities, in gymnastics classes, and especially in martial arts classes, you expose him to a positive group of friends with positive values. If you are too busy to pay attention to his friends and activities, he may not choose such a positive group, or may even be recruited by a negative group (or gang.)

    One aspect of your child's emotional life you don't have so much control over is his changing appearance. As he goes through puberty, he will be treated differently by his peers. Especially girls, but even boys will receive more and different attention when they start showing sexual maturity. This change in the attention they get changes their place in their peer society and can be very uncomfortable. It can be positive attention if your child becomes more attractive through puberty, even attracting the interest of older teens. It can also be negative attention because most kids grow more awkward in the early years, before reaching full maturity, and feel they are uncoordinated and less attractive. From their point of view, they are growing out of the golden age of childhood where their body was a great ally in having fun and gaining recognition, to now when their body seems to be their worst enemy in preventing them from doing many things they want to do well. Either way, they need your guidance on how to deal with their changing body and changing feelings. Help them understand that what happens to you in life is important, but it's much more important how you deal with it.

We don't always remember exactly what happened, but we tend to remember what we tell ourselves happened (our interpretation of the situation.) Help your child interpret situations positively, so when he remembers people and places, he tells himself positive stories that encourage him, rather than negative ones that discourage him.

If your child has a romantic interest, be interested. Help your child identify his feelings by asking, "What do you like about her?" If he is in love, he should want to talk about her endlessly. On the other hand, he may not be able to express his feelings verbally and need some guidance. Ask about the kinds of things they do together and offer to invite her over for dinner or some fun activities. If this person is important to your child, she should be important to you. Also, be available when they break up, and offer a shoulder to lean or cry on. It goes with the territory, and they need guidance on how to handle all the ups and downs.

Part of the movement toward separation will be a desire to spend more time with friends and less time with the family. Again, pick your battles. Don't schedule a family night on the night of the week when he has the most desirable activities with his friends. Pick a different night so he can do both. Try to keep the family together for dinner (if possible) as family time, and make the most of it by having positive discussions. Make family time fun. Family movie night is OK once in a while but doesn't compete well with movies or gaming with friends. Instead, go to fun places and do fun activities that he doesn't do with his friends, so it is unique and valuable. Schedule "dates" where he goes to specific activities with one parent or the other, and arrange your next "date" before leaving the first. This one-on-one time is especially effective in blended families.

As mentioned earlier, this will also be a time of moodiness brought on by fluctuating hormones, lack of sleep, and an immature brain.[173] To deal with your child effectively, you must first realize that it may be a chemical reaction that has nothing to do with you. Exercise a little patience and gentle guidance. Second, do your best to create a schedule that allows ample sleep. He will have a natural tendency to stay awake later, and lack of sleep will affect his ability to concentrate, which will affect his mood. Third, his still-developing brain leads to actions that are impulsive, hasty, and selfish. He simply doesn't have the adult capacity to think things through to the end, nor the experience of having made many common mistakes, yet he thinks he does. A little Socratic questioning will serve better than lecturing: Why did you do that? What did you think would happen? Why did you think that? Didn't you imagine anything else might happen? What could you do differently next time?

Try to keep these limitations in mind when dealing with his emotional outbursts while still maintaining rules of respect and decorum. This is an age where he may be witnessing disrespectful attitudes towards adults from his friends, and you need to reinforce that disrespecting ANYONE is not right, no matter how upset you happen to be. You have to keep perspective that he is learning by trial-and-error how to deal with puberty, yet still provide solid boundaries of acceptable behavior and the consequences of going outside those boundaries.

One final area of emotion your child may express is how to treat you around friends. Whereas a 7-year-old may not think twice about kissing you goodbye when you drop him off for school, an 11-year-old may find it embarrassing. Don't be afraid to ask, "How would you like me to treat you in front of your friends? Why?" Expand the discussion to other areas. Your idea of expressing your love may not be the same as your child's. "I want to be a better parent. How do you want me to show my affection?" "What can I do to make you feel more important in my life?" "Is there anything I do that you would prefer I no longer do?" You might even ask your child to imitate you when you are doing something he doesn't like – it will be enlightening. You don't need to obey his requests, but hear them, consider them, and respond with truth. You are still the adult, and you still have the responsibility to guide him the right way, but if you can guide him in a way he prefers, why not?

Raising 4 Dimensional Children in a 2 Dimensional World

Discipline

In his desire to express his grown-up identity, your child will try many different experiments to see what he likes, what his friends like, and what his parents like. He needs some freedom to try and fail, but you should not let him hurt himself. Here are some guidelines to establish ahead of time:
- Activities and choices must not be truly dangerous;
- They should not interfere with schooling or otherwise affect future well-being;
- They should not be irreversible (like tattoos);
- They should not contradict the family's most basic values.[183]

Don't be afraid to "put your foot down" when he crosses the line, but keep in mind the principle of Minimum Consequences (from Chapter 4) to achieve your goal.

One additional aspect of discipline I recommend is that you establish early that it's your house and your child does not have the right to lock the door to his room. He has a door that can be closed for privacy, and you should choose to knock before you enter, but he absolutely does not have the right to lock that door in an attempt to keep you out. Give him space when he needs it, but establish the rule now, rather than when he gets older.

Activities

There is significant research that shows that "soft skills" like getting along well with others in junior high school are more predictive of success like earnings, employment rates, and college attendance, than are the cognitive skills normally measured in school tests.[184] Do your best to help develop these soft, emotional skills.

Continue to use any activities from the previous chapter that your child found either difficult or particularly enjoyed, plus add these:

Read: Continue to read fiction to develop empathy as identified in the previous chapter's activities. Adolescents who are able to pick out other people's emotions accurately are better adjusted during middle school.[185]

Characters: Discuss books and movies to help identify what the characters are feeling – what emotions? Do you understand why they would feel that way? Have you ever felt that way? How do you feel about the way they feel?

Power of the Question: Teach your child how to ask questions to get to know someone (without grilling them), so they feel important. Practice on each other to learn some new things about each other, then ask your child to practice on the opposite parent or a sibling. Learning how to ask questions and really listen to the answers is one of the most powerful ways to "win friends and influence people," so this is a valuable social skill.

Compliment: Teach your child how to compliment someone else and then combine the compliment with a conversation starting question like, "Cool shirt! Where did you get it?"

Need or Want: Explain to your child the difference between a need and a want: A need is something necessary for survival, whereas a want is not necessary but only desirable. For example, people need food, but they don't need French fries (although they may want some.) Identify items and ask your child to classify each as a need or a want and discuss why.

Confidence: Ask your child to describe himself as accurately as possible. Some children will be shy and this will be a confidence building exercise, while others may brag, and you need to help them have a more realistic view and understand how bragging makes them unattractive. Help your child find a good balance using a combination of truth, humility, and perhaps humor.

Personal TimeLine: Give your child some paper and a pencil and ask him to draw out a timeline of his life, with today as the middle point.

Raising 4 Dimensional Children in a 2 Dimensional World

He should start with his birthday and identify events that were important to him up until today. From today forward he should identify events that he would like to achieve and the approximate date or age he wants to achieve them.

Wow: Whenever you have an emotional incident, check with your child – is he feeling the same emotion? Help him identify what he is feeling. If you find he is feeling a different emotion or drawing a different conclusion, ask, "Why do you think you are feeling that way? How do you know that? Let's play a game: What else could that mean?" Offer what you are feeling and the conclusion you are drawing and discuss it. You may be the one who is mistaken, or you may both be right.

Step Back: Whenever your child is upset, teach him to Step Back mentally from the issue. In his mind, he should close his eyes and picture himself feeling the way he feels. Then, he should mentally step outside himself and step back about ten feet to observe himself. What does he see about himself? How does he feel? How does he look? Is there another way to interpret the situation? How else could he feel about it? Then, ask him to step back into himself and open his eyes. Does he feel differently?

Procrastination: Discuss with your child what procrastination is (a delay of action) and then offer some examples of your own where you have procrastinated. Then ask your child to identify at least one thing he has delayed doing (either now or recently). Ask why. Point out that when you put something off, it weighs on you that you still have to do it, whereas if you do the hardest or least liked thing first, you have much better stuff to look forward to doing. See if you can get a commitment to stop procrastinating (you may offer one of your own as part of the bargain.)

Emotional Art: Ask your child to write or cut out large letters that spell an emotion, like LOVE, and then illustrate each letter to convey the emotion.

Preteens

Finish the Sentence: Ask your child to finish various emotional sentences, like, "What really makes me angry is _____," or "I really love to _____." Discuss the answers to get to know why he feels the way he does.

Strengths and Weaknesses: Have your child identify some of his strong talents and abilities, not only physically, but mentally, and emotionally. Next, have him identify some of his weak points. Finally, ask him how he intends to continue to develop his strong points and what he plans to do about his weak points.

Group Activities

Some of these activities are useful for carpools, restaurants, and rainy days. If you host a party for your child, Google some appropriate party games for tweens that put boys and girls together at close proximity but with safe boundaries like Twister. Of course, it's easy to let them play video games, but we are trying to raise four dimensional children, aren't we?

I feel: Ask each child to give a one-word answer to the question, "How do you feel?" When he gives the answer, he should illustrate the feeling with a physical movement.

Compliment: Ask each child to give one compliment to the person on his right. It must be true.

Predictions: Ask each child to predict what the person to his left will be like and what she will be doing twenty years from now. He must explain why he thinks that.

When I Grow Up: Ask each child to identify what he wants to be when he grows up and how he will know that he has grown up. Encourage them to discuss each other's answers.

Opinions: Ask two children to take opposite sides of any emotional issue (sports, politics, race), give them a few minutes to prepare, and then have them present their arguments to each other. You may need to referee to be sure each one gets a fair chance to present his position, emphasizing that only one person talks at a time. The goal is to practice preparing and presenting a convincing argument while practicing the rules of civil discourse. At the end, ask each child to comment on the effectiveness of the other's arguments and arguing style.

Skits: Give the group a situation to act out where each child has a clearly defined role. For example, two boys are in the bathroom at school: John is smoking but Ryan is not, and the principal walks in. Add as many characters as you have children or divide a large group into teams. You can even let the kids pick out the situation.

Peer Pressure: Ask children to take turns finishing the sentence, "I feel peer pressure to _____." After each statement all the children should discuss it – is there really any pressure to do that? From whom? What should the child do? When the discussion loses energy, have the next child finish the sentence and discuss her answer.

Embarrassing Moments: Ask each child to share a funny embarrassing moment with the others. Along with learning to laugh at yourself, this activity shows that everyone has embarrassing moments.

Harder for Whom: In a group of children that has both boys and girls, ask one child to take a position on the statement, "Boys (or Girls) have it harder because _____." Allow some polite discussion, and then the next child gets to give his opinion. Continue through the group until everyone has had a chance to give an opinion.

Spirituality

Starting at about 10 or 11 years of age children's appreciation of morality will change based on their ability to see things from other people's perspectives. Morality will become less based on authority figures' black and white rules, and more of what Piaget called a "morality of cooperation," where the rules are socially agreed upon for the benefit of the group. They still follow the rules, but view the rules more as negotiable guidelines meant to improve everyone's life. They think less about personal loss or gain (punishment/reward), and more about the social good.[186] Kohlberg used the term Ideal Reciprocity to describe the belief that is embodied in the Golden Rule: Do unto others as you would have them do unto you.[187]

At or near this age many cultures have a ritual that, at least in previous times, announced the child is becoming an adult and is ready to take on adult spiritual responsibilities. Catholic children make their Confirmation, Jewish children have their *bar mitzvah* or *bat mitzvah*, and some Muslims celebrate the *Khatam Al Koran*. Nowadays we have a longer life expectancy, so we shelter our children longer, and they do not need to take on the cultural responsibilities of an adult, but religious founders seemed to believe that preteens and early teens reach an age of understanding religious responsibilities.

You may witness your own child begin to question your family's religious beliefs, especially if she has been exposed to different religious beliefs in her friends' families. You may also witness a new level of religious fervor in your child as she becomes more committed by choice. Preteens often feel a personal closeness to God, where they feel God is their personal confidante with whom they can share thoughts and secrets they would not share with anyone else. Encourage the relationship.

If your child has been meditating, continue the practice. If she has not, you (or she) may consider starting to help her learn to focus, quiet her emotional unrest, and seek a deeper spiritual understanding. Yoga classes may also be a good option.

Activities

<u>Pick a Proverb:</u> Pick a proverb or common saying like, "Two heads are better than one." Ask your child what she thinks it means and how it applies to her life. Discuss it from your own experience and how it might apply to her and her future. You can pick a Proverb of the Day or of the Week (or Motivational Quote – maybe buy a motivational calendar) to have regular, value-based discussions, perhaps on the way to school each morning.

Raising 4 Dimensional Children in a 2 Dimensional World

Give Thanks: Ask your child to name something she is thankful for. Then you name something you are thankful for, and then take turns naming all the good things in your lives.

Rate Yourself: Children this age find it easy to criticize others (adults and other children.) Have your child "look in the mirror" and rate herself on a scale of one to ten on various qualities like honesty, loyalty, envy, etc. First, give an example by rating yourself on one of those qualities and explaining why, and asking your child if she agrees. Then ask her to rate herself and explain why she rates herself that way. After listening, offer your opinion as to whether she is too hard on herself or maybe too generous. Provide evidence of recent actions to help her get a better understanding of her behavior vs. her beliefs.

A Better Me: Ask your child to identify an area where she is weak. Then ask her what she could do to improve herself in that area. Help her make a plan to become a better person.

Luck: Discuss your beliefs on luck with your child. Is luck what it takes to succeed? What about hard work? Positive attitude? Does chance truly favor those who are prepared? Or do you believe in divine blessings?

Conservation: Discuss how people are damaging the environment and different ways you and your child can help conserve resources like saving water, recycling garbage, never littering, etc. Come up with specific actions that you can hold each other accountable for.

Good Deed: Ask your child what is at least one good deed she can do tomorrow. If she can't think of anything, make suggestions. Are there kids at school that seem lonely? Are there chores around the house that need to be done? Has she called Grandma or Grandpa lately?

If I had a Million Dollars: Ask your child what she would do if she suddenly had a million dollars. Help her realize that spending it all on herself would probably not make her happy, so what are some other things she could do with the money to help others? Can she do anything similar with the resources she currently has?

My Hero: Ask your child to identify at least one hero or role model she has and why she would like to be more like that person. How will she develop those qualities?

Stop the Bully: Ask your child what she would do if someone insulted her publicly. If someone threatened to beat her up if she didn't give him some money? If someone did that to her friend? Discuss positive, non-violent solutions. If you are not familiar with these techniques, attend a Stop the Bully seminar with your child so you both can learn how.

Group Activities

These are some activities you might use in the car during a carpool, at home on rainy days, or even at a restaurant to make better use of the time. Of course, you can use some of the individual activities above with one child taking your (the adult) part, or you might use these group activities with your child alone, with you taking the part of the first child.

Manners: Ask each child to identify proper manners when visiting someone else's home. After they have had a chance to agree or disagree on visitor's manners, ask them to discuss whether or not they should have the same manners at home and why.

Moral Dilemma: Introduce a moral dilemma like, "Mr. Jones' wife is sick, but he can't afford the medicine. Should he let her suffer or try to steal the medicine? What else might he do?"

Summary

The tween years are challenging physically, mentally, emotionally, and even spiritually. The onset of puberty will bring about significant physical changes in size, shape, and appearance that may be vastly different among friends and classmates. Some will become more attractive as their sexual traits become obvious, which creates one set of emotional issues. Others will not grow into their adult size smoothly, leaving them to look and feel awkward, which creates a different set of emotional issues. Toss in the release of a whole new set of hormones and a brain that has not developed the capacity nor the experience to handle all of this trauma, and life gets interesting, to say the least. Just be glad you are dealing with one tween, and not a whole classroom full of them like a middle school teacher. They are the true warriors.

      Your job will be a balancing act of initiating uncomfortable conversations, handling emotional meltdowns, dealing with childish attempts to act grown up, providing a shoulder to cry on, and guiding your child toward healthy, positive choices that also allow for establishing individuality while still caring about others. In addition, your child will be moving to a more mature spiritual understanding, so encourage prayer and participation in the appropriate religious rituals.

      One of the best things you can do is educate your child on the developmental stages of the brain, so that he understands scientifically how his brain will continue to grow into adulthood. When he talks with his friends, it's easy for them all to agree that "adults just don't get it." Fortunately, he still has some respect for science, so presenting scientific evidence may help him understand he is not as smart as he thinks he is. Google "tween brain function" or check out this site: https://www.greatschools.org/gk/articles/inside-the-preteen-brain-development/. It's important that he understands that one person's opinion is not automatically as good as another's, but things like evidence and experience are important. Ask him to compare his opinions to that of a little brother, a younger neighbor or cousin, or even to himself as a child. He will likely agree that he knows more now than he did then . . . so just maybe he will know more when he is older than he knows now.

Screen Time

      Screen time will become more challenging at this age. Be sure you have all the appropriate filters and limits on your child's phone, tablet, and computer to prevent viewing adult content, inappropriate sites, and making unacceptable purchases. Track the phone using GPS technology to know where she is when she says she is going somewhere. If your child doesn't know all the hacks, her friends do, so check her devices often.

As I recommended in the previous chapter, put off joining social media until high school. Why? First of all, most social media accounts have age restrictions, so you can use the regulations as your first defense. More importantly, according to Dr. Jonathan Haidt, a professor of Social Psychology at the NYU Stern School of Business, the number of American teens with depression anxiety drastically increased with the advent of social media. Older teen girls were 62% more likely to cut or otherwise harm themselves and 70% more likely to attempt suicide when compared to the same-aged girls from 2000 to 2010. Even worse, younger teen and preteen girls were 189% more likely to cut or harm themselves and 151% more likely to attempt suicide.[188] These kids are the first generation in history to get on social media in middle school, and the results are literally life threatening. Just because all their friends have social media accounts doesn't make it right or safe. Be strong.

Look at the Screen Time section in the previous chapter for some guidelines for setting limits of screen time, but much of her homework will be done on a screen and most of the communication with her friends will be done on a phone, and we have not even started to count time for entertainment. The goal is to have balance, where your child does not live her life in a two-dimensional world. If you find she has a problem, take the phone or tablet away, or limit the hours of use or the time of day she can use them. You can even allow her input as to how much time she thinks is acceptable – you will probably get a reasonable number, especially because most tweens radically underestimate the amount of time they spend on the phone. Push for more face-to-face time interacting with friends doing real world activities over staying home and hiding behind the screen.

Note: As all children are unique and develop at different rates, I recommend you read the next chapter to prepare for your child's

Raising 4 Dimensional Children in a 2 Dimensional World

growth and in case your child happens to develop more quickly in one area or another and the previous chapter in case your child happens to develop more slowly in one area or another. Specifically, some of the activities might well be continued into the older years.

Also please use your own good judgment in following any advice I offer. Research is subject to change and my advice may be based on research that has since changed or been updated since this publishing. Choose your actions based on your own beliefs, experiences, research, and judgment, especially during extenuating circumstances (like a pandemic.)

Recommended Resources:

https://www.helenfarabee.org/poc/view_doc.php?type=doc&id=37673&cn=1272 Introduction to Puberty - Child & Adolescent Development: Puberty (helenfarabee.org)
https://www.gov.mb.ca/healthychild/mcad/growingupok.pdf
https://www.gov.mb.ca/healthychild/mcad/helpgrowingupok.pdf
https://health.gov/myhealthfinder/topics/everyday-healthy-living/sexual-health/talk-your-kids-about-sex
https://www.edutopia.org/article/getting-creative-sel
https://littlehumans.com/
https://www.gamesofgenius.com/
https://mindup.org/
https://www.mindinthemaking.org/

References:

172. Healthy Child Manitoba; Child and Youth Programs; Middle Child and Adolescent Development; "Growing Up OK." https://www.gov.mb.ca/healthychild/mcad/growingupok.pdf. Accessed June 20, 2021.

173. Oswalt Morelli, Angela, MSW. "Mental/Emotional/Social Changes through Puberty." Helen Farabee Centers; Child & Adolescent Development: Puberty. https://www.helenfarabee.org/poc/view_doc.php?type=doc&id=38408&cn=1276. Accessed June 20, 2021.

Preteens

174. Oswalt Morelli, Angela, MSW. "Menstruation, Wet Dreams and Related Subjects." Helen Farabee Centers; Child & Adolescent Development: Puberty. https://www.helenfarabee.org/poc/view_doc.php?type=doc&id=38415&cn=1276. Accessed June 20, 2021.

175. Oswalt Morelli, Angela, MSW. "Primary Physical Changes Associated With Puberty." Helen Farabee Centers; Child & Adolescent Development: Puberty. https://www.helenfarabee.org/poc/view_doc.php?type=doc&id=38406&cn=1276. Accessed June 20, 2021.

176. Oswalt Morelli, Angela, MSW. "Secondary Physical Changes." Helen Farabee Centers; Child & Adolescent Development: Puberty. https://www.helenfarabee.org/poc/view_doc.php?type=doc&id=38407&cn=1276. Accessed June 20, 2021.

177. Oswalt Morelli, Angela, MSW. "Information for Girls; Managing Menstruation and other Vaginal Discharge." Helen Farabee Centers; Child & Adolescent Development: Puberty. https://www.helenfarabee.org/poc/view_doc.php?type=doc&id=38416&cn=1276. Accessed June 20, 2021.

178. Strauch, Barbara. *The Primal Teen: What the New Discoveries about the Teenage Brain Tell Us about Our Kids.* New York: Anchor Books, 2003, pp. 53-57.

179. Lumen Learning; Courses; Lifespan Development; Chapter 6 Adolescence; "Piaget's Formal Operaional Stage of Cognitive Development." Piaget's Formal Operational Stage of Cognitive Development | Lifespan Development (lumenlearning.com). Accessed June 20, 2021.

180. Baringa, Marcia. "How the Brain Weeds it's Garden." *Science,* March 4, 1994, 1225.

181. Bowman, Lee. "New Research Shows Stark Differences in Teen Brains." *Scripps Howard News Service*, May 11, 2004.

182. Oswalt Morelli, Angela, MSW. "How Do I Talk with My Child About Puberty?" Helen Farabee Centers; Child & Adolescent Development: Puberty. https://www.helenfarabee.org/poc/view_doc.php?type=doc&id=38411&cn=1276. Accessed June 20, 2021.

183. Oswalt Morelli, Angela, MSW. "Allowing Children More Autonomy." Helen Farabee Centers; Child & Adolescent Development: Puberty. https://www.helenfarabee.org/poc/view_doc.php?type=doc&id=38420&cn=1276. Accessed June 20, 2021.

184. Chetty, Raj. "Zip code Destiny: The Persistent Power of Place and Education." Interview on NPR; *Hidden Brain*; November 12, 2018. https://www.npr.org/templates/transcript/transcript.php?storyId=666993130. Accessed June 11, 2021.

185. Zaki, Jamil. "You 2.0: The Empathy Gym." Interview on NPR; *Hidden Brain*; July 29, 2019. https://www.npr.org/transcripts/744195502. Accessed June 20, 2021.

186. Oswalt Morelli, Angela, MSW. "Moral Development: Piaget's Theory." Helen Farabee Centers; Child Development Theory: Middle Childhood (8-11). https://www.helenfarabee.org/poc/view_doc.php?type=doc&id=37690&cn=1272. Accessed June 20, 2021.

187. Oswalt Morelli, Angela, MSW. "Kohlberg's Stages of Moral Development." Helen Farabee Centers; Child Development Theory: Middle Childhood (8-11). https://www.helenfarabee.org/poc/view_doc.php?type=doc&id=37692&cn=1272. Accessed June 20, 2021.

188. *The Social Dilemma*. Dir. Jeff Orlowski. Perf. Jonathan Haidt. Exposure Labs, Ardent Pictures, and Netflix, 2020. Documentary. The Social Dilemma | Netflix Official Site. Accessed June 20, 2021.

Chapter 9
Adolescence
Years 13 to 17

*"Adolescence is like having only enough light
to see the step directly in front of you."*
— Sarah Addison Allen, *The Girl Who Chased the Moon*

Adolescence and Emotions to Die For

Young Cheryn

(knock knock)

Mom: *May I come in?*

Cheryn: *Whatever.*

Mom: *What's the matter, honey?*

Cheryn: *Nothing.*

Mom: *It doesn't sound like nothing.*

Cheryn: *It's just that . . . sometimes I wish I had never been born!*

Mom: *Don't be ridiculous! You live a privileged life! You should be ashamed of yourself! There are kids your age right now in this city with no home who don't know where their next meal is coming from! You have your own room in a big, safe home with a full refrigerator, your own car, your own phone . . . you have nothing to complain about.*

Cheryn: *Yeah, right . . . you probably won't even miss me when I'm gone.*

Mom: *When I was your age, I had nothing! Let me tell you what it was like . . . .*

Young Jakki

(knock knock)

Mom: *May I come in?*

Jakki: *Whatever.*

Mom: *What's the matter, honey?*

Jakki: *Nothing.*

Mom: *It doesn't sound like nothing.*

Jakki: *It's just that . . . sometimes I wish I had never been born!*

Mom: *Oh, Baby, why would you say that?*

Jakki: *I'm not happy.*

Mom: *Come here, Sweetie. What makes you unhappy?*

Jakki: *I look like a giraffe! I'm too tall, too skinny, I have blotches all over my skin. Why can't I be like Lauren? She has a perfect body, perfect hair, and perfect skin!*

Mom: *Do you think if you had never been born you would feel better?*

Jakki: *I wouldn't feel anything, which is better than this depression!*

Mom: *Can I tell you a little secret?*

Jakki: *Sure.*

Mom: *When I was your age, I felt the same way.*

Jakki: *Did you want to kill yourself?*

Mom: *Sometimes, yes . . . but I didn't.*

Jakki: *How did you handle it?*

Mom: *I was tall and skinny and had bad skin, and there was this beautiful Italian girl in my class, Gina, who looked like a movie*

Adolescence

star. It was so depressing!

Jakki: *So, what did you do?*

Mom: *I grew up . . . slowly. I found out that being tall was nice once the other kids caught up with me. Gina is still only 5'2". I found out that being skinny was better than being fat. Gina weighed about 170 pounds the last time I saw her. I started taking care of my complexion and the zits all cleared up, and most of all I started being thankful for all I have.*

Jakki: *Yeah, what have I got to be thankful for?*

Mom: *First of all, you have me and your father, and we love you just the way you are. Second, you have your brain. You are a smart girl, and you can become anything you want to become. Third, look at all the things we have: A comfortable house, a refrigerator full of food, you go to a good school. Sure, some kids have a bigger house or nicer cars, but some kids have no house and don't know where their next meal is coming from. We are very blessed, and you have a bright future ahead of you.*

Jakki: *I guess you're right. It could be a lot worse.*

Mom: *Yes, it could. So, let's see what we can do about clearing up your complexion so you start to feel as beautiful as you really are.*

Which parent is more like you?

Both parents were kind enough to knock and ask permission to come in. Both parents were interested enough to push past the first response to get to the problem. Cheryn's mom took a hard-line approach that didn't acknowledge her daughter's feelings. Instead of asking further questions, she started a lecture. Her points were valid, but the presentation style probably prevented Cheryn from hearing them. Unfortunately, teen depression and even suicide are real problems that need to be taken seriously. Even kids that appear well-balanced and happy can entertain notions of suicide, so it's important to look for any hints.

Jakki's mom took a softer approach. She asked questions, not only acknowledging her daughter's feelings, but discovering the cause of the problem. Rather than lecture, she shared a personal story that showed she really did understand the feelings and the situation, and offered evidence that things will change and probably get better. She offered her daughter hope, which is exactly what someone who is depressed or contemplating suicide needs, plus she took a practical, positive step to better the current situation.

Adolescence

Adolescence is a difficult time for both the child and the parents. It is like going through the Terrible Twos again, but this time with a bigger body and more dangerous ways to act out. The adolescent brain is programmed by nature to reject living with his current family in order to create the desire and ability to leave the comfort of home, go out on his own, and establish a new family. Therefore, it is programmed for risk taking. Adolescents reject everything about childhood and embrace the external appearances of adulthood, often without accepting the responsibilities. The hormones that began to rage in preadolescence become a way of life. It is a natural process of growth, usually with a positive outcome, filled with mistakes, misconceptions, and many surprises along the way.

Many cultures have their rites of passage from childhood to adulthood. In the previous chapter I identified some religious rituals for preteens and early teens. Depending on the life expectancy of the culture, some time during the teen years there will be a ceremony from childhood to adulthood. More primitive cultures had hunting quests or mock battles; American girls have their Sweet Sixteen party; Hispanic girls have the *Quinceanera;* and several Eastern cultures celebrate the 20th birthday with a celebration.

Your child wanted nothing more than to be like you because in his eyes, you were perfect. Your adolescent wants to be nothing like you because in his eyes you are no longer perfect, and he is pursuing ideals. When he becomes an adult, he will realize that everyone is imperfect and appreciate all you did for him. Try to hang on until then.

Adolescence

Major Lessons: Progression from puberty to adulthood, development of the Pre-Frontal Cortex, reckless behavior, learning to drive, extreme emotions, and fascination with love.

Note: Please read the previous chapter(s), as all children develop at different rates and many of the advances at this age are built upon earlier developments. In case your child is a little slower in one area, or in case you missed some of the activities in the previous chapter (possibly because you just gained access to this book recently), it is always a good practice to review where you are coming from before advancing into new territory.

Physically

All the changes I identified in the previous chapter as beginning at the onset of puberty are continuing. The initial shock of changes should be over in the very early teens, and those changes should continue to progress throughout the teens. Boys will grow facial hair and may begin to shave. Girls will develop adult sized breasts. Obviously, there is a big difference between a 13-year-old and a 17-year-old, but adolescence is the common terminology until the age of adulthood, currently 18 in the U.S., but certain privileges like drinking alcohol are delayed until 21. Some taller boys may not reach full height until age 20 or even later.

As your child grows into his body, the awkwardness will disappear: He will experience a new level of strength brought on by his testosterone, and he can regain his coordination with training and practice. Resistance training may become an important part of physical development, but lifting weights should be limited to lighter weights while his bones and joints are still growing. Unfortunately, every teen boy wants to know what his "max" is, and that's where injury can occur. If your child chooses to lift weights, even if he is enrolled in a program at school with a coach, encourage him to do sets of medium to high reps rather than heavy weights to avoid injuring his joints. In his later teens he can begin to push a little heavier with fewer reps.

Raising 4 Dimensional Children in a 2 Dimensional World

Feeding

Healthy diets are healthy at all ages. If your child is heavy or breaking out in acne, cut down on the sweets and processed foods. If your child is skinny, encourage him to eat more. Teen boys seem like bottomless pits. Watch for signs of bulimia or anorexia, especially in girls – they sometimes get bad advice from their friends.

Everything boils down to habits. If they have good eating habits (healthy food in healthy amounts at proper times), everything should be fine. If they have started some bad habits (unhealthy foods in unhealthy amounts at the wrong times), do your best to have a discussion and start new habits. Although you have very little control over what they eat with their friends, you still have control over the groceries you buy and keep in the house. Availability is half the battle.

Sleeping

Teens need eight to ten hours of sleep a night, which may be challenging as their biological clock may have reset two hours later. Teens may naturally want to stay up later than children, but their school schedule may require an early rise, which creates a conflict. The common solution is to "burn the candle at both ends" during the week and try to make up the lost sleep on the weekend. Unfortunately, it doesn't work that way. Lack of sleep during any night leads to reduced focus, memory, and academic performance, as well as anxiety, depression, and aggression.[189] Sleeping late on the weekend doesn't hurt, but it is not the same. Do your best to get your teen to bed, without a phone, tablet, or laptop available, for at least eight hours a night. Habits matter.

Activities

<u>Keyboarding:</u> If your child has not learned how to keyboard properly yet, look into taking an elective course in keyboarding or programming at school. The ability to touch-type will save hundreds of hours in the future.

Adolescence

<u>Sports:</u> Hopefully, your child has chosen a sport or activity of interest by this time, but if not, he should pick one now. He can join school teams, neighborhood programs, or enroll in classes. The competition levels are increasing at this age, so the commitment to training also must go up to keep up. Find a good coach and maybe be the "home coach" to help him develop the discipline to practice at home. The choice of sport is not nearly as important as the discipline and dedication to train and improve. We do live in a competitive world, so learning how to compete is an important skill.

<u>Art:</u> Encourage your child to continue to develop artistic eye-hand coordination skills, whether it's drawing, painting, sculpting, playing a musical instrument, sewing, knitting, carpentry, or auto body repair. Creative outlets require physical skills to carry them out effectively.

<u>Gaming:</u> A limited amount of computer-based gaming is normal for teens in our culture. The manual dexterity required to play most games successfully is a fine motor skill and should be developed if he wants to get along well with his friends. The goal is to balance his two dimensional time with his four dimensional time to enjoy a balanced life.

Note: Use your good judgment in these and any physical recommendation I make. Take whatever precautions you think necessary for your teen in your unique situation (like a pandemic) to keep your child and everyone else safe.

Mentally

In adolescence the brain goes through a massive remodeling: It starts in the back with movement and vision and moves forward to the prefrontal cortex, which finally starts developing in earnest and begins hard wiring itself for the rest of her life. This part of the brain specializes in controlling emotions, behavior, and logical decision making. If that seems like a contradiction to the everyday impulsiveness, rebelliousness, and moodiness you see, please understand that the prefrontal lobe will continue to develop into the early 20s, so don't expect too much in the early teens.[189] The good news is that it is finally developing; the bad news is that it still takes time. Just for perspective, when your teen tries to explain how technology works to you, she probably thinks *you* are mentally impaired.

As her brain learns to process stimuli faster, her reaction time decreases. Her working memory increases, allowing her more "mental space" to solve problems and make plans. Her focus also improves, allowing her to filter out distractions so she can concentrate on the task at hand.[190] Your teen will also develop the ability to think more abstractly, which will show itself in an increased awareness of hypocrisy. Early adolescents are mostly still in the concrete stage, but as they mature, so does their thinking. They will first see hypocrisy in others (including you) yet may not see it in themselves. They may eventually become interested in philosophy and the meaning of life, which is why late teens (college students) can spend all night discussing philosophy, politics, and religion.

Brain development for those who score high on IQ tests seems to peak four years later than those with average scores.[191] Therefore, the smartest kids in elementary school may not be the smartest adolescents or adults. The brain continues to be plastic and adaptive into adulthood, so your child can continue to improve academic performance through training and focus.

Anders Ericsson, a psychologist from Florida State University who has spent over twenty years studying geniuses, prodigies, and other outstanding performers in sports, the arts, and entertainment, is convinced there are no special inherited qualities that distinguish people with expert abilities. In one of his studies, he found that "good" performers put in an average of 9 hours of practice a week, while "superior" performers put in an average of 24 hours of practice a week, which translated to about 10,000 hours of practice before the age of 20. He formed the "10 Year rule" which states that the highest levels of performance and achievement appear to require at least 10 years of intense prior preparation, and he believes that anyone who puts in the necessary time can achieve prodigy-level performance.[192] So if or when your teen finds her passion, she can become a world-class performer or expert as long as she maintains continued focus and dedication to practice.

Teens will begin being more self-directed, so instead of looking to you for a direction, they will increasingly look to their friends, and eventually to themselves, which is the outcome you should be working towards. Help your child learn to set her own goals, which usually entails setting a long-term goal (like becoming a doctor), and then setting short-term goals to achieve along the way (like going to medical school, graduating college with a high GPA, graduating high school with a high GPA, passing chemistry with a high grade, and passing tomorrow's test with a high grade.) An easy and effective way to learn to set goals is to set SMART goals:

> **S**pecific – to get a good job is not specific; to become an elementary school teacher is.
>
> **M**easurable – to look better is not measurable; to lose twenty pounds is.
>
> **A**chievable – to be able to fly is not achievable; to become a pilot is.
>
> **R**ealistic – to become the richest person in the world may not be realistic; to become a millionaire is more realistic.
>
> **T**imely – a dream has no deadline; a goal does.

For example, to graduate high school with her class is a specific, measurable, achievable, realistic, and timely goal. To graduate high school with her class with a 3.5 or better GPA is also a SMART goal, but a little more specific than the first one. Impress upon her that goals can change over time, and when you achieve one goal, you should set another. As another example, if she does become a millionaire, she may set a new goal to become a hundred millionaire, and possibly a billionaire. When she reaches that level, becoming the richest person in the world might be more realistic.

If she has goals that require academics, please re-read the previous chapters with advice on how to be a better student. Be available for her. Ask her to explain her studies to you – if she can teach it, she understands it well. Look online for tips and tricks on how to study better. Generally, people remember primacy and recentcy – the first thing and the last thing. Study in twenty-minute increments, then get up, move around, and breathe before studying some more. Posture can limit the oxygen in your lungs, so study with good posture. Study in spaced repetition: Learn it, review it later, and review it again. Study to remember; cram to forget.[152] Studying for an exam should be in the "review it again" category, not trying to learn it for the first time.

Should your child stay in school?

Professor James Heckman of the University of Chicago researched students in Texas who had taken the GED after dropping out of high school. He found that both the high school graduates and the GED graduates had similar scores on cognitive tests. In other words, the GED takers were as "smart" as the high school graduates. He also found that the GED takers were more likely to quit or get fired from their jobs, had less-stable marriages, and were much more likely to commit a crime. The ability to stay in school developed non-cognitive skills that led to more successful outcomes in life.[193] Once again, test scores seem to predict academic performance, but not success in life. If at all possible, have your child complete high school for the "grit" it takes to stick with something despite the challenges. That does not mean that if you do not finish high school, you have no chance of a successful life. The GED program provides exactly that opportunity. It's just that if you have the choice, staying in school has a track record of producing better results down the road.

Which colleges provide the best upward mobility? Ivy League colleges produce outstanding success rates for their graduates, but Ivy League colleges tend to be attended by students with a high socioeconomic background and high chances of success. The odds of a poor student who gets a scholarship to an Ivy League school graduating are not as high as the odds of that same student attending a mid-tier state college, graduating, and making a good life for herself. Mid-tier state colleges seem to have the highest rate of socioeconomic mobility.[194]

Adolescence

Communication

Listen. Your teenager will complain that nobody understands her. If she talks, listen first before talking. Repeat back to her things she says to show you are listening. Ask questions if you don't quite understand. If she doesn't talk, ask questions that show you are interested. Reach out.

The temptation will be to lecture her, perhaps as your parents lectured you. If so, do you remember those lectures being effective when you were a teen? Probably not. Instead, follow the wisdom of Socrates and ask questions whose answers lead in the direction you want to go. Questions show you are interested in her opinion, plus they make her think and come up with her own conclusions. At the end of the conversation, if you did it well, she will have convinced herself instead of you convincing her.

Talk About Drugs

When you see an opportunity, initiate another conversation about smoking, drinking, and drugs. The conversation you had years ago in Chapter 7 was fine for the time, but a lot has changed since then. The facts about the effects of smoking, drinking, and drugs on the teenage body and mind haven't changed, but your child's attitude probably has. More of her friends may be involved to one degree or another. Have a conversation at least once a year, but more often if you notice anything suspicious: You may smell smoke, vape fragrances, or pot on her clothes or in her hair. You may see other signs like some questionable new friends. Stay involved.

Make your opinions heard, but emphasize your concern for her health and safety first. Point out that these choices are still illegal for her, and now that she is interested in getting a job or getting into a good college, how a criminal record makes both much harder. Avoid lectures and employ searches for evidence and Socratic questioning. Enforce the rules you have set. You are still the adult, and she still lives in your house. You have the right to establish the rules. Of course, you will get better "buy in" if she has some input in the rules, but the responsibility is still yours. Don't be afraid, and don't put it off.

Raising 4 Dimensional Children in a 2 Dimensional World

Talk About Sex

As I said in the puberty discussion about sex in the previous chapter, the talk about sex is not "one and done," but should be an ongoing conversation. At least every six months initiate a conversation, but more often if you see any warning signs. As your teen gets older, it is more likely she will want to become more sexually active, whatever that means among her peers. One of the things you can do is try to keep her involved with friends who are likely to have opinions similar to your own. Peer pressure can work in your favor if her peers want her to be a "good girl."

It's been a long time since I have been a teenager, but I have heard it said that oral sex is the new French kissing. Find out what your daughter's friends think is acceptable and unacceptable . . . by asking her. Ask her opinion on the matter. At some point during her teen years, you will probably need to have the protection talk about condoms and why they are so important. Review the potential negative consequences of sexual contact like pregnancy, STDs, and broken hearts. As she gets older, move your approach away from childlike fear to a more rational fear, so that the precautions she takes are a rational decision – just remember she may not be so rational when in a hot state.

Talk About the Law

Review the talk you had in Chapter 7 about treating police officers and other authorities with respect. Now that your child will be driving and riding with other teens in their cars, the chances to have a run-in with the law have increased dramatically. Reinforce the idea that treating a police officer disrespectfully or just not cooperating fully is asking for trouble, and possibly a life-or-death choice. Impress upon her to do what she has to do to get out of the situation, then report any behavior she believes is illegal to a superior officer. She may not get immediate satisfaction, but she will have survived and been able to enter her objections on the officer's record.

Adolescence

Activities

Much of your child's mental education has been assumed by the school and it takes up a significant amount of her day. Help her keep focused on school achievement while still making time to develop the other three dimensions of her life. One area that might be helpful outside her classroom assignments is preparing for college entrance exams like the SAT, and you may want to consider a special training course to help improve her score on the test.

In addition, help your child with life skills that aren't always taught in academic schools, like;
- How to apply for a job (practice the interview)
- How to open a bank account or PayPal account
- How to write checks and balance a checkbook
- How to get and manage a credit card
- How to pay online or in person electronically
- How to balance saving money vs. spending money
- How and when to buy an expensive item on credit

Journaling is also a good activity for teens, sometimes in the form of a diary. Writing in general provides an opportunity to make her thoughts objective. When she writes thoughts down, first of all, she needs to organize them either when writing, or after she has a chance to see them and evaluate them. Second, writing is an artistic expression. It is a creative outlet. Encourage your child to write a diary, poetry, lyrics to songs, short stories, or just scenes. Writing can also be emotionally therapeutic.

One other academic area you may wish your child to explore is dual enrollment. If your child is a good student, she can enroll in the local junior college or other institution while still in high school and take online classes. It is possible to graduate high school having already earned her first year of college credit (or more). Just make her aware of investing too much of her precious time in her mental dimension, at the possible cost of the other three. High school students tend to get so focused on graduation or building up a good resume to get into a good college, that they may miss some of the important lessons of becoming an adult like independence, integrity, and self-reliance.

Emotionally

Adolescence is not a time for him to attend to your needs, but for you to attend to his. Evolution has programmed him to become a creature motivated to leave a safe home and move into unfamiliar territory. In order to accomplish this illogical feat, the teen brain becomes very sensitive to dopamine and oxytocin.[195]

Dopamine is a neural transmitter that primes and fires reward circuits in the brain. It is the "feel good" hormone that also provides the ability of rapid learning and the extreme emotions attached to winning and losing. Teens love the thrill, always looking for something new and exciting, unusual, or unexpected. Thrill seeking peaks around age 15, but dopamine continues to be a driving force until about 25, especially when other teens are around.[195] Despite being a driving force, dopamine levels have been shown to fall in the teen years, leaving some teens to feel "dopamine deprived." Some psychologists have said that teens may engage in high-risk behaviors to increase their levels of dopamine.[196] (The military takes advantage of this tendency by primarily enlisting soldiers from 18 to 25.) You can help your child get some healthy thrills by enlisting him on sports teams or in other competitions, or just planning exciting, adrenaline-producing activities that are relatively safe like roller coasters or water slides – plus, it's a great way to become the "cool parents."

Oxytocin is not a neural hormone, but it produces the good feelings you get from bonding. It is what motivates your teen to fall in love, to make best friends, and to be part of a group. It also can cause "us vs. them" feelings, where the "us" are him and his friends, and all adults, including you, are the "them."[195] However, research has shown that families who eat dinner together have higher levels of oxytocin, and teens who eat dinner with the family show reduced signs of stressed behavior.[197] That's something simple you can do.

The combination of the two hormones makes adolescents very active socially, sensitive to peer pressure, and open to meeting new people and sharing new experiences. They are developing the same cognitive processes as adults, but tend to weigh risks and rewards

Adolescence

differently because the dopamine creates a higher payoff to the reward.[195] I mentioned in Chapter 1 that video games are actually designed to create small releases of dopamine with each point, goal, or kill, so it is no wonder that teens develop a real addiction to gaming because their brains are more sensitive to dopamine. Actually, teenage brains are more susceptible to all addictions (including drugs), so as I've said before it's a good idea to get them addicted to something healthy, like sports or music.

What else can you do? Well, if you have done your job well up to this point, it should all come together during adolescence. Your time and effort should be paying off compared to the children of your friends, who may not have been so involved. Regardless, your teen needs a framework to operate within. He needs room to experiment, but he has to have solid boundaries. If you are too confining, you will activate his territoriality and get rejection. If you are too permissive, he may hurt himself. Use a light, guiding hand, enforcing rules and consequences, but give him input on the rules and review them every six months or so. As he gets older, permissible actions may change, and he will understand that if you do not agree to something today, you will re-negotiate six months from now, which gives him hope.[195]

In Chapter 3, I described high-reactive and low-reactive infants, their personality traits, and the most likely personality traits they would have during their second year and during adolescence. At 18, adolescents who were high-reactive infants tend to report more unrealistic worries, including visiting new places, meeting strangers, entering crowds, and brooding over possible harm. They are at only a slightly higher risk for developing anxiety or depression, but their risk aversion makes them less likely to drive at high speeds, experiment with drugs, engage in sex at an early age, or cheat on exams. It also makes them suitable for valuable professions like computer programmers, historians, scientists, and mathematicians. 18-year-old adolescents who were low-reactive infants are at a slightly higher risk for asocial behavior. Their sociability and willingness to take risks make them valuable members of our society, and more likely to leave home to attend a faraway college or leave one job for another that appears more interesting or challenging.[198] However, as has been researched and proven over and over, people are born with tendencies, but those tendencies may or may not develop in a given environment. If your teen seems to want security and certainty over freedom and uncertainty, that is not a life sentence. Both tendencies produce valuable and happy adults, and adolescents have the power to evaluate themselves and their tendencies, and take positive steps to change if they so desire.

Sex hormones also affect mood and can vary by the time of day or the time of the month. Teen girls will go through PMS as part of their menstruation, but the effects can be minimized by taking moderate snacks through the appropriate days to even out levels of blood sugar. Teen boys might experience fits of violent male testosterone (VMT), which can be treated by engaging in a tiring, non-competitive physical activity like going for a run.[199]

At any age, habits are the key, but the habits developed during the teen years have a better chance of carrying over into adulthood. First you create your habits, then your habits create you. As I cited in a previous chapter, about 43% of everyday activities are done repeatedly, almost every day in the same context.[200] Help your child reduce stress and reduce the chance of impulsive decisions by creating consistent daily habits.

> **Ways to Form a New Habit**
>
> 1. Make a decision.
> 2. Set a SMART Goal.
> 3. Make it fun or at least reduce friction.
> 4. Devise a reward.
> 5. Continue until it becomes automatic.
>
> **Other Tips:**
> Add it to an old habit.
> Establish cues to remind you.

Adequate sleep is important. Sleep deprivation leads to a bad attitude, so try to establish a daily routine that allows for enough sleep.

Establish wake-up habits: Don't hit the snooze button. When he hears the alarm, he should get up, go to the bathroom, take care of

Adolescence

personal hygiene, make his bed, get dressed, eat breakfast, perhaps make his own lunch, and prepare for school.

The school day should be organized by a schedule of classes. After school may be an athletic activity, school club, an after-school job, or a ride home. Once home, he should have a generic schedule of physical activity, homework and study time, and perhaps chores. Each child will have a different schedule depending on his individual needs, family needs, membership in various activities, whether those activities are in season or not, and any upcoming special events. Allow him to set his own schedule, but don't be shy about asking why he is devoting so much time to this or that, and asking why not try a different way that you think might be better.

Also take a close look at specific habits that lead to trouble, or what psychologists call automaticity. If someone calls your child a bad name, how will he react? Will he get in a fight? (Boys tend to fight physically more than girls, but girls can get into word fights or social media fights.) Will he withdraw and get depressed? If his friends are all doing something illegal, will he just follow along? Research on the infamous south side of Chicago showed that certain interventions like the Becoming a Man (BAM) program could reduce arrest rates of troubled youth in the program by 44%, while increasing their chances to pass their classes and stay in school. Unfortunately, the results were not permanent as once the youth were no longer in the program, their results reverted to the average.[201] Your child needs to form habits that last, and the earlier he ingrains those habits, the longer they will last. Although these are emotional reactions, in the Spiritual section of this chapter I will present some strategies for helping your child develop an internal locus of control so that he is not so easily influenced by the words and actions of others.

As I mentioned in previous chapters, disrespect for authority may start showing up, especially now in the teenage years. It is part of their mechanism for being able to break away and establish their own identity, so lack of respect for authority will seem cool and probably be encouraged by their friends. Your best defense is to remind your son what it feels like to be treated that way, and to appeal to his sense of "treating others how you would like to be treated." If your child demonstrates leadership qualities, he might even be able to convince his friends that respect is cool, and disrespect is not.

One special technique you can teach your teen for better emotional balance is the Heart Lock-In technique, which is designed to promote sustained positive emotional states. On a regular basis (perhaps at a specific time each day – before going to sleep?) and whenever your child is upset, ask him to focus his attention in the area of his heart while intentionally remembering a positive feeling like appreciation or love for someone special for about five to fifteen minutes. This emotional restructuring technique can reinforce a baseline positive outlook that leads to physical efficiency, mental sharpness, and emotional stability.[202]

Two final pieces of emotional advice:
1. Jewelry doesn't make you valuable
2. Tattoos don't make you beautiful.

Your child's value and beauty come from within. If he feels worthless, all the gold chains he can carry won't change that. If he feels ugly, a fully tattooed body won't change that. Depending on your family's culture, advise him on how to groom himself to present the proper image like an actor preparing for a role: Choosing the proper wardrobe, hairstyle, posture, and gestures to communicate his unique personality.

Adolescent Myths

The Imaginary Audience

First coined by the psychologist David Elkind, the imaginary audience is a mistaken belief in that the adolescent imagines that he is so important that there is an audience focused on his every move and hungry for every bit of information about him. Social media like Facebook and Instagram feed into this fable by allowing people to take pictures of their lunch, their pets, and themselves grocery shopping, as if it were celebrity news. Social media provides the perfect outlet for the belief, and if you get a few "likes" on your post . . . then maybe people really are interested?

Adolescence

The downside of this myth is that it causes teens to engage in attention-getting activities, including outrageous dress and actions. If you notice your child acting out to get attention, first of all, give him some attention. That may be his way of saying that he really needs more attention from you. Second, remind him of some of his good character qualities. Any idiot can do something shocking. Wearing or doing something outrageous may get him momentary attention, but in a short attention span world, it won't last. Instead of LOOKING interesting, he should focus on BEING interesting by being honest, faithful to his friends, and genuinely caring about people – those are characteristics really worth paying attention to.

The Personal Fable

Also coined by David Elkind as a corollary to the Imaginary Audience, the Personal Fable goes something like, "I am the center of attention because I am so special and unique. No one else has ever suffered the depth and intensity of my emotions." Of course, everyone is unique, but very few are so unique that they are the center of everyone else's attention. More likely, everyone else is thinking about themselves, and you are only important to yourself. Another part of the personal fable is the Superman Myth explained below.

Help your teen understand that although he is important to you and the center of your world, he is probably not the center of everyone else's. Just because HE never experienced the intensity of his emotions before, doesn't mean no one else ever has. Most likely, other people have loved as intensely, if not more so, and have suffered greater hardships than he has. He may be exceptional in some ways, but in most ways, he is very normal.

The Superman Myth

Teens tend to think they are never going to die. The line of thinking goes something like this: "Sure, other people may get sick, get killed in car accidents, or become addicted to drugs, but that could never happen to me. After all, it hasn't happened so far, so I must be doing something right." And although it may be true that he is doing something right, that doesn't give him the license to do something riskier or more dangerous. Actions have consequences.

Raising 4 Dimensional Children in a 2 Dimensional World

Take time to discuss with your teen every time you see a news story of a teenager who gets hurt or dies doing something risky. You don't want to depress him or make him afraid to live, but it's important to impress upon him that he is not Superman, and he can get hurt or die by making bad decisions, and sometimes even by accident. He must do his best to avoid dangerous situations and dangerous people, and not listen when others try to goad him into doing something risky.

Vampire Friends

Vampires who drink blood are not real, but there are people who seem to feed on others emotionally like vampires. They talk about themselves incessantly and don't care about anyone else. They think nothing of dumping a load of emotional garbage on you and then driving off feeling better.

First of all, make sure your child is not an emotional vampire (and you, yourself, are not one either, as he may have learned it from you.) Second, help him identify the signs. Friendships should be mutual. Friends help each other through rough times, but if he has a friend that always takes and never gives, that is not a healthy relationship. It may be time to find another, more positive friend.

Frankenstein Envy

Comparison is natural for adolescents but can lead to either motivation or envy. Discuss the positive and negative of comparisons with your teen: When someone else does or has something good, it could motivate him to also do or earn something good. If, instead, he becomes jealous, it only leads him down a dark road.

As your child moves into the teenage years, especially girls will begin to make the illogical emotional mistake I call Frankenstein Envy: I wish I had Susie's hair, and Juanita's complexion, and Mary's car, and LaKeshia's personality, etc. The obvious flaw is taking the best parts of each girl and assembling them into one ideal individual, so monstrous that no one, not even the list of gifted friends, can compare favorably.

Help your child understand that she may not have Susie's hair, but she is good in math; she may not have Juanita's complexion, but she actually has better hair than Juanita. If she expresses this kind of

Adolescence

envy, first help her to admit and identify the feelings, and then help her understand that everyone has their own strengths and weaknesses, and if looking at others motivates you to take better care of your hair or complexion, that is a good thing – and then show her how to do it.

Social media also provides a tough place for comparisons. She shouldn't compare herself to a Photoshopped image of one of the most beautiful models in the world. It's just not realistic. Even her friends tend to post only their highlights on social media, and if your daughter compares her life to the highlights of her friends lives, she is likely to come up short. The missing piece of information you need to provide is that her friends have the same problems that she is having, but they just don't post them, so their lives are likely no better than hers. The constant comparison to others' highlight reels along with the fear of missing out (FOMO) are two reasons why living a two dimensional life can be emotionally draining.

If I sound too depressing, I apologize. I am trying to help you identify problems you and your child may be facing. The teen years are filled with land mines that may explode at any moment, but they can also be a joyous, fun-filled time. As the awkwardness of puberty develops into a more adult-like body, your child's self-image will improve. A combination of hormones, improved cognitive ability, and undeniable physical ability will boost most adolescents' confidence. It is a time of increased freedom and fun with friends before taking on the responsibilities of adulthood. Adolescence can be totally awesome!

Activities

Continue using the emotional activities from previous chapters (especially if you did not use them when your child was that age) and upgrade the sophistication based on your teen's cognitive and emotional development. Also try these:

<u>Soup Kitchen:</u> Volunteer to help at a local Food Bank or Soup Kitchen (perhaps on a Thanksgiving) and bring your teen along. First of all, it makes clear all the things he should be thankful for by showing him up close and personal those who don't have his advantages. It's powerful

medicine for depression. Second, it develops compassion. Third, it provides a good feeling of self-worth to help those less fortunate than you. Discuss with him whether he would like to make it a regular practice.

Play the Part: Your teen's school probably has a Drama Club or will put on a play. If he is interested at all in entertainment, encourage him to join the club or be part of the production either as a performer or perhaps as part of the stage and support crew.

YouTube: As an alternative to traditional stage performance, YouTube has made it possible for anyone to be an international performer, producer, or director. Help your child develop his own YouTube channel by discussing what to produce, how, and how often. Social media trends change rapidly, especially among young people, so platforms like Instagram, Snap Chat, Tic-Toc, or something else might be more desirable for your child and his friends than YouTube. Just be sure to be a subscriber so that you can see what he posts.

Motivation: Help your teen become more positive by taking advantage of programs by motivational speakers like Anthony Robbins, Zig Ziglar, Joel Osteen, and others. If your child is a reader, buy some motivational books. If he is a listener, get some audio presentations for him to listen to instead of music when working out so he can feed his mind and emotions while he is exercising his body. Alternately, you can play them in your car when traveling together and then discuss what they say.

How to be a Motivator: Point out that motivational speakers are not the only motivators in the world. Ask your teen how he could motivate classmates, teammates, friends, and even other family members. Discuss techniques like complimenting others, cheering them on, getting commitments, and following up with them. Then switch the discussion to how he could motivate himself using similar methods.

Leadership: Discuss leadership with your teen by analyzing politicians, teachers, coaches, and other leaders you both know.

Adolescence

Adolescents are always complaining about some authority figure, so when he starts, help him understand why they are doing what they are doing and maybe ask how they could have done it better. If your child has a leadership role on his team, club, or class, ask questions about decisions he has to make and what he is considering while making them. Push a little deeper to ask how he might lead himself a little better. Leaders are not born, but developed through experience, so help him gain the experience.

<u>Active or Passive:</u> Explain the difference between being active and passive. Passive people feel like victims, as they feel they have no control over things that happen to them. Active people become victors because they don't wait for things to happen; they make things happen. Ask your teen how he can become more active in getting something he wants, for example, the best way to have a friend is to be a friend.

<u>Problem People:</u> Adolescents love to complain. Explain to your teen that there are problem identifiers and problem solvers. Problem identifiers are important because they can see what's wrong. Problem solvers are *more* important because they not only see what's wrong, but they also do something about it. Ask your teen if he thinks he is a problem identifier or a problem solver. Then, the next time he complains about something, ask the question again.

<u>What Else Could It Mean:</u> Building on the activity <u>What Else Could It Be</u> from Chapter 8, move the game into emotionally charged events like, "I sat down next to Sally at lunch, and she got up and left." "OK, what do you think that means?" "Sally hates me." "OK, what else could it mean?"

<u>Frame Shift:</u> Help your teen shift the frame away from himself when his personal fable makes him feel inadequate. For example, if he is upset because his girlfriend cheated on him, instead of framing the situation only on himself, expand or shift the frame to include the girl, who is a cheater and doesn't love him the way he loves her. Help him change his perspective to see the bigger picture.

Raising 4 Dimensional Children in a 2 Dimensional World

<u>The Thought Police</u>: When your child is upset ask, "Why do you feel that way?" He will probably assign the responsibility to someone else by saying they did something to make him feel that way. Dig deeper, to help him understand that what someone else did was just the stimulus. The Thought Police would say that he has control over how he reacts to that stimulus. He probably made some interpretation of their action, then he had an emotional response to that interpretation. Help him understand that (1) he may have misinterpreted the action, and (2) he could choose to respond in another way or with a different emotion. It won't be easy, but if he imagines the Thought Police catching him when he doesn't accept responsibility for his reactions, over time he may realize that he has the power to interrupt the process and actually choose his emotional reactions.

<u>Thoughts on Trial</u>: When your child is upset, for example he didn't make the baseball team, teach him to (1) Identify the thought that is upsetting him (I'm no good). Name it to shame it. (2) Present the evidence to defend the thought (he didn't make the baseball team). (3) Present the prosecution of evidence against the thought (he's good at science and has good friends). (4) Make a rational, not emotional judgment on the thought (It's not that he's no good, it that he was not good enough *at baseball* to make the team. If he practices, he might make the team next year, or he could focus his time and energy on something else he also enjoys.)

<u>Take Action</u>: Upgrade the <u>Compassion</u> activity from Chapter 7. Instead of just imagining the bad guys when they are being good, brainstorm on what you could do in various situations to show compassion to these poor, unhappy souls. What kinds of things can you do to prevent people from becoming bad people, and what kinds of things can you do when confronted with an angry, aggressive, or dangerous person? Your child has probably experienced some "Stop the Bully" lessons (if not, search online for strategies), so discuss these with two goals in mind: (1) how to deal with bullies, and (2) developing a creative habit to find more imaginative actions to take to prevent or diffuse potentially dangerous situations.

Adolescence

Group Activities

These are some activities you might use in the car during a carpool, at home when your child's friend(s) come(s) over for dinner or to watch a game, or even at a restaurant to make use of the waiting time. Of course, you can use some of the individual activities above with one teen taking your part, or you might use one of these group activities with your child alone, with you taking the part of one teen.

I Feel Stressed: Ask each teen to complete the sentence, "I get really stressed when _____." You might even share a stressor of your own to be part of the discussion. Let them discuss each answer by identifying a first impulse reaction to the stress, and rating that reaction on a scale of one to five, with five being the best and one being the worst. Then, everyone in the group should brainstorm some other ways to cope with the situation that might be worthy of a five.

What did you see: When your teen has at least one other friend with him, be on the lookout for something interesting to see. Point it out so they both watch it, then ask them to describe exactly what they saw (this is a good activity to try after seeing a big play in a game.) Chances are good both eyewitness accounts will not be exactly the same. Point out the differences and help them understand that two people can see the same event and see it differently, which should help them realize they should not rely so heavily on what other people say.

How would You Do It: When your teen has at least one other friend with him, think up any imaginary project and ask, "John, if you were going to make a _____, how would you do it?" When he answers, then ask the other one how he would do it. Then say, "Those are both good ideas, but pretty different. If you two were going to build it together, how would you work with each other?" Listen as they compromise (or not) and offer advice on how to work together, and at the end, offer commentary about leadership principles one or the other demonstrated to get the job done.

Raising 4 Dimensional Children in a 2 Dimensional World

<u>If You were the Coach:</u> While watching a game, ask one teen, "If you were the coach, what would you do next?" A couple of plays later, ask the same question to another teen. The point is to give them imaginary leadership practice, weighing what to do in a particular situation with the materials (or players) at hand.

<u>Difficult Conversations:</u> Start difficult conversations about emotionally upsetting subjects like race, drugs, or sex. Help your teen understand that he shouldn't be afraid of feeling vulnerable, but should be grateful that he has an opportunity to learn how to handle different feelings and situations. We all have blind spots and difficult conversations help us learn what we didn't see or didn't know.

Spiritually

Your child is starting to look like an adult. She is starting to claim she is an adult, with adult rights. It's time for her to start accepting responsibility like an adult. Rights don't come without responsibilities. Maturity is not measured by age, but by willingness to accept responsibility. She doesn't need to get a job and pay for her own apartment yet, but she should accept responsibility for her decisions. Ideally, in her teens she should develop an internal locus of control and realize she has control over certain things in her life. If you make all of her decisions for her, she will feel (rightly so) that she has no control over her own life, which may lead to depression, and almost certainly will lead to an inability to handle the challenges of life on her own. If she looks to you, teachers, coaches, or friends to tell her what to do, she will never gain experience at making decisions. On the other hand, if she learns step-by-step to take control of her schedule, her emotional reactions, and her adolescent life, she will be better able to make decisions when life throws the inevitable curve ball.

Let me put it this way: If your daughter is used to being told what to do and obeying, what will she do when her boyfriend tells her he expects her to have sex with him? On the other hand, if you have taught her to make her own decisions and always question the opinions of others, she will be more likely to be guided by her beliefs rather than his. The same principle applies to any future decision your teen

Adolescence

will make, especially when pressed by peer pressure, and the earlier she gains that locus of control, the less stress you will have over her decisions.

During the teen years your child may (or may not) advance to Kohlberg's highest level of morality, moving from the social contract mentality of ideal reciprocity to one of universal ethical principles. In the previous chapter, I pointed out that ideal reciprocity meant that you would do unto others as you would have them do unto you. This level of morality is no longer self-centered, as it focuses on how to treat others, but it is still self-based, as it uses your own desires as the guiding principle for behavior. Universal ethical principles move away from the self, identifying principles that are simply right or wrong, regardless of how they affect you. For example, sacrificing your life for someone else or for a worthy cause obviously does not benefit you – you die and are gone – but those who believe in universal ethical principles may be willing to make that sacrifice.

Why? One reason is the belief in an afterlife. If your religion believes you will be rewarded or punished for your actions in this life by going to heaven, hell, or being reincarnated, then acting rightly is more important than living or dying. Sacrificing this life is an investment in the next life, and just a good business decision. If you are a secularist who doesn't believe in an afterlife, it becomes harder to justify sacrificing your own life. However, when it comes to moral decisions, even secularists may believe in separating effort from outcome. When we develop physical, mental, and even emotional skills, outcome is the feedback we need to improve our technique. We look in the mirror to improve our dance moves. We take tests to measure our ability to study and learn. We view another's emotional reaction to what we say. The outcome helps us improve what we do.

However, in the spiritual realm of universal principles, the question is no longer what we do, but why we do it. We must act rightly – we must do the right thing, even if we may not like the outcome. If someone is dying, we do our best to comfort them – not because it will keep them from dying; not because we would want them to comfort us; but because it is the right thing to do. If a cashier accidentally gives you too much change, you give the extra money back – not because you would get caught; not because you would want her to do the same for you if you were the cashier; but because it is the right thing to do. For the things within our control, we try our best, and then learn from our failures. For those things beyond our control, we do the right thing regardless of the outcome.

The biggest challenge in doing the right thing becomes determining the principles at stake. Morality isn't always an obvious choice between right or wrong. There are often fifty shades of gray. For example, killing is wrong. Does that mean you cannot kill someone who is trying to kill you or your family? Or could you stop him without killing him? Is there another option?

Lying is wrong, but what is truth? Which truth? When your grandmother says, "Does this dress make me look fat?" one truth might be that the dress doesn't make her look fat, but the constant diet of cookies, candies, and cakes makes her look fat. Another truth is that she definitely looks like a fat old lady no matter which dress she wears. Another truth is that you love her and to you she looks beautiful. Each of these statements is true, so which truth would you tell her? There really are alternative truths.

Because identifying the principle is so important and yet so difficult, we need practice and education on identifying the relevant principles. Take abortion as an example: Is the proper principle the woman's right to do with her body as she pleases, or is the proper principle the baby's right to life? Depending on your religion or your own morality, you may choose one principle over the other.

Have some difficult discussions with your teen about moral issues that come up in news stories, things that happen at school, situations in movies, and whenever possible. Education is the process of replacing inaccurate beliefs or assumptions with more accurate ones. For your teen to enjoy and value these conversations, you must listen to her and take her opinions seriously. You don't have to agree with her, but if you assume that you are right and she is wrong, she will shut you out. If you listen carefully, you may actually learn something in the process and share with each other some deep

Adolescence

connections that can continue for a lifetime. After all, she probably doesn't have those kinds of discussions with her friends.

Encourage your teen to pray to get answers to her most pressing questions. Children pray to get something like a new bike; adults pray for guidance to understand something and make the right choice. Get her to move away from wanting "things" and more toward wanting to be better. Also encourage her to continue to say prayers of appreciation every night before going to sleep and every morning before getting out of bed. Gratitude is a powerful antidote to the depression many teens feel.

Encourage her to read scripture and to attend religious services with you and the rest of the family. Teens are searching for answers in a confusing world. Religion can provide those answers and give meaning to her insecure life.

Her questioning of authority may lead her to question your family's religion. Answer her questions the best you can and refer her to a religious leader if you don't have all the answers. Your faith and your example still have a powerful effect from your spirit to her spirit, even if you can't supply logically or emotionally correct answers.

Encourage your teen to meditate to achieve a sense of calm and well-being. Even if you don't believe in meditation, she can achieve a similar feeling of well-being just by closing her eyes as if she were going to sleep and resting for a few minutes.[203]

Activities:

Values vs. Feelings: Help your teen distinguish between values and feelings to help her make decisions on morals and not emotions. For example, say a word like, "Revenge." Your teen should identify it as a feeling, not a value. Some words like "compassion" and "empathy" can be both feelings and values, so the explanation would be more important than the answer.

Dinner Guest: Ask, "If you could invite anyone to dinner, alive or dead, who would you invite?" to start a discussion of heroes and role models, and to discuss their values.

Raising 4 Dimensional Children in a 2 Dimensional World

<u>What's His Agenda:</u> When watching television commercials or political ads, ask your teen, "What are they trying to do?" Watch one of the biased opinion shows like those on Fox News or MSNBC, and ask, "What's his (or her) agenda?" Help her realize that not everything you read, see on TV, or see on the Internet is true, and most are just the opinion of someone with an agenda. Being able to identify the agenda helps create a healthy dose of skepticism, which will help her make better choices.

<u>Shift Attention:</u> An important meta-cognitive skill is the ability to shift attention away from a temptation and toward a more positive feeling or action. Many of the mental, emotional, and spiritual activities presented in previous chapters helped develop this skill, but now your teen is old enough to develop it on her own by sheer focus. An undisciplined mind will continue to think the same thought over and over, whether that thought is anger, depression, or lust. A disciplined mind realizes what is happening and intentionally shifts attention to a more positive thought, possibly with the aid of some physical action. In other words, instead of feeling depressed, go for a run, or dance, or shoot some hoops.

<u>Cheerleading:</u> All the great teams have cheerleaders, so why not your great teen? You can be her cheerleading captain, but she needs to learn how to be her own best cheerleader. Help her identify her best qualities – physical qualities are important to combat Frankenstein Envy – but character qualities like courage, resilience, and determination are more important to develop self-worth, especially in the face of emotional trauma. She needs to understand her strong points and be able to say them out loud with confidence. Practice with her. Then, whenever she feels down, she can motivate herself by replacing a negative thought with a positive one, and recounting her specific strengths that will help her overcome the current challenge.

<u>Reduce Friction:</u> When your teen sets a goal, discuss with her how to make that goal happen. Give her the lead in the discussion to make her think things through, but ask questions and identify potential problems that can be solved with a better plan. Friction in this sense is anything

that slows down your progress. If your teen wants to set aside two hours to study every night but keeps getting distracted by texts from her friends, a way to reduce friction would be to turn off the phone for those two hours and then check her messages when she is finished studying. Discuss creative ways to reduce friction to help her achieve her goals.

Love: Teens are obsessed with love, so help your teen understand the difference between emotional love and spiritual love. Emotional love is a feeling about a person that can change according to their behavior: You can even hate someone you once loved. Spiritual love is more a belief than a feeling, and it does not change according to a person's behavior. Spiritual love is expansive: It wants to grow to encompass more and more people. You can love those who hate you. You can love those who want to hurt you. The opposite of spiritual love is contractive: It is afraid. It excludes. It hides. Help your teen not only understand spiritual love, but experience it.

Driving

Driving a car is a complex activity: It takes physical skill and practice, it takes mental concentration and knowledge of the law, and it takes emotional self-control. The average car weighs over 2,000 pounds and has over 100 horsepower, which makes it a potentially lethal machine not only for the driver, but for the passengers, and anyone else on or near the road. The leading cause of death among adolescents 15 to 19 years old in the U.S. is auto accidents (followed by suicide and homicide) according to the CDC.[204] If your child's high school has a driver's education course, it is a good investment of time. If not, there are plenty of online courses, and you should spend some time yourself teaching your teen to drive safely and offering advice during practice.

Practice off the road first, in an empty parking lot, if possible, before attempting to drive on empty roads in quiet neighborhoods. Only go into traffic after you both have a lot of confidence. Emphasize that accidents happen when you least expect it – when a child runs out into the road chasing a ball, or a drunk driver wanders over the center line. Activate your adolescent's multi-tasking brain to think about what dangers could happen and constantly be on the lookout in case one does happen. Of course, texting or even looking at a phone is a no-no. Whoever is calling or texting is not worth dying for . . . or killing someone else. Never drink and drive. If his friends want to drink, suggest your child be the designated driver to solve two problems: (1) it keeps your teen from drinking, and (2) it protects him and his friends from alcohol related accidents.

The reason teen auto insurance is so high is that most teens will get into a accident in the first few years of driving. Choose the safest car you can find that provides the most protection. Motorcycles offer almost no protection, so they are a recipe for disaster, but you will have to make your own decision there. I recommend avoiding all high-performance machines until after the thrill-seeking age has passed. However, if you can find and afford a performance driving school that teaches some higher-level driving skills, especially driving on ice and snow, it could prove invaluable. Wet or icy roads and blown out tires can happen to anyone, so learning how to control your vehicle if it starts to slide could be a lifesaver.

Finally, emphasize to your teenager that professional race car drivers operate in a controlled environment: A racetrack with no access, one that the driver has studied extensively, and the only other people on the road are professional drivers. Street racing has none of these safeguards. Remind your teen that public roads have other cars, pedestrians, dogs, and lots of other surprises, and the other driver is obviously someone willing to take dangerous risks . . . and may be alcohol impaired. Before being drawn into someone else's Fast and Furious dream, he has to think, "What could possibly go wrong?"

Summary

Adolescence is a time of innocence and insolence, when the best and worst impulses struggle for possession of your teen. It is a time of contradictions, when no adolescent really wants to be understood, yet they constantly complain that no one understands them. If you follow Maslow's original hierarchy of needs, your teen may advance to the self-actualization level, may not reach that level until he becomes an adult, or may never reach that level at all. Of course, you want to move him to the highest level you can, but this is an area where you can only control your effort and not the outcome.

There are massive differences between a 13-year-old and a 17-year-old, physically, mentally, emotionally, and spiritually. Depending on how well you have been educating him, and continue to do so, the both of you will make it to adulthood – but that's not the finish line. The umbilical cord may have been cut at birth, but the connection between children and their parents (especially their mothers) continues for a lifetime. You share the same blood and many years of shared experience. After he has successfully managed to break away and become independent, he will return and appreciate all you did.

Nature has programmed him to be rebellious – how else would he be able to leave the comfort and safety of his home to venture out into the world to make his own home and family? Don't take it personally. He's probably not rebelling against you; he's rebelling against everything (the proverbial rebel without a cause) to muster the strength he needs to strike out and find himself and his place in the world. You just happen to be in the way.

It's still your job to keep him safe. Set boundaries that allow him to get his thrills in a safe way. Help him learn to think more logically. Help him learn to think before acting or reacting. Help him find out about love (and maybe get a broken heart) without causing a pregnancy or catching an STD. Help him find a safe way to handle his emotional impulses, possibly in sports or other physical activities. If he has found his passion, encourage him to pursue it. World-class ability takes years of training and thousands of hours of practice, which usually begin in childhood or early adolescence. Adolescent brains are prone to addiction, so see if you can encourage an addiction to sports, music, art, or academics.

Help him take responsibility for his feelings and actions. Help him get his first job, learn how to earn and control his money, so that it doesn't control him. Teach him how to drive safely. Keep him on track to graduate high school and perhaps get accepted into college. Help him form healthy habits and set SMART goals. Be on the lookout for his belief in some of the common teenage myths, and continue to talk with him about drugs, sex, and ethics.

Raising 4 Dimensional Children in a 2 Dimensional World

After a lot of care and commotion, you will have helped produce a valuable adult who will one day raise well-balanced, 4 Dimensional children of his own.

Screen Time

Now that you probably have to allow your child onto social media, it's also a good idea to become at least a friend on her social media accounts, but even better to have her passwords so you can log in and monitor her accounts whenever you want. She may be upset that "big brother is watching her," but she will behave much better knowing that you can see what she sees, and she will tell her friends to keep the content clean, too. She may complain that she wants privacy, that you are cyberstalking her, but (a) it is your phone that you pay for, and (b) she is still a minor and your responsibility. Give her room and respect, and only intervene when you see a real problem. The less you comment and question, the better she will accept your monitoring, but as cited in the previous chapter, what your child sees on social media can mean the difference between life and death.

Continue to discuss the amount of time she spends on social media and understand that she may not be rational about it. Social media companies have dozens of engineers creating algorithms, sometimes even artificial intelligence algorithms, designed to keep her attention with steady shots of dopamine. Because teenage minds are susceptible to addiction in general and dopamine specifically, it's easy to understand how they get addicted to social media, and why someone like you needs to be the voice of reason by setting and enforcing limits. Computers and phones are wonderful servants, but harsh, unfeeling masters.

Research shows that teens who spend more time on social media are more prone to anxiety[205] and young adults who spend more time on social media feel more isolated.[206] Of course, your child thinks she is the exception to the statistics (Superman Myth), but why fight the odds? She should go with the flow and follow the path of least resistance by spending less time in the 2 dimensional world and more

Adolescence

time face to face with people.

Note: As all children are unique and develop at different rates, I recommend you read the previous chapter in case your child happens to develop more slowly in one area or another, or in case you gained access to this book after your child became a teen. Specifically, some of the activities might well be continued into the older years.

Also please use your own good judgment in following any advice I offer. Research is subject to change and my advice may be based on research that has since changed or been updated since this publishing. Choose your actions based on your own beliefs, experiences, research, and judgment, especially during extenuating circumstances (like a pandemic.)

Recommended Resources:

https://www.babygaga.com/17-coming-of-age-ceremonies-from-other-cultures/
https://www.helenfarabee.org/poc/view_doc.php?type=doc&id=37673&cn=1272
https://www.gov.mb.ca/healthychild/mcad/growingupok.pdf
https://www.gov.mb.ca/healthychild/mcad/helpgrowingupok.pdf
https://health.gov/myhealthfinder/topics/everyday-healthy-living/sexual-health/talk-your-kids-about-sex
https://www.edutopia.org/article/getting-creative-sel
https://littlehumans.com/
https://www.cebc4cw.org/program/helping-the-noncompliant-child/detailed
http://www.incredibleyears.com/
https://www.gamesofgenius.com/
https://www.child-encyclopedia.com
https://toolsofthemind.org/
https://mindup.org/
https://www.mindinthemaking.org/
https://www.vroom.org/
https://parentsasteachers.org/

References:

189. Strauch, Barbara. *The Primal Teen: What the New Discoveries about the Teenage Brain Tell Us about Our Kids.* New York: Anchor Books, 2003, pp. 103-104.

190. Luna, B; Garver, K; Urban, T; *et. al.* "Maturation of Cognitive Processes from Late Childhood to Adulthood." *Child Development,* September/October 2004, pp. 1357-1372.

191. Brynie, Faith Hickman. *101 Questions Your Brain has Asked about Itself but Couldn't Answer . . . until Now.* Minneapolis: Twenty-First Century Books, 2008, p. 137.

192. Restak, Richard, MD. *The New Brain – How the Modern Age is Rewiring Your Mind.* Rodale and St. Martin's Press, 2003, p. 23.

193. Heckman, James. "What's Not on the Test: The Overlooked Factors that Determine Success." NPR; *Hidden Brain;* May 13, 2019. https://www.npr.org/templates/transcript/transcript.php?storyId=721733303. Accessed June 22, 2021.

194. Chetty, Raj. "Zipcode Destiny: The Persistent Power of Place and Education." NPR; *Hidden Brain;* November 12, 2018. https://www.npr.org/templates/transcript/transcript.php?storyId=666993130. Accessed June 22, 2021.

195. Caremans, Gregory. *"Neuroscience and Parenting."* https://www.udemy.com/course/neuroscience-and-parenting/ Section 5.30. Accessed May 29, 2021.

196. Brynie, Faith Hickman. *101 Questions Your Brain has Asked about Itself but Couldn't Answer . . . until Now.* Minneapolis: Twenty-First Century Books, 2008, p. 85.

197. Howard, PJ. *Owner's Manual for Happiness.* p. 50. https://paradigmpersonality.com/wp-content/uploads/2017/08/OMH-Ch-2-Boosters-Downers-Myths.pdf. Accessed June 22, 2021.

198. Kagan, Jerome, PhD. "Temperament." Encyclopedia on Early Childhood Development, updated 2019, pp. 13-14. www.child-encyclopedia.com/temperament/complete-topic. Accessed June 22, 2021.

199. Howard, PJ. *Owner's Manual for Happiness.* p. 73. https://paradigmpersonality.com/wp-content/uploads/2017/08/OMH-Ch-2-Boosters-Downers-Myths.pdf. Accessed June 22, 2021.

Adolescence

200. Wood, Wendy. "Creatures of Habit: How Habits Shape Who We Are – and Who We Become." NPR; *Hidden Brain;* December 30, 2019. https://www.npr.org/transcripts/787160734. Accessed June 15, 2021.

201. Ludwig, Jens; and Pollack, Harold. "On the Knife's Edge: Using Therapy to Address Violence Among Teens." NPR; *Hidden Brain*; January 6, 2020. https://www.npr.org/transcripts/794016613. Accessed June 22, 2021.

202. Arguelles, Lourdes; McCraty, Rollin; and Rees, Robert A. "The Heart in Holistic Education." HeartMath Institute; Assets; Uploads; 2015. https://www.heartmath.org/assets/uploads/2015/01/heart-in-education.pdf. Accessed June 15, 2021.

203. Howard, PJ. *Owner's Manual for Happiness.* pp. 51-52. https://paradigmpersonality.com/wp-content/uploads/2017/08/OMH-Ch-2-Boosters-Downers-Myths.pdf. Accessed June 22, 2021.

204. Curtin, Sally C, *et.al*. "Recent Increases in Injury Mortality Among Children and Adolescents Aged 10-19 Years in the United States: 1999-2016." Centers for Disease Control; *National Vital Statistics Reports*; Volume 67, Number 4. National Vital Statistics Reports Volume 67, Number 4, June 01, 2018 Deaths: Recent Increases in Injury Mortality Among Children and Adolescents Aged 10–19 Years in the United States: 1999–2016 (cdc.gov). Accessed June 22, 2021.

205. Raudsepp, Lennart; and Kais, Kristjan. "Longitudinal Associations between Problematic Social Media Use and Depressive Symptoms in Adolescent Girls." *Preventative Medicine Reports*, September, 2019. https://doi.org/10.1016/j.pmedr.2019.100925. Accessed June 22, 2021.

206. Primack, Brian A; Shensa, Ariel; *et. al*. "Social Media Use and Perceived Social Isolation Among Young Adults in the U.S." *American Journal of Preventative Medicine*, July, 2017 53(1):1-8. https://doi.org/10.1016/j.amepre.2017.01.010. Accessed June 22, 2021.

Chapter 10

Closing Thoughts

"All journeys have secret destinations of which the traveler is unaware." – Martin Buber

The Destination or the Journey?

Willie was invited by his grandfather to go to the store to get some groceries. It was a long walk in the snow, but he always enjoyed his grandfather's company. As they walked across the countryside, Willie ran over to his neighbor's barn to pet the cow, and then returned back to the road with his grandfather. Then, he ran over to the other neighbor's tree that had a swing hanging from one of the branches. He took a few swings, and then ran back to catch up with his grandfather. A little farther along the road, he saw Sally, a girl from school, sitting on her front porch. Willie ran over to say, "Hi," and then came back to the road.

When they finally reached the store at the top of the hill, the grandfather said to Willie, "Turn around and look at our tracks in the snow. Do you see how my tracks go straight down the road from our house to the store, while yours go left and right and everywhere? When you have a goal in life, it's best to stay focused on where you are going and not get distracted."

"But Grandfather," Willie replied, "If I stayed on the road, I wouldn't have petted the cow, or swung on the swing, or said, 'Hi!' to Sally."

There are those who focus on the journey and those who focus on the destination. Each has its value. If you follow every distraction,

Closing Thoughts

you may never reach your goal. On the other hand, if you focus only on your goal, you may miss out on life. There are times when we must focus on our goal, but there are other times when we need to stop and smell the roses. Achievement requires sacrifice, but we must always be aware of how much we are willing to sacrifice. We are not human DOINGS, we are human BEINGS, and sometimes it's more important to BE than to DO. Life has more than one dimension.

Although we all have 4 Dimensions to our lives, we do not all have an equal balance in each dimension: Some are more physical and may become professional athletes. Some are more mental and may become brilliant scientists. Some are more emotional and may be more concerned with the relationships in their lives than their accomplishments. Others are more spiritual and may dedicate their lives to religious pursuits. No one way is better or worse than the others.

My goal is to make you aware of the 4 Dimensions and help you develop your child in each dimension to live a well-balanced life. If your child chooses to focus on one area over the others, that is her right. I just recommend that you instill in her a desire to be balanced rather than one-sided. Even a brilliant scientist can have a healthy body, loving relationships, and a fulfilling spiritual life.

Once again, please remember that although you are responsible for your children, you do not own them, and you cannot control them. They are unique beings who are not here to re-live your life as you would have liked it. They are here to live their own lives, make their own mistakes, and create their own futures.

You are the gardener who helps the tree bear fruit.

You are not King Arthur; you are Merlin.

You are not the hero of their story . . . you are the teacher or coach who helps the hero make history.

Take joy in your role and the journey you take together.

Appendix
Psychological Integration

"If I have seen farther, it is by standing on the shoulders of giants. . ."
– Sir Isaac Newton

The Right Tool for the Job

Mary: *John, what are you doing with that hammer?*

John: *The computer is broken and I'm going to fix it.*

Mary: *With a hammer?*

John: *Well, that's the only tool I have!*

    I offer the following information and opinions of how the 4 Dimensional Theory fits in with or apart from various psychological schools of thought. I do not have a degree in psychology, so these are just the results of my research and opinions. There are many tools available to psychologists, but as the above story illustrates, choosing the right tool is paramount. I respectfully ask qualified psychologists and psychology students to construct experiments to either prove or disprove what I say – in this chapter and throughout the book – that's how we all learn.

Secularism

    Since the Age of Enlightenment, secularism has replaced religion for many. The development of the scientific method based on observation and repeatable results enamored mankind – after all, if our ability to think rationally is what separates man from the rest of the animals, then why not set rationality as the ultimate way to judge everything in our world? Tempting, but not exactly a sound logical conclusion.

Judging religion through the lens of reason is as faulty as judging science through the lens of religion. To use a more familiar example, can you explain emotion rationally? Scientists study the endocrine system and identify hormones and chemical reactions that create the feelings associated with emotions, but what causes the release of those hormones? To be blunt, what is the actual scientific explanation of love?

I don't believe you can explain love rationally – nor do you need to, and I don't believe you need to explain religion rationally. I believe they are separate dimensions of our human experience. Spiritual knowledge and truth are different from rational knowledge and truth, and one should not be subjected to the rules of the other. I am not saying there is no overlap, nor that certain aspects of religion cannot be explained rationally. What I am saying is that you should not expect to be able to explain all aspects of one in terms of the other – just ask Galileo.

Rationalists like to believe that the brain rules the body. However, recent scientific evidence shows that the heart, traditionally identified as the seat of emotion, sends more information to the brain than the brain sends to the heart.[207] In some people, at least at some times, emotions are clearly in control when committing crimes of passion.

Am I saying that the heart rules the mind? No. I am saying they are separate dimensions that affect each other, but none is "supposed to" control the others. They are supposed to work together.

I believe that logic and reason are the tools of the mind, but not the tools of physical, emotional, and spiritual realities. You should always use the right tool for the right job.

Epigenetics – Nature or Nurture?

Genetics are the hardware, while upbringing is the software. You inherit genes with certain traits, but those traits are activated or not by your environment. About the turn of the century, DNA had 2 identities: (1) the inherited identity and (2) the identity formed during embryogenesis, the time the fetus spent developing in the womb. An obvious trait, like having two arms, is hardwired into our DNA. But during the time in the womb, its expression can be altered, as we saw in the thalidomide babies born with extreme deformities.

Now, people like Moshe Szyf of McGill University believe there is a third identity, the experiential identity, where experiences influence the programming of genes.[208] Where the child of a professional athlete may inherit certain capabilities in his DNA, those capabilities may or may not be activated by his upbringing. The son of a great baseball pitcher may have the genetics to become a great baseball pitcher himself, but he might also become a computer gamer who can't even make the high school baseball team if he never takes up an interest in baseball. The genetic potential never gets expressed.

Piaget

As my references indicate, I relied heavily on Jean Piaget's stages of childhood development for my assertions and discussions of the mental dimension. His theories, at least as I understood them and described them, still seem to be largely accurate.

Kohlberg

As my references indicate, I also relied heavily on Lawrence Kohlberg's stages of moral development for my assertions and discussions of the spiritual dimension. His theories seem to be largely accurate in the childhood and adolescent years. Other theorists have expounded on higher levels of the spiritual dimension, but they do not seem pertinent to my subject of educating children.

Appendix

Carl Jung

Carl Jung developed a psychological theory that included archetypes supposedly common to all people. It was drawn from the study of myths and legends from different cultures, and has been used in dream interpretation as a window into the unconscious, with the goal of integration.

Because he divided the mind in to conscious and sub-conscious, one could say that everything he developed was in the mental dimension, as the conscious and sub-conscious are both areas within that dimension. However, he was also ridiculed by some psychologists for proposing concepts like the collective unconscious, which seemed more mystical than scientific. In that sense, he may have alluded to a spiritual dimension of the human experience.

Another way to look at his theories is to update them slightly so that the four basic archetypes in myth and especially in dreams (the Id, Ego, Anima, and Superego) actually represent the four dimensions of every person. What he called the Id might actually represent the physical dimension of man – our physical instinctual desires driven by the amygdala, without rationality to inhibit them. The Ego could actually represent the rational mind, the pre-frontal cortex imposing logic and order on our world. The Anima could actually represent our emotional dimension, centered not in the mind but rather in our heart and perhaps the endocrine system, providing the source of artistic inspiration. Finally, the Superego could actually represent our spiritual dimension, that quiet still voice inside that guides us on matters of morality, and is more a con*science* than either the conscious or sub-conscious mind.

Jung believed that we spend our lives trying to achieve integrity, and dreams were the language of the subconscious mind trying to work out and/or communicate how to do it. That makes sense, but rather than integrating the conscious and sub-conscious minds, I believe we need to integrate all four dimensions of our beings, and perhaps re-interpret certain dreams with the characters representing the 4 dimensions rather than his 4 archetypes.

CBT and NLP

Cognitive Behavioral Therapy is a very effective method of correcting mistaken beliefs that cause emotional distress. It provides psychological techniques to help a person overcome crises in a relatively short amount of time. When a patient trusts a therapist, in a few sessions they can identify the underlying problem of the emotional issue, discover the belief that causes the distress, understand that the belief may have been formed in their childhood (when they had an incomplete understanding of the world), and then change that belief, thereby reducing or eliminating the current distress. CBT is results-based and generally does not require years of therapy. I incorporated some basic CBT in advice and activities designed to help children correct erroneous beliefs or interrupt the stimulus/emotional response reaction by inserting a rational step between the stimulus and response.

Neuro-Linguistic Programming identifies thought patterns that lead up to certain actions. It provides a basic way of understanding behavior that underlies Cognitive Behavioral Therapy, but can also be used to model successful strategies. In addition to overcoming emotional distress like CBT, NLP can be used to develop excellence in many different disciplines by modeling the behaviors of outstanding performers and then copying those behaviors. I believe I incorporated some basic NLP in some of the activities designed to help program the children's minds to better handle emotional issues.

My only caveat is that these are effective techniques of the mind: They are not all-encompassing philosophies. I personally disagree with a basic tenet of NLP in that there is necessarily a rational step between the stimulus and response. Their very names indicate that they use the mind to control the emotions, which can be very effective for people whose emotions are controlling their minds and bringing undesirable results. However, they are limited in that they do not take into account the other two dimensions of being human, so they do not provide the answers to every question. In the physical dimension, there are some responses that are not fed through the regular mind, but are amygdala level survival responses that are very difficult to control. On the other hand, I do like the idea of the Wise Mind being the integration of reason and emotion. I would just suggest that a Wiser Mind would integrate the body, mind, heart, and spirit.

I do believe they are the right tool for certain jobs, but not the right tool for every job.

Multiple Intelligence Theory

Howard Gardner's multiple intelligence theory has not found a lot of empirical evidence to support it. It is an attractive idea in response to the traditional SAT test scores or even older IQ tests that measured verbal and mathematical ability, and some basic logic. He addressed a serious issue at the time that labeled some people "unintelligent" because they lacked abilities in one dimension but may have had extraordinary abilities in another dimension. The judgment placed on them from test scores seemed to make them "less than" others who scored higher on the tests.

To me, the issue is the actual definition of intelligence. If intelligence means mental capacity, then everything tested in an Intelligence Test should be an aspect of the mental dimension. If intelligence means capacity or affinity for any endeavor, then we can separate out mental intelligence from physical intelligence, emotional intelligence, and spiritual intelligence. With that understanding, specific skills and talents would require overlapping dimensions of intelligence. For example, musical talent requires some emotional intelligence to communicate feelings, some physical intelligence to play the instrument, and some mental intelligence to learn the notes, patterns, and interplay. Perhaps this is why some psychologists define musical intelligence as a talent, rather than an intelligence (reserving the word intelligence for only academics.)

The "G Factor" theory supports a single, dominant type of intelligence, but this, again, I would relegate to the mental dimension. The question remains: Is intelligence only a mental capacity, or can there be intelligence outside the cognitive realm?

In the 1990s Daniel Goleman popularized the idea of Emotional Intelligence, which adds support to my position that not only is emotional intelligence separate from cognitive intelligence, but that physical intelligence exists separately, as does spiritual intelligence. I believe the 4 Dimensional Theory goes a long way in solving the original problem that Gardner was trying to address: High scores in one area are a very limited measure of human value, as there are other areas that can and should be measured. SAT and IQ scores seem to accurately predict academic success, but not success in life. Emotional Intelligence and "grit" seem to be better predictors of economic and social success. Olympic Medalists and other champion athletes do not necessarily score well on IQ tests, but their success in the physical arena is undeniable. Then there is spiritual success, which is not easy to measure by rational standards. I believe it can only be measured by spiritual standards. Fortunately, many religions have divinely inspired scriptures containing guidelines to achieve spiritual success, making God the ultimate source (and final judge) of spiritual matters. Far be it from me to say I know better.

Wilber

Ken Wilbur's Integral Theory is an attempt to put everything into one theory, which is necessarily more complex than my goals here, yet remarkably simple considering he is putting the entire universe into one neat package. He seems to agree with the concept of different types of intelligence, and that education should teach the different types at each stage of development for the child. On that point I believe we can agree. The 4 Dimensional Theory is more streamlined or simpler than I suppose he would like, but my goal is to communicate an understandable system that the average mother can use, which naturally would be more limited. Because he believes that "everybody is right," I will assume he would take my theory and Integrate it.

His Great Chain of Being goes well beyond our purposes here. He understands the spiritual dimension far better than most psychologists, who are naturally focused in the mental dimension. The big advantage Wilbur offers are in the higher levels of spiritual development, which are probably not appropriate for children. Adults

Appendix

interested in going beyond the basics offered in this book are invited to research his work and seek higher levels of spirituality.

References

207. Arguelles, Lourdes; McCraty, Rollin; and Rees, Robert A. "The Heart in Holistic Education." HeartMath Institute; Assets; Uploads; 2015. https://www.heartmath.org/assets/uploads/2015/01/heart-in-education.pdf. Accessed June 15, 2021.

208. Szyf, Moshe. "How Do Our Experiences Rewire Our Brains and Bodies?" NPR; *Hidden Brain*; August 25, 2017. https://www.npr.org/templates/transcript/transcript.php?storyId=545092951. Accessed June 23, 2021.

www.ingramcontent.com/pod-product-compliance
Lightning Source LLC
Chambersburg PA
CBHW071805080526
44589CB00012B/699